holson : drawings and painted reliefs

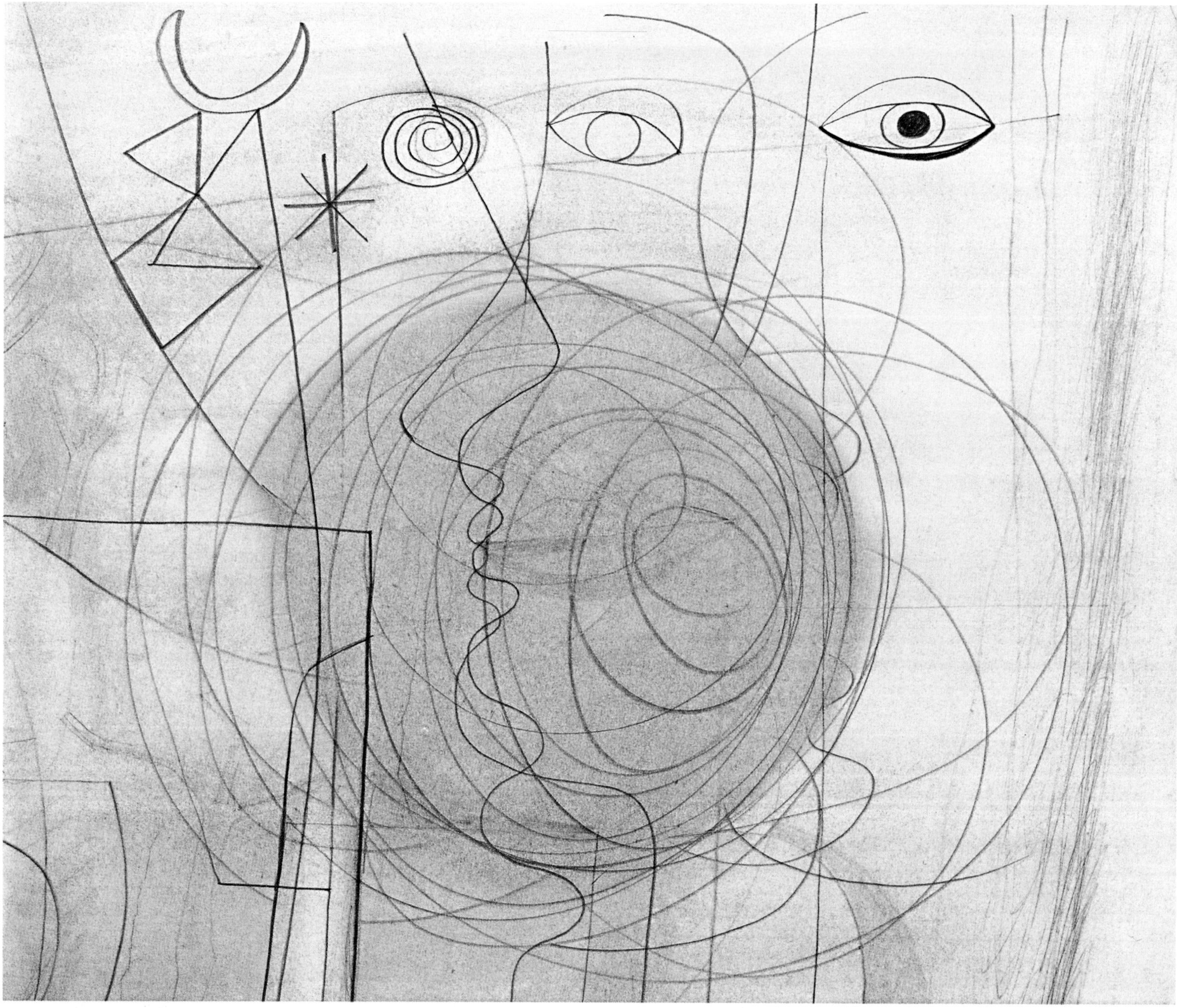

May 1954 (portrait of the artist)
oil wash and pencil on paper
29 × 34 cm (11½ × 13½ in)

Ben Nicholson : drawings and painted reliefs

PETER KHOROCHE

Lund Humphries

This paperback edition first published in 2008 by
Lund Humphries
Gower House
Croft Road
Aldershot
Hampshire GU11 3HR

and

Suite 420
101 Cherry Street
Burlington
VT 05401-4405
USA

Lund Humphries is part of Ashgate Publishing

British Library Cataloguing-in-Publication Data
A catalogue record for this book is available from the British Library

Library of Congress Control Number: 2001038875

ISBN 978-1-84822-004-1

Designed by Sally Jeffery

Origination, printing and binding in Singapore
under the supervision of MRM Graphics

CONTENTS

Introduction

The main focus of this book is on the drawings and reliefs executed by Ben Nicholson between 1950 and 1975. Together they stand as his most assured, most characteristic achievement, and, with the white reliefs of 1934–9, are the works by which he himself wished to be judged.[1]

Yet neither the late reliefs nor the drawings have received the attention they deserve. The drawings have mistakenly been treated as somehow subsidiary to the paintings and reliefs when in fact they have qualities of wit, poetry and spontaneity quite special to themselves – qualities which, added to their variety and sheer virtuosity, entitle them to fully equal status. Far from being a side-issue, they are perhaps Nicholson's most personal expressions. Certainly they are the most approachable, while the late reliefs are generally felt to be the least so. By placing the two together in context, and examining the qualities of each, I hope to show them simply as two complementary aspects of a single artistic sensibility, while also exploring the 'idea', the peculiar interiorized vision, that underlies all Nicholson's work.

Reliefs and drawings are the two poles between which Nicholson's imagination went 'chasing out something *alive*':[2] the universal sensed by way of the particular; the three-dimensional object expressing one facet of reality, the two-dimensional image another. This lifelong search to express the inner life of things is my true subject.

Nicholson's own published statements on art and artists are sparse.[3] He was not fond of 'explanations', preferring to let the work speak for itself. How was it possible for him, or for anyone, to analyse what had been created, and could only be appreciated, intuitively? For him any attempt at such analysis was not only largely irrelevant but, far worse, destructive of the living thing. He much approved Braque's dictum: 'Il n'est en art qu'une chose qui vaille. Celle que l'on ne peut expliquer', which he rendered as: 'One can explain everything about a painting except the bit that matters'.[4]

To appreciate Nicholson's contemplative, non-literary, inward vision, it may be that detailed analysis is inappropriate and description superfluous, since neither touches on what is most important: the power of the work to move the heart and mind. Conscious of these pitfalls, and of Nicholson's strictures, I have refrained from picking his works to pieces and tried instead to determine the essential nature of his art, through each shift of style and change of medium; to suggest continuities in technique and aesthetic ideal; and, generally, to provide a background, in the belief that, though there is no substitute for *looking*, and though a work stands or falls according to its ability to move the viewer without any sort of intermediary, yet some idea of the artist's expressed aims, his temperament, his circumstances – the places, people and period of time that affected him – can help towards a fuller appreciation of what one sees.

The first peak of Nicholson's achievement, the white reliefs, may at the time of their making have seemed to abolish all the works that went before. But elements of those earlier works were to resurface throughout the rest of his career and provide a key to understanding it as a consistent whole. This is why I devote much of the first chapter to tracing the long evolution that led up to the reliefs. Without a knowledge of that background one may fail to appreciate the works of his maturity for what they are: a brilliant synthesis of previous discoveries. I am thinking especially of the painted reliefs dating from the mid-1950s to the mid-1970s, in which Nicholson reached an entirely original solution of how to convey his experience of the world around him.

Several people who knew Nicholson well have remarked on how much the work was the image of the man.[5] Yet his dislike, often repeated, of the cult of the artist's personality and his consequent shunning of all publicity have led to misunderstanding both about him and about the nature of his art. To redress this I have made a point of frequently quoting his own words from letters (most of them previously unpublished) even more than from his published writings (which are by now fairly well known). The tone and style of these, almost as much as their content, should make clear what many pages of exposition might fail to do – the character of both man and work.

1919–39

from illusionistic painting to abstract carving

Looking back to 1911 and his student days at the Slade School of Fine Art, Paul Nash remembered one incident very clearly.

> The Slade Life Class, for the most part astride donkey easels, had been absorbed for some time producing their own or the Professor's view of the male model – mostly passable imitations of the natural form – when I was shocked to notice that Ben Nicholson was not conforming to the general attitude. Upon a large sheet of paper, on a drawing board of Imperial size set upon a painting easel, he had drawn in heavy pencil a small dark figure, a sort of manikin, bearing no resemblance whatever to the model. It was, of course, simply his personal equivalent for the model, characteristically presented and, I need hardly add, not the kind of equivalent approved of.[6]

With hindsight we know that this search for a personal equivalent rather than a literal representation of the thing seen would become central to the work of Nicholson's maturity. But it is startling to see him already so early holding true to an inner vision which he had not yet the means to express. Small wonder that this refractory attitude should baffle his drawing-master at the Slade, when even among his own family he met with incomprehension. In a letter written to Ben late in 1912, his mother tempers praise with advice, again about drawing: 'I think your still life at Rottingdean is *very very* good in very many ways & if you'll only work at *drawing* a bit you'll be all right I'm quite sure.' The final sentence of her letter suggests that she is writing to someone unsure of himself and misunderstood by others: 'I have the greatest faith in you & know you will do something splendid some day.'[7] Many years later, his sister Nancy could still remark that of all William Nicholson's children, 'Ben was the only one who couldn't draw'[8] – a preposterous statement unless we interpret 'couldn't draw' as 'couldn't copy'. To his father, whose art, for all its poetry and sensitive regard for medium, was grounded in illusionism, Ben's early efforts could only have seemed like perverse fumblings lacking in skill. One might well question whether William ever really understood, or sympathised with, Ben's aims or achievement. As late as the 1930s, when Ben's work was being shown in international exhibitions, William's pride was mixed with puzzlement.[9]

To be born into a family of artists and to grow up in a lively artistic environment was undoubtedly an advantage, but it soon came to feel more like imprisonment. So much so that it seemed the only way to affirm his own personality might be to break away altogether. Ben Nicholson in his teens and early twenties appears to us as someone gradually, hesitantly, almost reluctantly coming to terms with his artistic heredity – an impression that may seem at odds with the fierce dedication of his maturity – but there were powerful reasons, both personal and historical, for this slow realization. By his mid-twenties, when he had to recognize that art had finally claimed him too, he was faced with the double task of inventing a pictorial language that would convey his personal way of seeing things, while at the same time discovering what that personal vision was. A further fifteen years of constant experiment lay ahead until, at the age of forty, he produced his first fully mature work, which was also his most extreme reaction to all previous influences: the reliefs carved out of wood and painted a uniform, luminous white.

At the time of Ben's birth on 10 April 1894, William and Mabel Nicholson were living in a roomy, Dutch-gabled cottage (formerly the Eight Bells pub) in the village of Denham, Buckinghamshire, not far from Hubert von Herkomer's art school at Bushey where they had first met six years earlier. In unconscious forecast of things to come, William made a print of Ben's baby foot in lampblack on white paper, and hung it in a place of honour.

With his first breath Ben absorbed the atmosphere of the painter's studio (even the fox-terrier who guarded his cot was called Whistler), and was soon familiar with the artists, writers and theatre people who were his parents' friends. As an infant he sat on the shoulders of Edward Gordon Craig while he careered up and down the quiet, leaf-shaded village street at Denham, pretending to be a horse. And when William Nicholson designed the costumes for the first production of *Peter Pan* in 1904, Ben took a water-colour he had made two years earlier, of a Red Indian and
1 two horses, one walking into the picture, one walking out of it, and enlarged it into

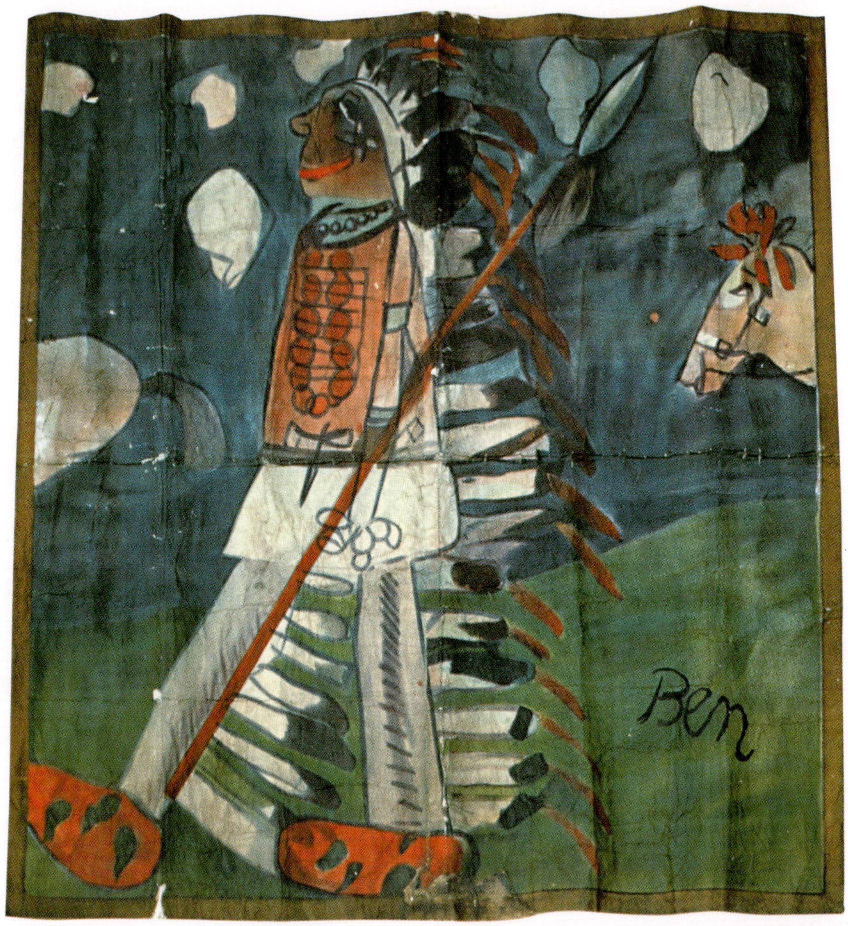

1 *1904 (Peter Pan poster)*
poster paint on paper backed on cloth
*c.*152 × 137 cm (60 × 54 in)

a poster for the play (though he felt a lasting grievance against Barrie, supposed expert in the psychology of little boys, for not paying him so much as sixpence for it).[10] Holidays at Dieppe, a meeting place for artists English and French in the 1900s, immersed Ben still more thoroughly in the artistic life of the Belle Epoque.[11]

With such surroundings and personalities influencing his boyhood, only a very strong pull in another direction could have prevented Ben, at the age of sixteen, from entering the Slade School of Fine Art at University College London. Among his fellow students were Stanley Spencer, William Roberts, David Bomberg, Edward Wadsworth, C. R. W. Nevinson, Mark Gertler and Isaac Rosenberg, but he had nothing to do with any of them and had no great opinion of their work, though later he came to admire Bomberg's painting. The only real friend he made there was Paul Nash.

Nicholson always claimed that he learnt more about form and spatial relationships in the billiard-room of the Gower Hotel, a few minutes' walk away,[12] than at the Slade which, under the triumvirate of Fred Brown, Henry Tonks and Wilson Steer, had reached its apogee in the early years of the century, but was now out of touch with developments in France: Tonks and Steer were openly hostile to post-Impressionism and did not understand Cézanne. Tonks even made it clear to his students that, though he could not actually forbid them, he would far rather they did not go and see the exhibition *Manet and the Post-Impressionists*, organized by Roger Fry, which opened in November 1910. Despite this, or because of it, Nicholson did go, to judge for himself. So, independently, did his father. Afterwards it turned out that each had liked the same Cézanne still life best, and Ben even went back several times to see it (though it would still be some years before he fully understood Cézanne).[13] The Slade could not provide him with what he needed: the discovery within himself of his own particular vision, as well as the confidence to cultivate it. After three and a half terms' unenthusiastic attendance, he abandoned the place at the end of 1911. Comparing his situation at this time with that of Paul Nash, he later wrote: 'I was in the painting world & trying to get out & he was out & trying to get in.'[14] To be the son of an accomplished and successful painter and to feel in himself the same instinctive urge to paint – however uncertain its actual realization – meant inevitably that to find his own path would not be easy.

Nicholson's rejection of Tonks and preference for billiards was not just an anti-establishment, anti-academic stance, though it was that as well. It was part of his sense of alienation from the accepted teaching of the schools, pointedly illustrated by Paul Nash's reminiscence of him in the life class, part also of an as yet obscurely felt reaction to the elegance and finish of his father's painting, its easy satisfaction with the outward appearance, the surface of things.

In later years he attributed this reaction to his mother's influence. Herself descended from a long line of painters and engravers, she was an artist in her own right.[15] Most of her surviving pictures are portraits – the sitter presented boldly, even starkly, against a dark or neutral background or in a dimly lit interior. She shared with her brother, James Pryde, a passion for the theatre, and like him could create in her paintings a sense of drama and mystery. But it was not so much her painting that influenced Ben, as her powerful personality. Assessing, many years later, what each of his parents had contributed to shaping his work, he wrote:

> I think chaps when they try & account for the severity in my work overlook the fact that it is the logical outcome not only of reaction against father's 'accomplishment' – but of an intense sympathy & admiration for my mother's strength of character & Scotch *purpose* – she gave up her promising painting career for her children & put all her creative powers into this & *I owe her absolutely everything*. Father's painting is at its best (in his still life & some of his small landscapes) *very fine* – I admire it v. much – but I don't think it contains in itself alone the seeds of a new development & without mother's fierce balancing contribution it would have fizzled out in the following generation ... It is this direct approach set off against father's brilliance & elegance (which of its kind was v. good) which meant so much to me. ... I think it's *all* and not part of this background which made me produce my brand of work.[16]

After the Slade the next few years were a period of vacillation and, somehow connected with it, of ill health: the asthma, which had brought his schooldays to a premature end when he was still only fifteen, now reasserted itself. He went first to Tours then to Milan for a stay of several months in each, to learn French and Italian, then tried Madeira and eventually Pasadena as a cure for his asthma (which at least had exempted him from war service). News of his mother's sudden death, in July 1918 from the Spanish influenza epidemic, brought him back to England.

Writing fifty years afterwards, Ben described her as 'the rock on which my whole existence has been based'.[17] She had in truth been his mainstay, always encouraging, even when not always comprehending, his tentative steps towards personal expression. At this critical stage of his development her loss was devastating. He seems to have coped with it by at last committing himself wholeheartedly to being a professional artist.

Soon after he returned to England in September 1918, he found a studio of his own at 67 Cheyne Walk on the Chelsea embankment, and his more positive attitude is reflected in the number of paintings he now completed and was prepared to exhibit. In the seven years since leaving the Slade he had completed very few works and exhibited just four. Now, in the course of 1919, he showed no fewer than ten works in four separate exhibitions. Of these ten, only three can at present be located, and it is hard to see in them anything more than docile echoes of his father's still-life formula – the uninspired result of patient toil against the grain of his own instincts.

One still life painted in 1919, but apparently not exhibited, is of interest because
2 it does seem to be a beginning as well as an end. *Blue bowl in shadow* has the fastidious elegance, the rich paint surface, the strong contrast of light and dark that one finds in a still life by William Nicholson, but where the father's juxtaposition of objects might be odd or whimsical, the son's combines apparent simplicity with mystery, a powerful contrast of colour with an attention to the abstract play of forms. The position in space of the orange-framed rectangle is ambiguous and the object itself not immediately identifiable – a frame, or mount perhaps, enclosing the

prepared ground for another still life? The curve of shadow answers the curve of the bowl. The paler orange of the left-hand bottom corner of the frame corresponds to the division of the two greys of the inner rectangle. Circle is played off against rectangle. Though there is a danger that with hindsight we may read too much into this early work, still so heavily indebted to the elder Nicholson, hints of the future are unmistakably there.

It was not that Ben was unaware of the need to turn his back on his father's virtuosity and the highly-finished vacuity of so much Edwardian painting, so as to begin again from the beginning. The problem was to find a model that would unlock his own gifts. And in this he was not alone: his contemporary, Ivon Hitchens, was faced with the same problem at exactly the same time. T. S. Eliot, six years older than Ben Nicholson, found himself in a similar impasse: 'The kind of poetry that I needed, to teach me the use of my own voice, did not exist in English at all; it was only to be found in French.'[18] For Nicholson and Hitchens, as for Eliot, the revelation was to come from France, but that still lay ahead. Despite several visits to the post-Impressionist exhibition of 1910, Nicholson had been too young to absorb and be influenced by what he saw. Nor, if he saw them, was he inspired by the Cubist and Futurist works exhibited in London (and Milan) in the years before the War, as were some of his fellow-students at the Slade – Bomberg, Wadsworth, Nevinson and Roberts – and the slightly older Wyndham Lewis. Only after the war did he identify with Lewis's aim to shake British art out of its provincial stagnation. But it is safe to assume that none of the pictures he exhibited in 1919 betrayed this new alignment.

Friendship with the sculptor Frank Dobson, whose studio was around the corner from his own, proved to be Nicholson's first step towards prising himself free from his father's influence. Through Dobson he came into contact with Wyndham Lewis and briefly looked to him for guidance. As he later recalled: 'the contact with vorticism & Lewis . . . enabled me to break away from my family ptg [*ie* painting] tradition – the contact with vorticism didn't do much more for me than that, because my interpretation of it was aggressive & the biggest urge was to bust up the sophistication all round me – I soon realized that this was also a dead-end if one continued with it.'[19] By 'vorticism' here we must understand the work of those who had once been Vorticists, alias Cubo-Futurists, in 1913–15. Nicholson could never have been drawn to the abrasive, anti-romantic, urban aesthetic of Vorticism, nor been a dupe to the foolish belief that paintings inspired by steel girders, dizzying architecture and the speed and violence of machinery are necessarily more 'modern', more 'progressive', than paintings of landscape or still life. But in the less radical post-war work of Dobson, Lewis and Bomberg he thought he could see a way forward.

Three portraits by Nicholson, exhibited at the Goupil Gallery in November–December 1920, marked this passing phase. In the words of a contemporary review: 'Benjamin Nicholson, in his efforts to escape from the parental complex, has suffered a transference of his affections to the newest school of painting. He has vigorously blackened the noses of his sitters, hollowed their cheeks, and endowed them with

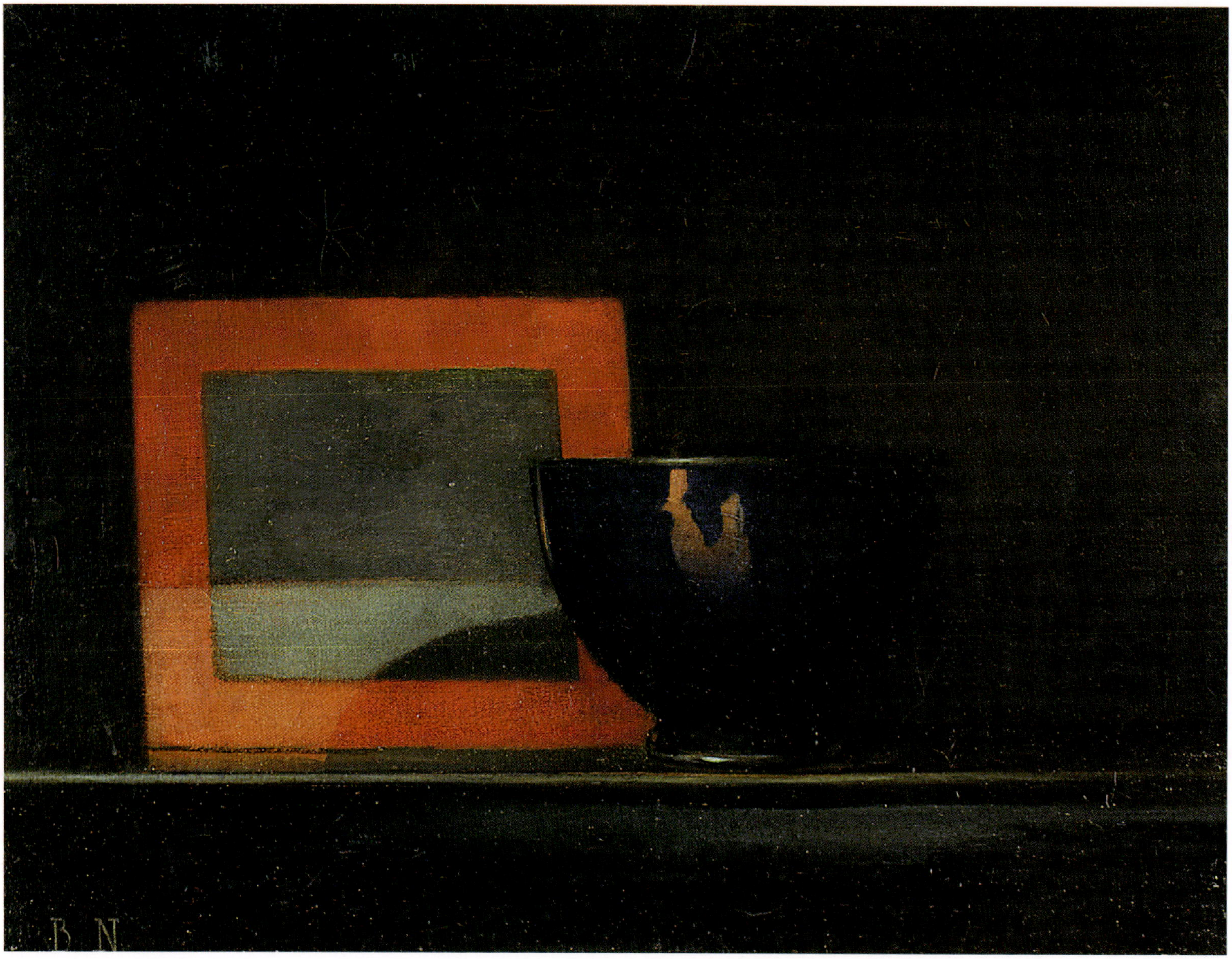

2 *1919 (blue bowl in shadow)*
oil on canvas
48 × 65 cm (19 × 25½ in)

sorrowful expressions; they are now quite up-to-date.'[20] But the influence on Nicholson of the ex-Vorticists, some of whom had rallied in March 1920 to exhibit as *Group X*, was predictably short-lived. 'Once I'd tried out a strong-man Wynd. Lewis phase I decided *hard* & strong led nowhere whereas *sensitive* even if temporarily weak *could lead* somewhere eventually & indeed if handled properly could lead anywhere.'[21]

One of the three portraits Nicholson exhibited in 1920 was of Robert Graves, and was reproduced as the frontispiece to his book of poems, *The Pier Glass*, published in 1921. Graves had married Ben's sister Nancy and they were now living at Boar's Hill outside Oxford. It was through them that Ben met Winifred Roberts who was on a visit to her aunt at Boar's Hill in the spring of 1920. Winifred too was an aspiring painter, encouraged in this by her grandfather George Howard, ninth Earl of Carlisle, whose main interest was painting. She had been one of the first students at Byam Shaw's newly opened art school on Campden Hill and had been trained in his brand of late Pre-Raphaelitism for several years until his premature death in 1919. Recently she had spent several months with her father and sister in India – an experience of colour and light that was to have a profound effect on her painting.

Ben and Winifred were married that November and spent their honeymoon on a month's tour of Italy, ending up at Lugano, just over the Swiss border, early in December. Above the town, among the terraced vineyards of Monte Brè, they soon discovered a villa for sale. Snow-capped mountains surrounded it and there was a wonderful view across the blue expanse of the lake below to where another great mountain range rose out of the water. The air was clear, the light radiant. To the Nicholsons the place seemed magical.[22] They persuaded Winifred's father to buy the Villa Capriccio (which they learnt had previously belonged to the chef of the late Tsar) and agreed to pay him rent for it. Thus began a three-year period in which Ben and Winifred would spend from late autumn to spring at Castagnola above Lake Lugano, and the summers in London and Cumberland with Winifred's parents.

At first Nicholson painted Dobson-inspired heads, but this was soon to change. On their way to and from the Swiss canton of Ticino they would spend a week or more in Paris where they not only visited the few galleries showing contemporary painting but fed their enthusiasm for the Italian Primitives at the Louvre. Years later Nicholson described how 'the real revelation came on a visit to Paris ... in Spring 1921 ... I remember suddenly coming on a cubist Picasso at the end of a small upstairs room in Paul Rosenberg's gallery – it must have been a 1915 ptg – it was what seemed to me then completely abstract & in the centre there was an absolutely miraculous green – v. deep, v. potent and absolutely real – in fact none of the actual events in one's life have been more real than that – & it still remains the standard by which I judge any reality in my work.'[23] This was no exaggeration: the works of Picasso in the period of synthetic Cubism (1912–15) were to be the greatest single influence on Nicholson throughout his subsequent career. Here at last he had found the model that would eventually elicit his own personal form of expression. As he explained, 'for the 5 months in Lugano immediately following the terrific adventure of a week in Paris we were completely isolated from all paintings & painters. ... During those 3 winters I ptd dmd [sic] nearly a picture a day (still life & landscapes) ... although only a fraction of the work done during this experimental period remains, it was a very important period of fast & furious experiment.'[24]

In this Winifred was the ideal companion. Her spontaneity and freshness of vision, her sensitivity to light and her colour sense, all contributed to wean Ben finally from the toilsome execution and old-masterish sobriety of his earlier still lifes. And her poetic awareness and appreciation of their idyllic surroundings were equally stimulating. For both of them it was a beginning, and though each developed differently, each making their own separate discoveries, they could share their excitement and growing sense of purpose. Both made a practice of working out-of-doors.

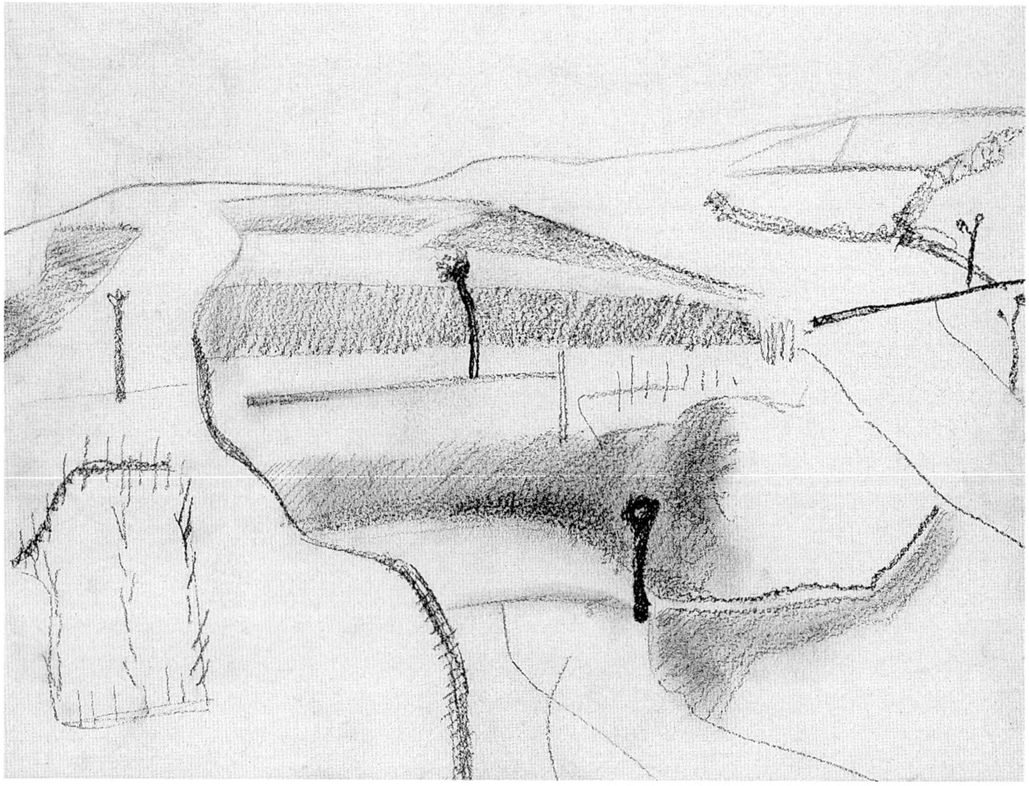

3 *1922 (willow trees)*
pencil on paper
23 × 30 cm (9 × 11¾ in)

Winifred, in her eagerness to capture her sensations in paint, would work fast and often complete a picture at one go. Ben, for whom painting was always a much slower process, would make drawings which he could later use as a basis for painting in his studio.

When the Nicholsons returned to England in April 1923, they left the Villa Capriccio for good, partly because the cost of living there was too high, partly because, having now found themselves as painters, they felt the need to be more continuously in touch with what was going on in London. A sign of this growing confidence was that immediately on their return, in May, they had a joint exhibition of their recent work at the Paterson Gallery in Bond Street. One visitor recorded his reactions to it: 'There are about fifty specimens – half the husband's and half the wife's – mostly oils, but with some dozen water-colours of hers. I came to the conclusion that she was by a long way the better artist of the two. Poor Ben is struggling to find a future which will reconcile his past and present. He is emerging from Vorticism. She is quite a good painter of flowers, and one of her watercolour landscapes is really attractive.'[25]

The visitor was Herbert Asquith, former Liberal Prime Minister, under whom Winifred's father had served as Under-Secretary of State for India. In finding Winifred's work more approachable than Ben's, he expressed the general verdict. Ben's forbidding portraits, stark landscapes and still lifes 'with a peasant flavour', as Winifred described them, attracted no one, whereas Winifred's flower pieces all

found buyers. To Paul Nash, though, the whole show, with its fresh and original use of colour, seemed full of promise,[26] while the critic Frank Rutter singled out Ben's
4 *Cold Fell* for its effective simplicity.[27] In it the north-country light and temperature are captured by lively handling and bold colour contrasts: patches of brilliant emerald green against the green-ochre of a spatially ambiguous foreground; fields in pale pink and pale yellow against the brown fellside; slate-grey, louring sky against white clouds and rifts of pale blue.

Soon after their exhibition closed, Ben and Winifred visited Paul and Margaret Nash at Dymchurch on the Kent coast.[28] Though they stayed only a few days,
5 Nicholson painted a seascape, tackling the subject head-on, with a view straight out to sea. Again it is the painterly quality of this small picture that is most striking. If the grey-green of sea and sky, divided by the darker line of the horizon, is relatively naturalistic, the shore in the foreground certainly is not: thickly brushed-in patches of colour draw attention to themselves as paintmarks but can only partially be resolved into pools, channels or shelving beach, while the black rod rising vertically on the picture surface is only gradually deducible as a breakwater. Clearly Nicholson is more interested in the quality of the paint surface and the contrast of ochre and brown with grey and green. The rough, scraped ground, most clearly visible in the left- and right-hand portions of the sky, will become a familiar characteristic of subsequent works. Apparent already at this early stage is Nicholson's predilection for disposing space in two dimensions with little or no recession – a clear debt to Cubism, as is his wish to stress rather than disguise the object quality, the aesthetic autonomy of the work: initially at least, the response must be to what it is, not to what it is about.

Nicholson all the while felt the need somehow to paint the inner life of things rather than their outward and material appearance. This interest in what at the time he
6 called 'the abstract stuff'[29] led him in 1923–4 to paint several 'abstractions' of still-life themes, clearly indebted to the Cubist collage technique of overlapping planes of colour and pattern.[30] In the parochial context of British painting in the 1920s such experiments met with scant appreciation, or even comprehension, from the critics. Yet they did testify to an awareness of what was happening elsewhere. That he himself felt he had gone too far too fast in these paintings may be deduced from the more representational still lifes he produced during the rest of the decade – more representational, yet concerned to express the inner life rather than the outward aspect.

Among the first to recognize this deeper concern was Helen Sutherland, whom Nicholson met towards the end of 1925. She soon became, and remained, his most important patron, giving quite as much support by her sympathetic understanding of his work as by her commitment to buying it at the outset of his career. A remarkable person with an exacting, fastidious ideal of life, a finely discriminating intelligence and great moral sensitivity, her insight into the nature of Nicholson's art was immediate and instinctive. Unfortunately for us, she recorded very little of her reactions to specific works of his. However, partly because they are among the earliest

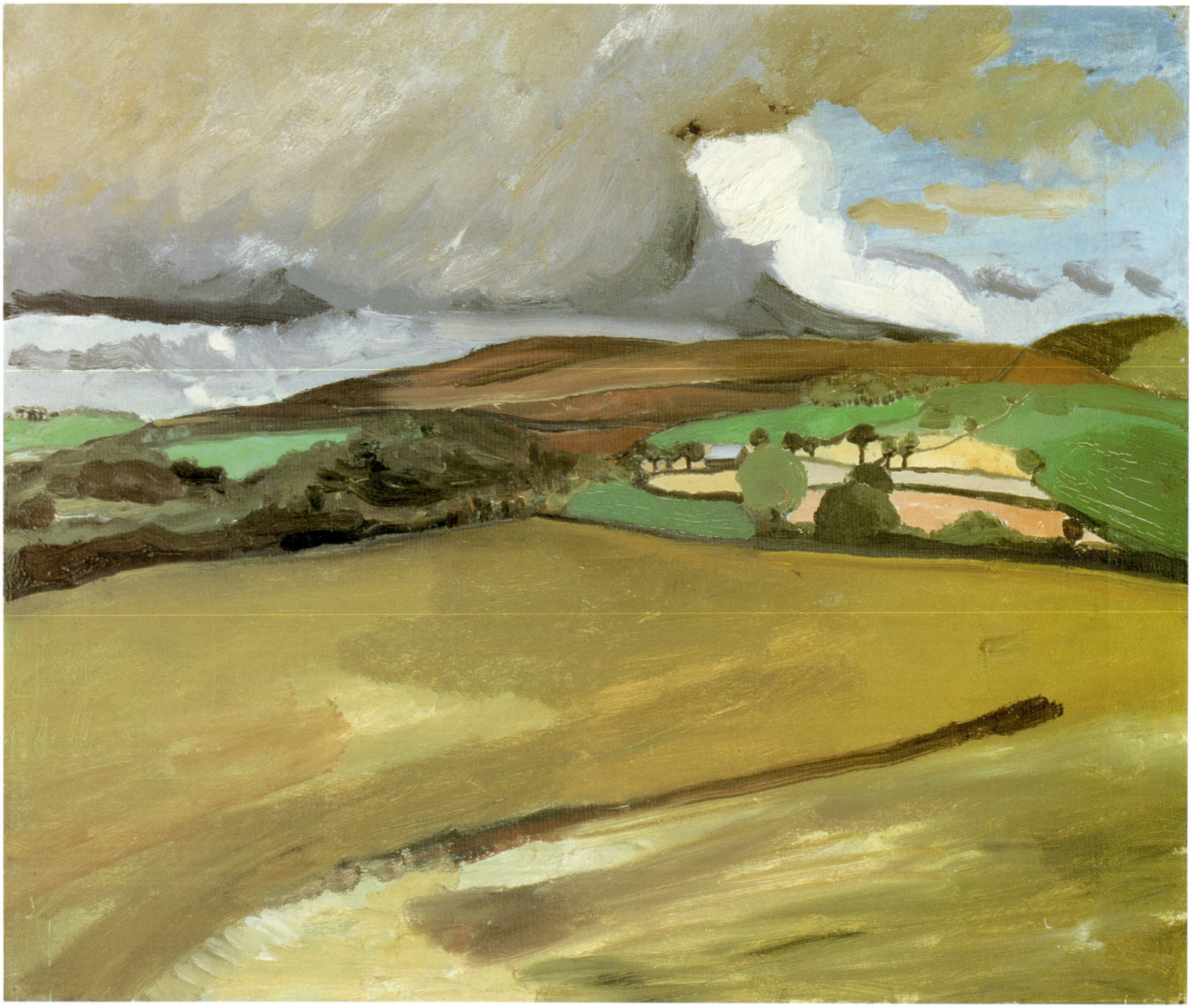

4 *1922 (Cold Fell)*
oil on canvas
51.5 × 63 cm (20¼ × 24¾ in)

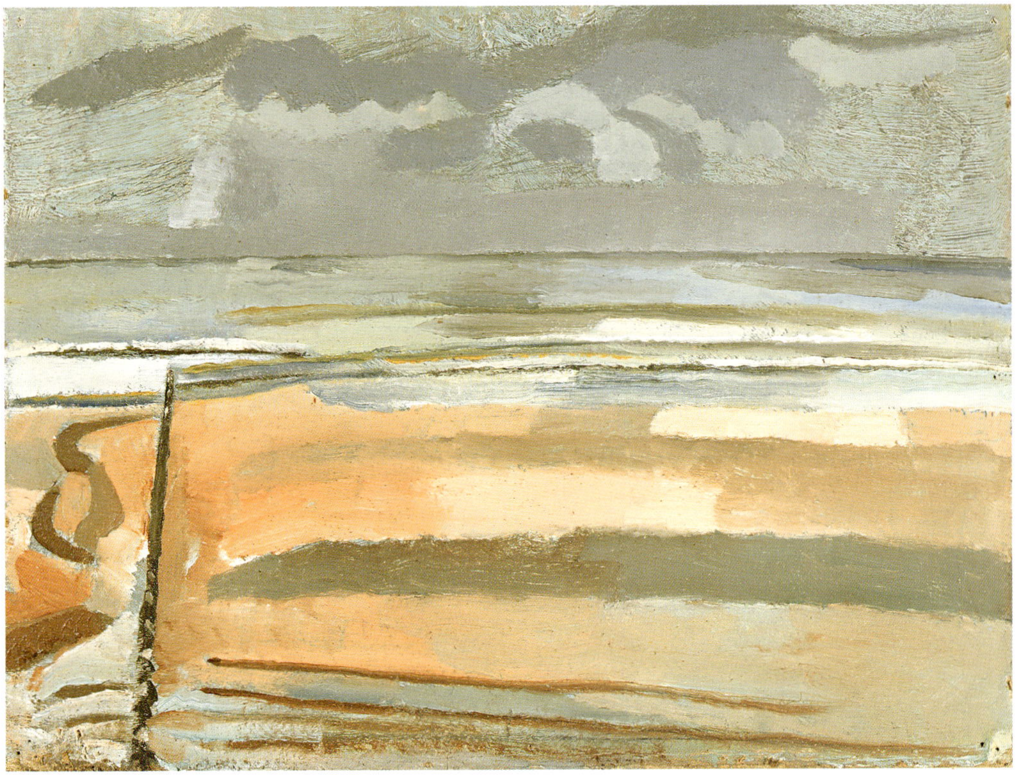

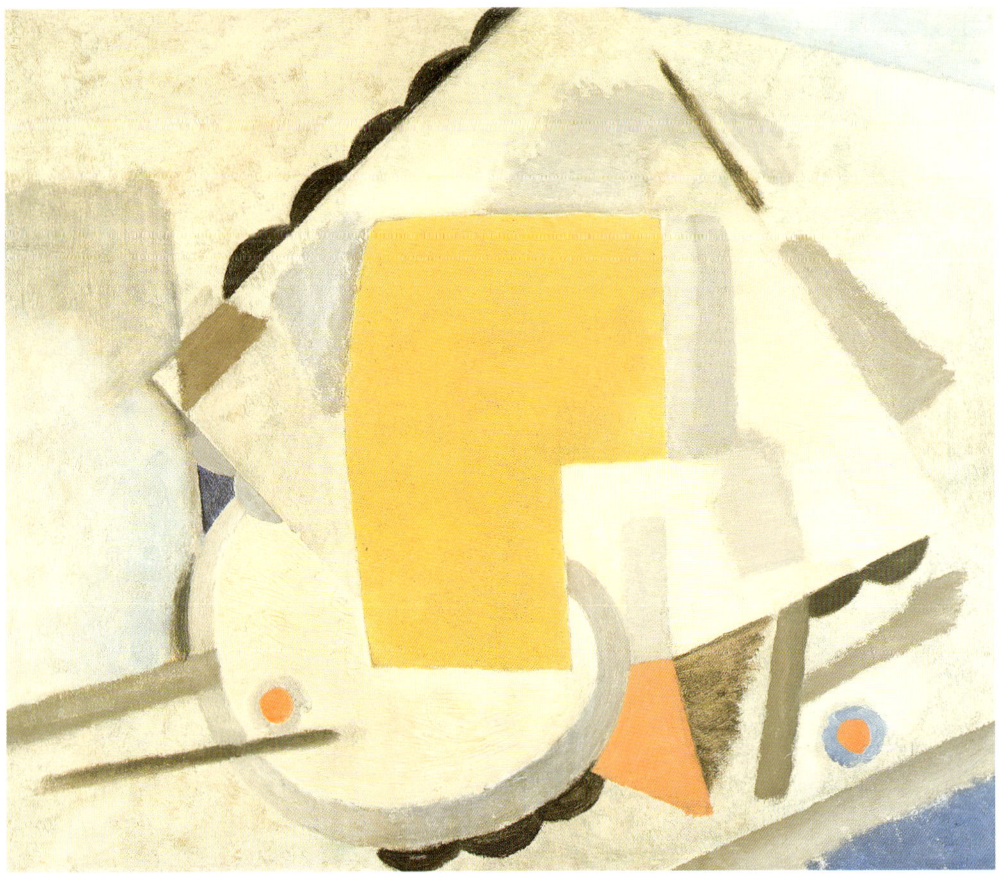

5 *1923 (Dymchurch)*
oil on canvas mounted on board
29 × 38.5 cm (11½ × 15¼ in)

6 *1924 (abstract painting – Andrew)*
oil and sand on canvas
63.5 × 76 cm (25 × 30 in)

critical appreciations of Nicholson's work, partly because they remain among the most perceptive, I reproduce here three extracts from her notebooks, dating from 1926. First, on the general character of his painting:

> He has subjected reality so intensely to imagination that there seems very little ordinary reality left in his pictures – he creates a world of his own & quite apart – but this imaginative world has a universal character & it is *there* that what seems to have been taken away is given back to us.

7 Next, a series of entries about one painting – actually *1925 (still life, bottle and goblets)*, not '3 goblets' – in which she tentatively explains it to herself.

> (Bamburgh, July 1926) I've brought up a still life of Ben's 3 goblets – blue, black, red – the red a queer very opaque red with a little spot of light in it – & they've all got very odd interesting shadows behind them. They are strange. One, the blue, is apparently a glass goblet but they are not painted in the least in a representational way – in a way they are absolutely unlike what they are supposed to be, i.e. they are unlike the *common* experience of these objects ... but they are a *vision* – by someone who thinks in paint & thinks originally. Most artists paint a common human experience when they paint objects or persons. This artist seems to be seeing these goblets for the first time – as if they've never been seen before – and his *inward* vision – his most personal vision has taken on impersonality – has got actualised.
>
> ... Why, if we can ever really like objects, if we can ever really disinterestedly enjoy shapes and colours, why should we not like these? Because they are not painted as we are accustomed to see things painted – nor do they look in themselves like things we are accustomed to see – they look rather like a child's painting. I suppose because this struggle to paint a personal & inward vision of an outward object is absolutely new.
>
> Watts painted inward visions – but indirectly by analogy – by translation. His wasn't direct or a painter's vision. Blake came much nearer. Watts told a story & his inward vision & his painting had no *vital* connection with one another, whereas with Ben the inward vision is directly seen *in* the painting he produces – the outward thing stammers & staggers a little in its new birth as the body of a new vision.
>
> Ben's Goblets remember what we've forgotten. His aren't seen in their individual finite useful character but some universal character is expressed in them ... And this is the nature, the significance of Art – to bring to light things belonging to the human spirit but which are largely still hidden from us.

Her diary entry for 7 December 1926 records: 'Cooie [*ie* Constance Lane, the painter] and Mr Hitchens to dine talked ptg all the evg – very interesting'. The corresponding notebook entry makes a tantalizingly brief reference to Ivon Hitchens' comment on the same '3 goblets' that evening.

> The difference I think between Ben & Winifred's painting is this – Ben begins with the inward thing – the spiritual value – & lets the outward expression take care of itself. Winifred begins with the outward reality & *presses through* to the inward life.
>
> My 3 goblets are impressive bec. the inward idea – life – is big, weighty – tho' it is puzzling to say how or why or what this spiritual thing, life, idea has been & is expressed in 3 goblets & their shadows ... What this picture says is spiritual & *said* in paint. Mr Hitchens showed me how the paint says it: the study of tone – painting the bottle not in a

materialistic way to show the very stuff of the glass bottle, but . . . as a tone & as part of a scheme of a related harmony of tones.

It was an almost casual word of Mr Hitchens which made me see the difference between *materialistic* painting & spiritual painting. He showed me how differently a materialistic painter wd have treated the bottle etc in Ben's Goblets. He pointed out that Ben was exploring tones & tone harmony – an almost musical phase in painting . . .

The spirit in painting is always the interesting thing. Even in materialistic painting it's present & makes the *choices* of light & colour & subject – & the more spirit is present the more it chooses & materialism is changed to realism.[31]

To see 'the difference between *materialistic* painting & spiritual painting' we have only to compare *Still life, bottle and goblets* with *Blue bowl in shadow* painted six years earlier. The inward and informing vision described by Helen Sutherland – what Nicholson called his 'idea' – is crucial to a true appreciation of his work, and we shall return to it.

In the winter of 1923 the Nicholsons, while staying with Winifred's parents in Cumberland, found an old farmhouse for sale, which was built on and partly out of Hadrian's Wall. The high ground fell steeply away to the south, down to the wide valley of the Irthing. Beyond there were views to the fells at the north end of the Pennines and to the outlying peaks of the Lake District. Banks Head answered their need and they bought it at once. It was the beginning of a new phase in their lives and in their painting.

Winifred felt a special affinity with the light and colour of her native Cumbrian landscape. In her best work one feels she is pushing the frontiers of what can be perceived ever further back, to reveal a spiritual world. Her desire to express the numinous behind the material was intensified by her faith in Christian Science to which she held firmly from the mid-1920s to the end of her life. Its insistence on the spiritual reality behind material appearances had a significant and lasting effect on Ben's outlook too. Not that he ever subscribed to Christian Science unconditionally. As with the painting he admired, he took from it only what suited his purpose, which was to paint the living reality inside of things.

Closely allied with this wish to objectify the pure essence of what he saw was his love for immediacy and directness of execution. From his father Ben had inherited a freshness of perception, a visual appetite, such that he could see a jug, a cup or a horse in a field as if for the first time, and convey his delight in its singularity by a painting or drawing. This childlike wonder was liable, in the long process of making a painting, to become self-conscious and so lapse into the knowingly childish, but it was nonetheless a fundamental part of his creative impulse: as in his father, a streak of childishness coexisted with elegance and sophistication. The challenge was to integrate this appealing naivety with a fastidious care for the design and physical texture of a painting.

It was not only the childlike vision that inclined Nicholson towards the consciously naive (a stylistic trait that recurs throughout his work, right up to his latest

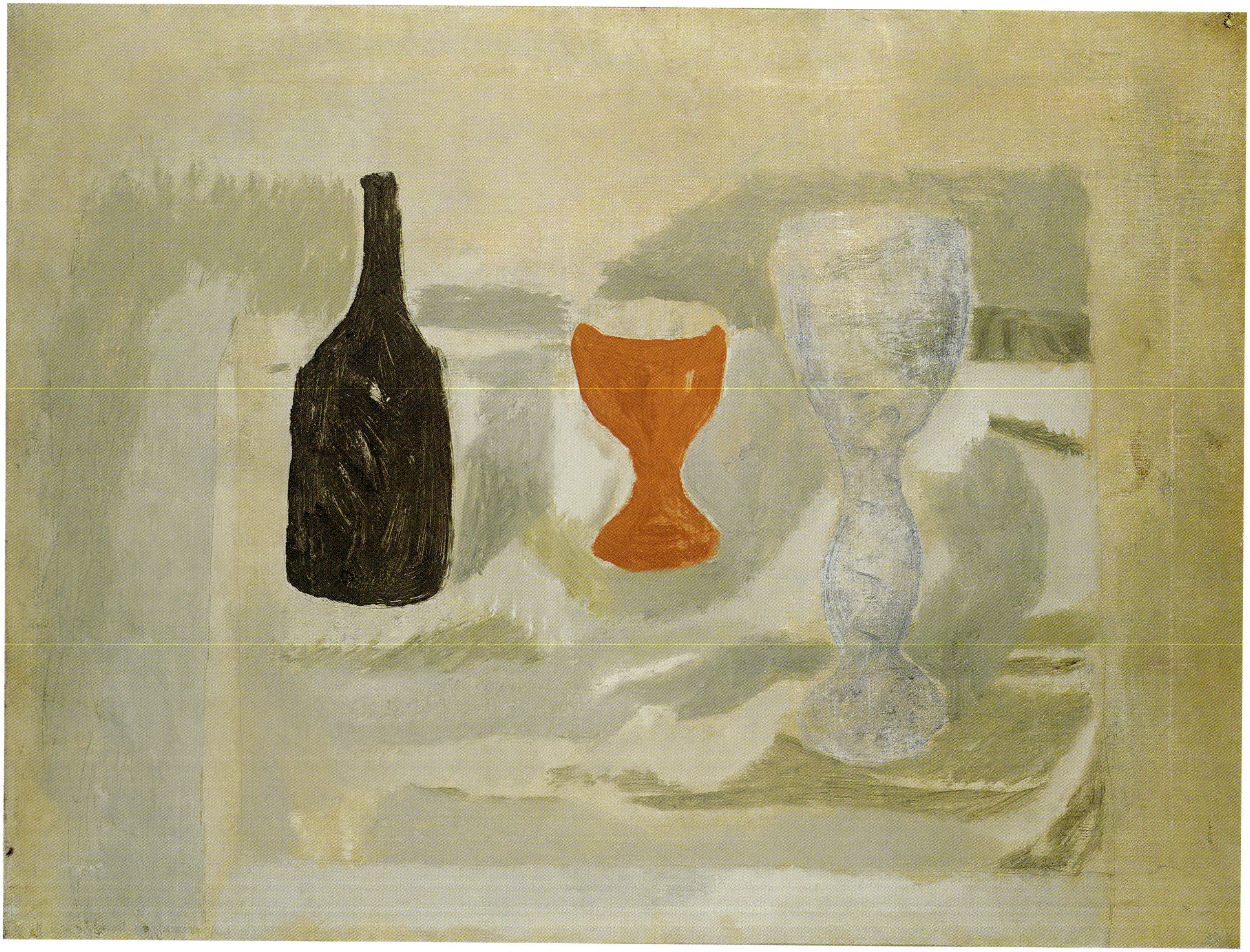

7 *1925 (still life, bottle and goblets)*
oil on canvas
55.5 × 76.5 cm (21¾ × 30¼ in)

drawings). There was, outside himself, a historical influence too – the subjective revolution in art which, in the last quarter of the nineteenth century, had increasingly forced every serious artist to question first principles, to become a child, a primitive, and slowly create his own language. This in turn was part of a larger reaction against the weight of tradition and the complexities of European civilization in favour of an invigorating mixture of the primitive, the exotic and the childlike. On their honeymoon in Italy, and later in the Louvre, it was the Italian Primitives that Ben and Winifred sought out. At the same time they were attracted to the poetic naivety of Henri Rousseau's paintings of Paris and its suburbs, and equally to African sculpture, to St Francis and to Tibet.[32] Some of these enthusiasms would have been confirmed, if not originally inspired, by reading Roger Fry's *Vision and Design* early in

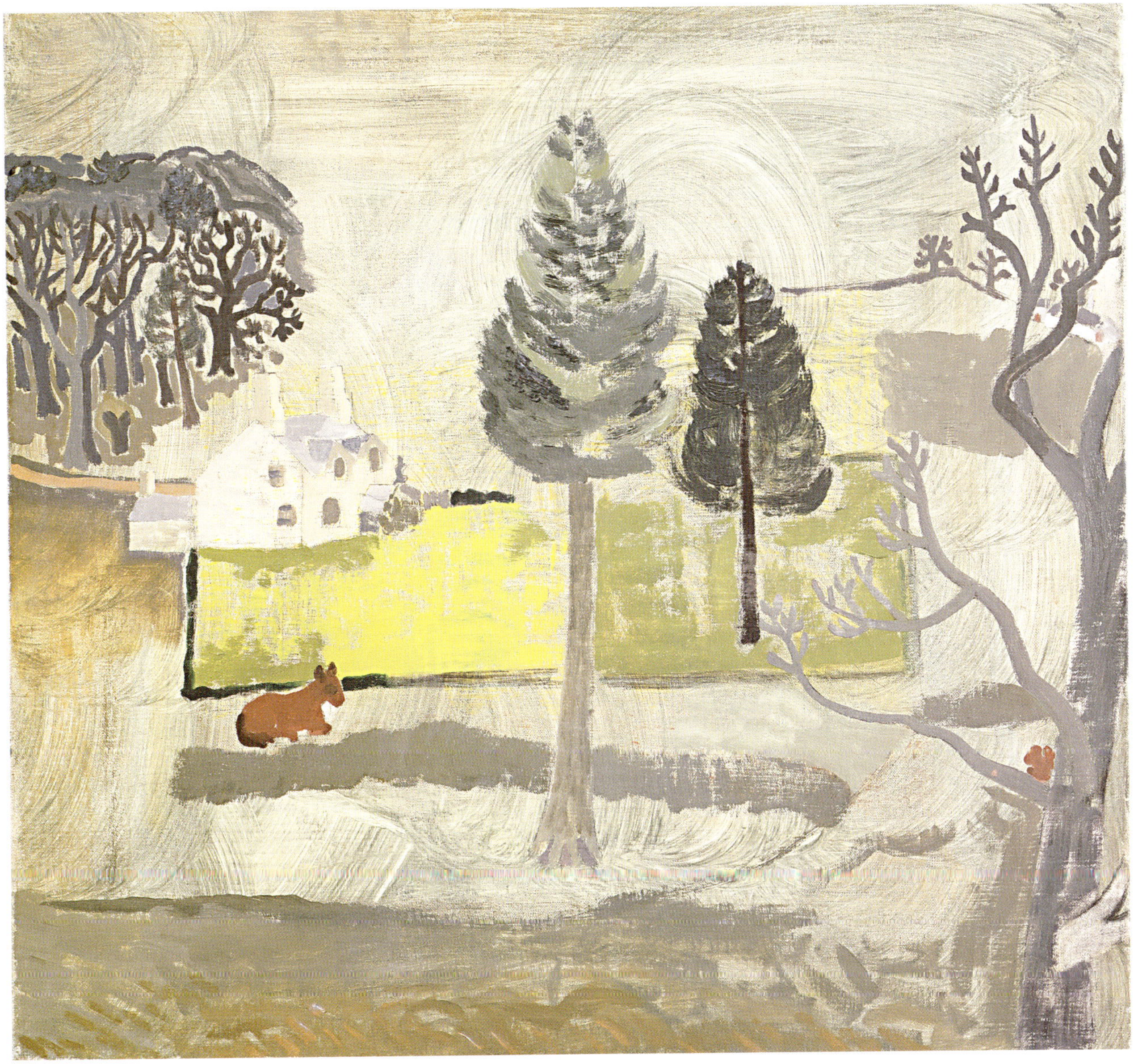

8 *1928 (Walton Wood cottage, no.1)*
oil on canvas
56 × 61 cm (22 × 24 in)

1922. In these essays, first published between 1901 and 1920, Fry lays special emphasis on the formal element in painting, partly as a corrective to the symbolic, the anecdotal and the slickly representational which, in English painting, had come to predominate, partly in an attempt to embrace non-European art within one universal aesthetic theory. To the Nicholsons, and to all their contemporaries with a live interest in art, Fry's persuasive arguments were a stimulus visual, intellectual and creative.

Doubtless his ideas were in the air, if not actually discussed, when Ivon Hitchens came to Banks Head for a two-month stay early in 1925. Hitchens, like Winifred Nicholson, was a natural colourist, but he was also concerned with the more abstract principles of rhythm and formal structure. Like Ben, he was still coming to terms with Cézanne. All three were united in their rejection of the outworn teachings of the art schools and in their realization of the need to begin again at the beginning. Only then would they be in a position to understand and absorb contemporary artistic developments across the Channel.

For Ben sophisticated naivety was the necessary first step in slowly building up a personal language which would eventually go beyond the *faux-naïf* and, by an ever
8 greater refinement of complexity, regain the 'simple'. In *Walton Wood cottage, no.1*, which he painted in spring 1928, the swift execution is one facet of his deliberate primitivism. The perspective created by the trees – one in the foreground, one in the middle ground – is contradicted by the two rectangular paddocks in the centre of the picture, tilted up in approved Cubist fashion to emphasize the picture plane and in turn contradicted by the lie of the white cottage. If there is naivety, it consists in these engagingly awkward juxtapositions and in the childish rendering of the red pony (characteristic of Nicholson's animals at all periods of his work). But however much an expression of the child in him, it is a knowing playfulness, baffling for the critics who could not understand that this apparently wilful mixture of the childlike with the sophisticated was a way of achieving immediacy in his painting and purging it of dead convention.[33] In the same spirit and at the same time his brother-in-law, Robert Graves, was taking a keen interest in nursery rhymes, claiming, in his enthusiasm, that 'the best of the older ones are nearer to poetry than the greater part of the *Oxford Book of English Verse*'.[34]

In August 1928 the Nicholsons stayed with friends at Feock, on the Falmouth estuary in Cornwall. They were joined there by Christopher Wood who, earlier in the year, had spent an inspirational few weeks painting with them at Banks Head. Now they explored together that 'Sleeping Beauty's countryside of southern foliage,
10 sheltered creeks and wide expanse of placid water'.[35] Nicholson's moonlit evocation of the nearby Pill Creek is as remarkable for the technique involved in its making as for its atmosphere of poetry and mystery. The effect of moonlight reflected on the water and peeping through the trees is produced by scraping the thin covering of paint back to the gesso ground – a favourite device for achieving variety of texture and the weathered effect, as of a time-worn object, which he sought. Noteworthy also is the amount of pencil in the rendering of the trees, forest floor and sketchy flight of steps down to the shore. The painting is saved from prettiness by animated, and animating, brush marks of thin paint sweeping up through the forest and up from the foreground towards the ghostly sailing boat in the creek. As so often in his future work, culminating in the late reliefs, Nicholson is at his best working within a limited range of colour, preferring instead to exploit surface texture and tonality.

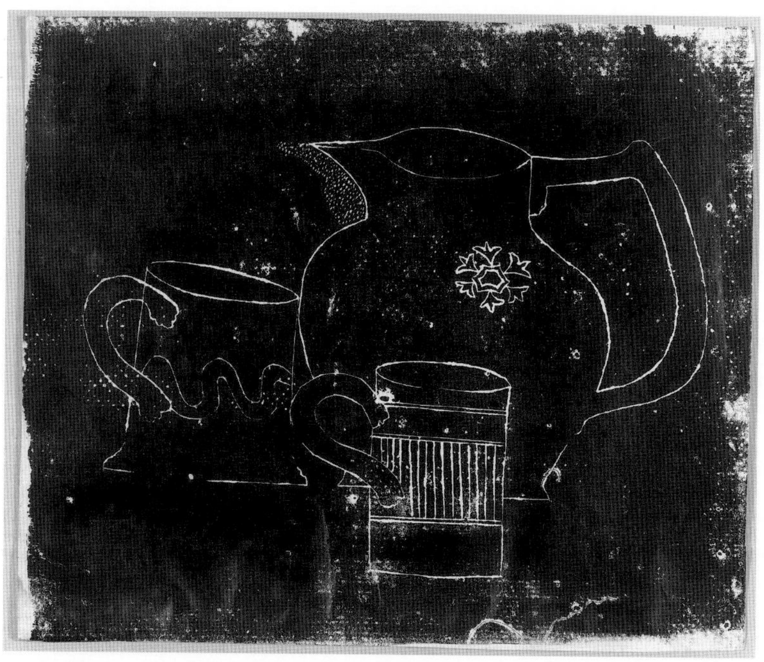

Later that August Wood and Nicholson went over to St Ives for a day's outing. Wood had painted there in 1926 but this was Nicholson's first visit. He later recalled:

That day's visit from Pill Creek (Truro) in a hired open Ford —— we left this in St Ives with its driver at once and went all over & around St Ives drawing & agreed to meet some hours later. The place in those days was comparatively unspoilt & v. dramatic (especially coming from the sleepy Falmouth creek). Really I suppose my desire was to record as many
11 impressions as rapidly as possible in that time & prob. on odd sheets of paper or v. small sketch book. I remember trying to draw a large ship in full sail with the aid of a telescope ... most difficult bec. one had to find the ship between each pencil stroke ... This was an exciting day, for not only was it the first time I saw St Ives, but on the way back from Porthmeor Beach we passed an open door in Back Road West and through it saw some paintings of ships and houses on odd pieces of paper and cardboard nailed up all over the wall, with particularly large nails through the smallest ones. We knocked on the door and inside found Wallis.[36]

Alfred Wallis was a seventy-three-year-old retired fisherman who, since his wife's death, had taken up painting, 'for company' as he said. His subjects were scenes from his early life at sea as well as the streets, the harbour and the surrounding country of St Ives.

He would cut out the top and bottom of an old cardboard box, and sometimes the four sides, into irregular shapes, using each shape as the key to the movement in a painting, and using the colour and texture of the board as the key to its colour and texture. When the painting was completed, what remained of the original board, a brown, a grey, a white or a green board, sometimes in the sky, sometimes in the sea, or perhaps in a field or a lighthouse, would be as deeply experienced as the remainder of the painting. He used very few colours, and one associates with him some lovely dark browns, shiny blacks, fierce greys, strange whites and a particularly pungent Cornish green.[37]

Clearly Wallis appealed to Nicholson's romantic (and modern) valuation of the primitive and childlike. But more specifically he was excited by Wallis's ability to make his pictures come alive, partly by the sheer intensity of his feeling, partly by his method of working, which allowed the material make-up of the painting to be undisguised yet, through the viewer's eye, to be transformed into a vivid experience. This confirmed Nicholson in his tendency to stress in his own paintings the process of their making, so that they should be artefacts to be appreciated for themselves as much as for whatever they might refer to outside themselves. The balance between these two demands would shift dramatically in the next few years.

The impact of Alfred Wallis on Nicholson was not evident in a change of style but in this confirmation, just when he was open to it, of an outlook and practice he had already adopted (unlikely though Wallis's bits of painted cardboard may seem as a reinforcement of Picasso's *tableaux-objets*). Just as importantly, Wallis's pictures exemplified that imaginative freedom to which Nicholson aspired. He never lost his enthusiasm for Wallis's work (as he did eventually for Christopher Wood's), and in later years he was instrumental in preserving and promoting it.

← 9 *c.1928 (jug with two mugs)*
linocut
28 × 32 cm (11 × 12¾ in)

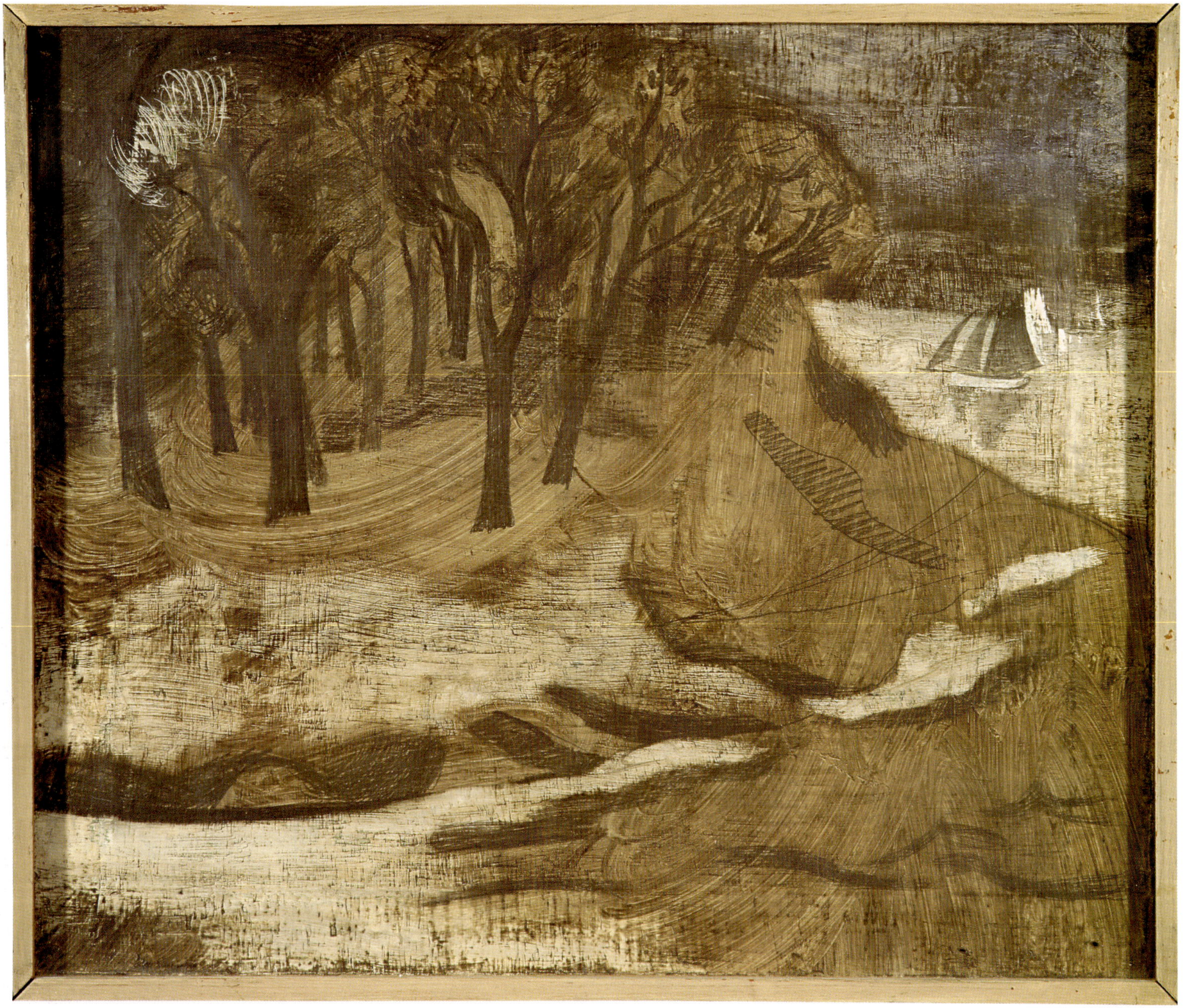

10 *1928 (Pill Creek, Cornwall)*
oil, gesso and pencil on canvas
49 × 61 cm (19 × 24 in)

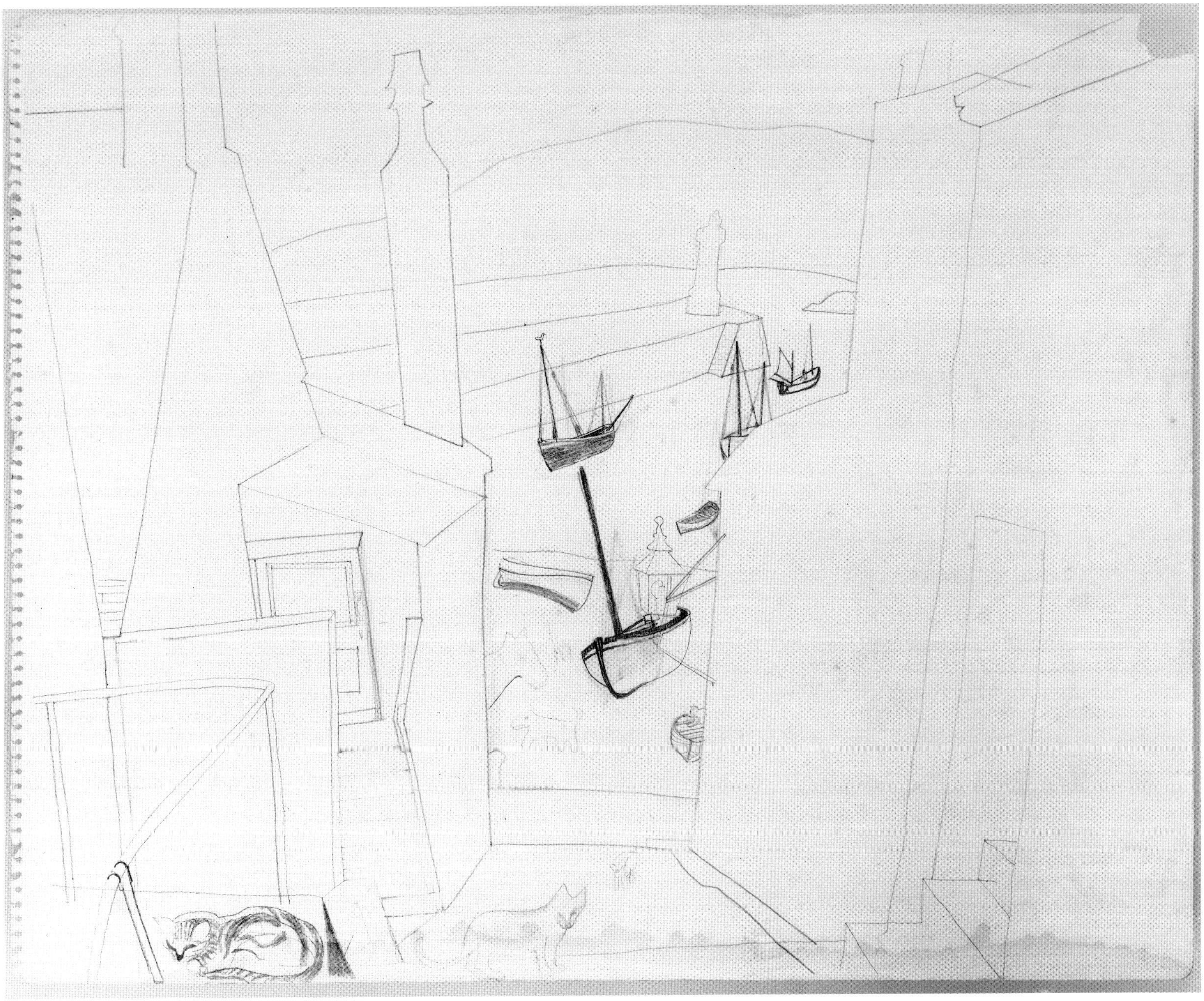

11 *August 1928 (St Ives)*
pencil on paper
33 × 42 cm (13 × 16½ in)

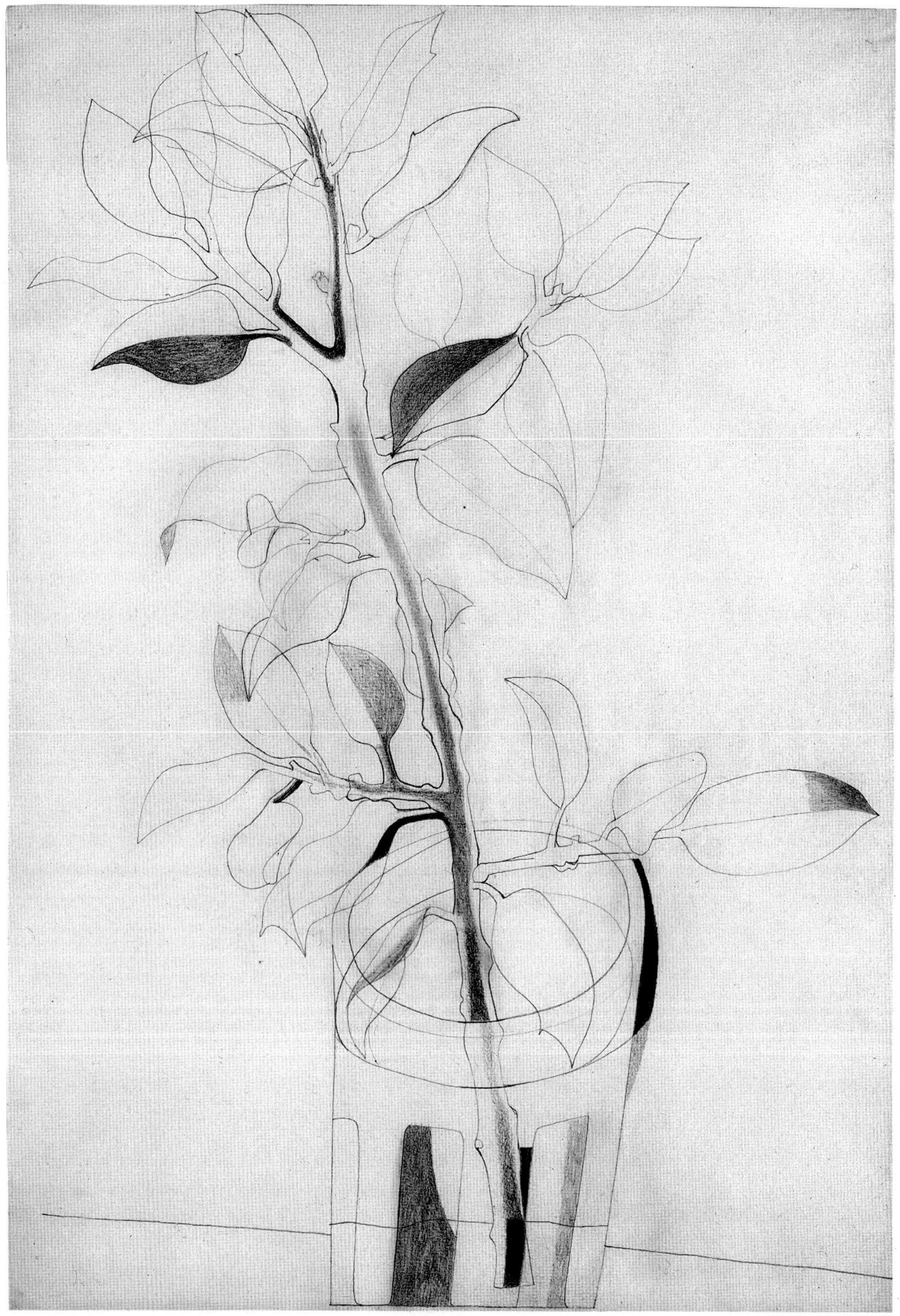

12 *c.1928 (camellia)*
pencil on paper
50.5 × 35 cm (19¾ × 13¾ in)

Already for some years Ben had spent long periods in London by himself, working in a studio in the King's Road, while Winifred remained where she felt happiest, in Cumberland. In truth it is hard to imagine how Ben could have been content to stay indefinitely in a place so out of touch with ideas, people and events in the art world. That he continued so long with his brand of nicely judged primitivism shows how strongly he must still have felt the need to break with the past – his rebellious attitude

seems manifest in the vigorous brushwork of his 'blunderbusts' as he called them – but by 1931 he had surely exhausted that vein. Looking at one of the best of the
13 Cumbrian landscapes, *1930 (Birch Craig, winter)*, we may take stock of what by now have become Nicholson hallmarks: the abraded priming in some places showing through, in others covered with thinly diluted paint, to suggest depth and give variety of texture; the use of blue in a non-naturalistic way to evoke the cold of winter; conventional perspective subverted to gain immediacy; the use of buildings, deftly readjusted, to animate and articulate the landscape: the dovetailed facets of grey and off-white culminating in a triangle of pure white from which the eye rebounds to the nursery horse embossed on the hillside, then out to explore the rest of the picture. There is no attempt to conceal the fact that this is an object made of paint and canvas, materials at the service of poetic evocation, not descriptive illusionism.

Yet for all their subtlety of tone and texture and space composition, these landscapes are still gestures of revolt. Once the preliminary ploy of self-conscious naivety had served the purpose of overturning accepted attitudes and techniques, it was time to go forward and forge a new, more fully personal language on the basis of what Cézanne and Cubism had revealed.

In this Winifred could not give Ben the support and single-minded comradeship he needed. Like Kit Wood (to whom she had become close before his self-inflicted death in 1930), she remained largely unaffected by the discoveries of Cubism, and in a letter written almost forty years later Ben is still taking her to task for this: 'What was really the point of Cézanne tipping that fruit bowl, if the early Cubists who came out of this 'discovery' were to be ignored by others who came after them? The whole contemporary movement in painting surely grew out of this – Of course it takes us into a different world – but why not – we can't stand still however nicely we do so?' Winifred, in her reply, protests: 'Colour, light, the interplay of the seven rainbow hues so that they create light – so that the picture becomes a lamp – a luminosity – a transparent entity – something so exciting that I for one have no time to bother about how the great masters play with space, shapes, with measurement and their balances.'[38] Which perhaps merely reflects the two artists' different gifts, temperaments, aims: Winifred, swift and direct, trying to capture the freshness of things seen and, through colour and light, to transfigure them; Ben, slow and painstaking, gradually eliciting an inner vision and adjusting the painting in terms of its own aesthetic demands. Witness another telling comment by Ben on Winifred's painting: 'About construction – NOTHING EXISTS – without this. I much admire your inspired flights of imagination but unless they have structure they do not fulfil themselves – as I see it.'[39]

These differences were certainly not such as to bring about a complete rupture, though a gradual estrangement led to Ben's departure from Banks Head in the autumn of 1931. Until their divorce in 1938 Ben regularly saw Winifred and their three young children – Jake, Kate and Andrew – and they exchanged letters and ideas about painting right up to Winifred's death fifty years later, in 1981. But the only permanent tie Nicholson acknowledged was with his work.

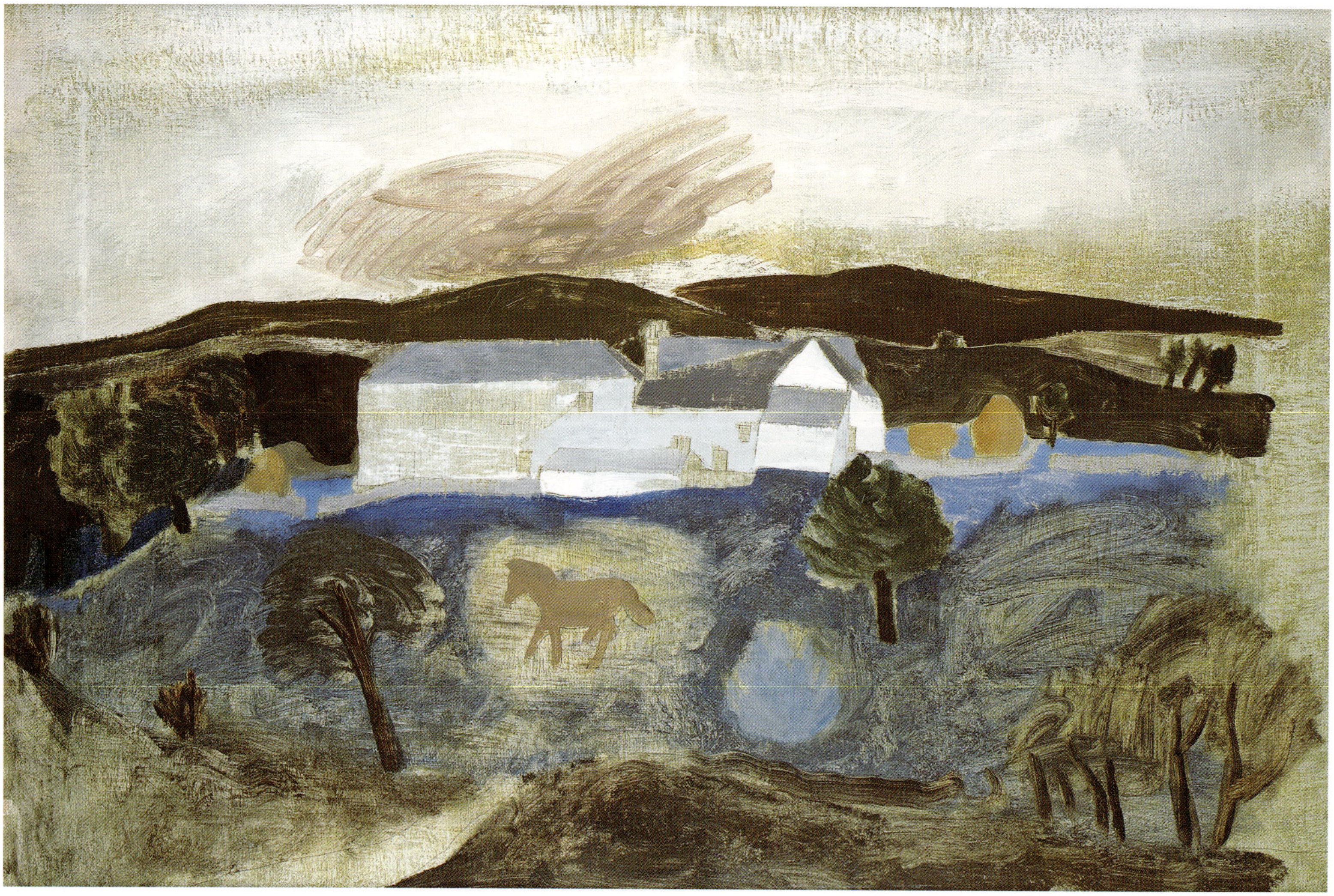

It was probably in April 1931 at the Bloomsbury Gallery, where he was showing thirty-four of his paintings and she one of her sculptures, that Ben Nicholson and Barbara Hepworth first met. She had already seen, and been excited by, his work early that year at an exhibition of the *Seven and Five Society*,[40] and in September she invited him, as one of a party of friends which included Henry and Irina Moore and Ivon Hitchens, for a fortnight's holiday in a farmhouse she had rented at Happisburgh on the Norfolk coast. By the end of November he had found rooms in Hampstead, close to where Hepworth was living (having by now parted from her husband, John Skeaping), and from March 1932 he had begun to live and work with her in her studio, at first for short spells only, interspersed with brief visits to Winifred and the children in the unrealistic expectation that they would accommodate themselves to his new relationship with Hepworth.

In June he was writing to Helen Sutherland about an exhibition he was planning to share with Hepworth at Tooth's Gallery in November: 'It is going to be very exciting the show because each carving has its 2 or 3 ptgs which were done at the same

13 *1930 (Birch Craig, winter)*
oil on canvas
61 × 91.5 cm (24 × 36 in)

→ 14 *1932 (girl in mirror)*
pencil on paper
38 × 31 cm (15 × 12¼ in)

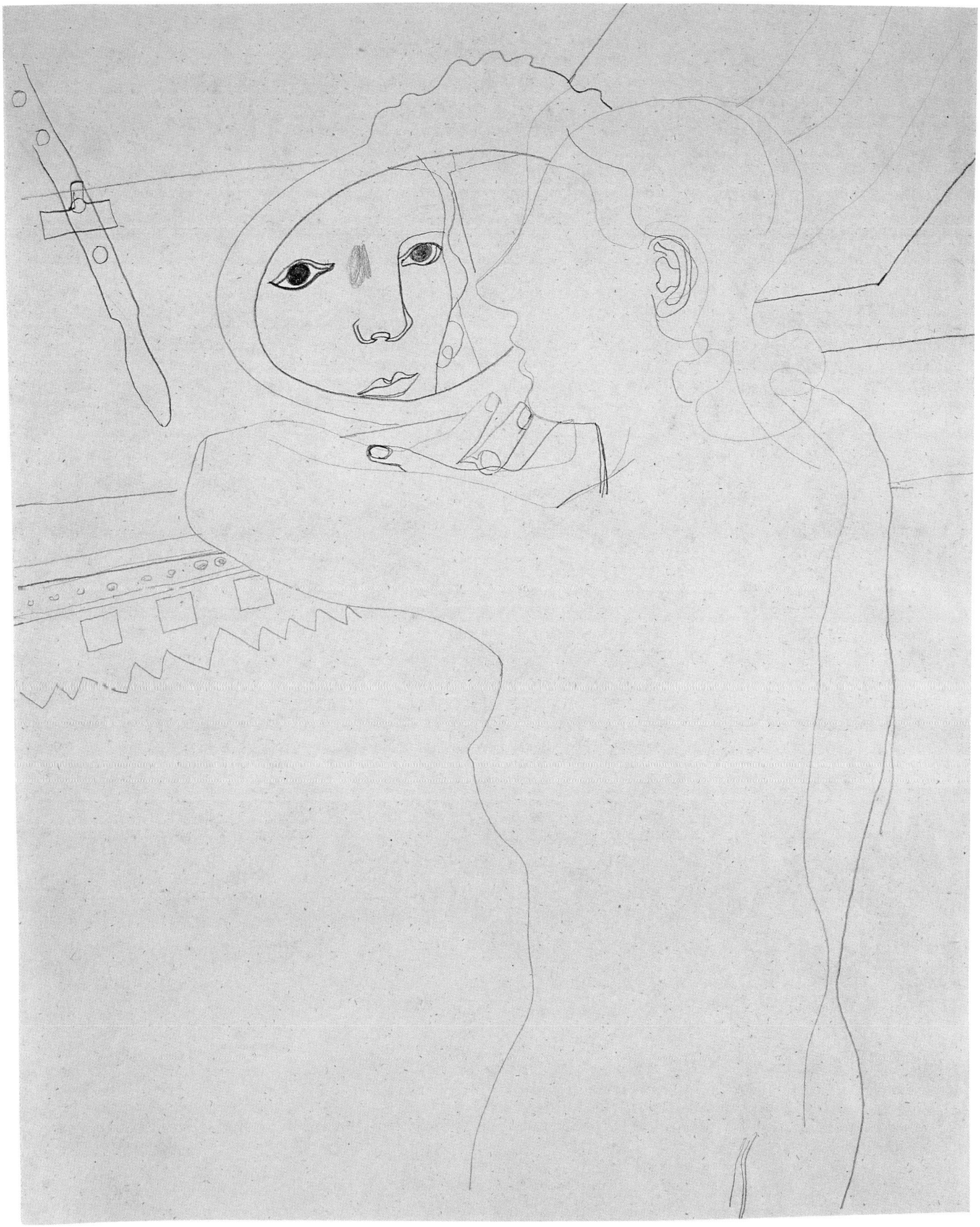

15 time, & the connection is very close. The big picture [*ie Profile – Venetian red*] has a most lovely dark rosewood carving [*ie* Hepworth's *Kneeling Figure*] that goes with it – & each comes most beautifully to life with the other.'[41] *1932 (profile – Venetian red)*, even apart from its large dimensions, is a painting of monumental beauty. In its compositional structure of bold, rectangular blocks, it has links with the primitive reliefs made thirty years later, in its colour and textures too. A five-inch band of canvas has been cut away at the bottom, and the backing board painted a cool, dark green – perfect complement to the rich browns, spotted creamy greys and Venetian red above it – with a border of pale dots marking the former presence of tacks. The combination of refinement and deliberate lack of finish, of subtle judgement and insouciance, are quintessential Nicholson. It is left to us to ponder the relationship of the objects on the upturned table-top: the ghostly white sculptural profile; the mug hitched up to it, so that its handle cheekily echoes the throat (or the bosom, if you reverse the profile) of the delicately pencilled silhouette; and the 'moon jug' making one of its earliest appearances in a work by Nicholson, still to be a source of inspiration almost fifty years later. Leaving the handle of this jug to play its game of hide-and-seek, one is drawn to the magical luminosity of the area to the left of the mug, where layers of paint have been partially scraped back to the ground, producing an effect of patina. Nicholson liked to scrape down a previously painted canvas to provide a rich ground for a new painting. The grain of the canvas and the colours and textures that remain after the scraping have their own beauty and 'atmosphere' which influence the choices he makes as he works towards expressing his idea.

It was the effect of patina or decaying fresco in Nicholson's paintings of the early 1930s that first intrigued and attracted John Summerson, the architectural historian, who was later to write an incisive essay on Nicholson in the Penguin Modern Painters series; and Paul Nash, reviewing the 1932 exhibition, noted how Hepworth's sculpture also assumed a weathered, time-worn appearance.[42] This shared concern for texture was part of a more profound similarity between the paintings and the sculpture: the quality they both had of self-consistent objects whose meaning and beauty stood in no need of outside reference or validation.

The excitement of discovery as he worked together with Hepworth was still fresh in Nicholson's memory over thirty years later: 'I remember the feeling of vitality in no.3 at that time was terrific – you could almost *touch* it. One felt that if it escaped out of the window it could cover all London.'[43]

Winifred too played an important part in this ferment. She had moved to Paris with the children in the autumn of 1932 and taken a flat overlooking the Seine, where they spent half of every year (the other half in Cumberland) until their permanent return to England in 1938. Ben went over to see his family in December 1932, the first of many visits to Paris during the next four years, which provided the stimulus that London could not give. Through her friends, among whom were Braque, Giacometti, Arp, Hélion, Calder, Mondrian and Brancusi, Winifred provided a vital link with the Parisian art world (backed up by Ben's membership in

→ 15 *1932 (profile – Venetian red)*
oil and pencil on canvas mounted on board
120 × 88 cm (47¼ × 34½ in)

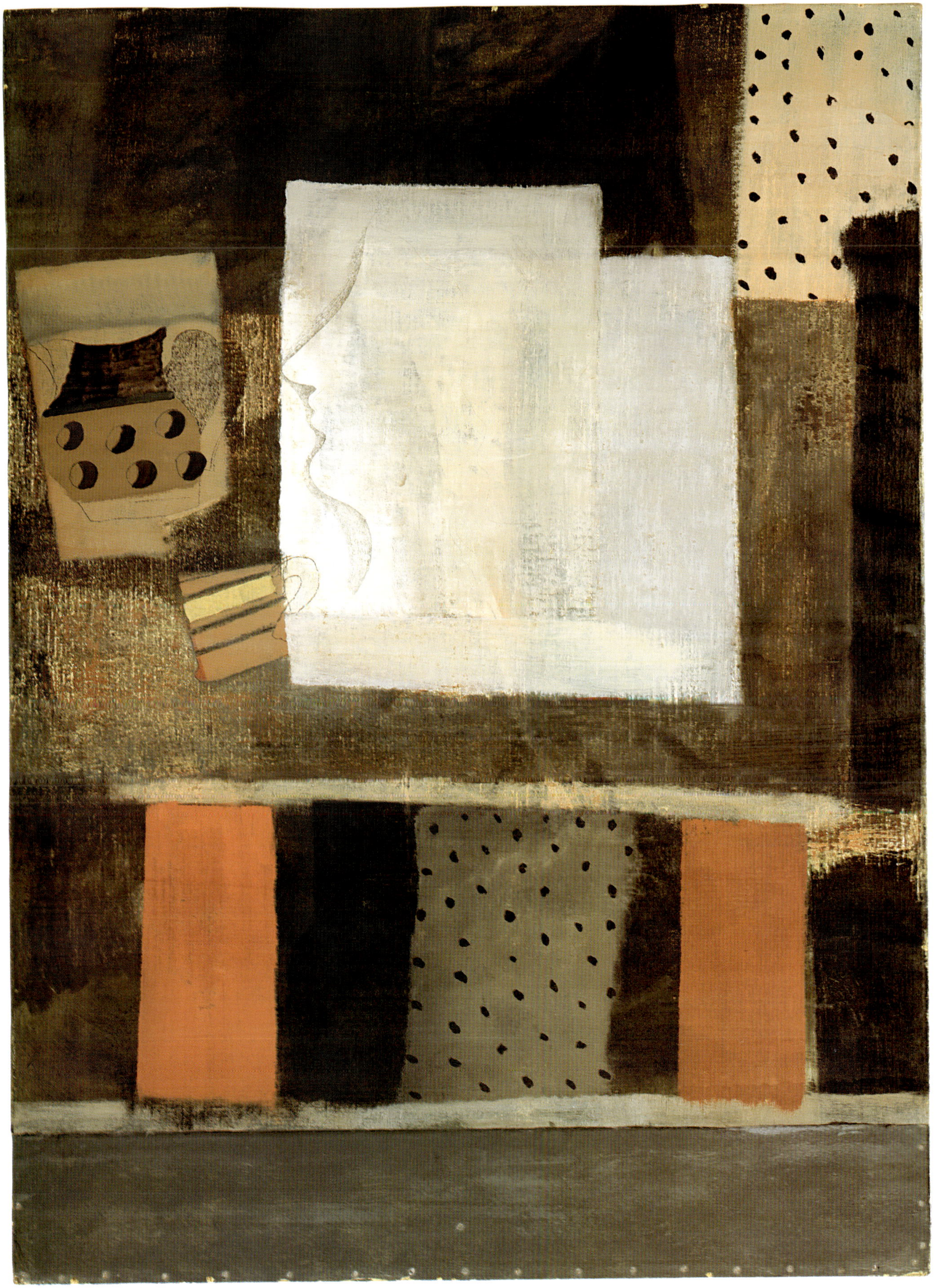

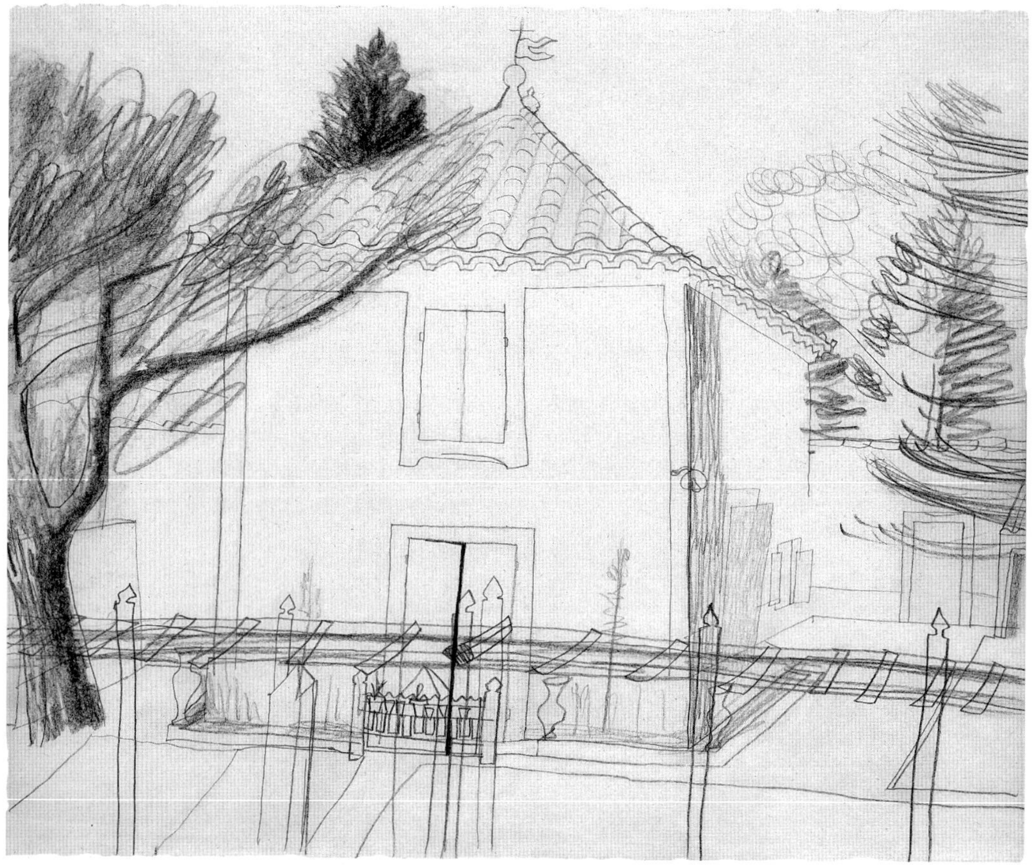

16 *1933 (Café Robinson, St Rémy)*
pencil on paper
30.5 × 38 cm (12 × 15 in)

1933–4 of the *Association 'Abstraction-Création'*, a large and indiscriminate grouping of non-figurative artists). For his longer stays of about a month, she would find Ben a studio in the *quartier* so that he could continue to work out his ideas even when away from London.

In the course of 1933 Nicholson, like an ever-quickening vortex, sucked in a number of influences which, combined and transformed, would propel him towards the radical new synthesis of the white reliefs early in the following year. There was the shock of an abstract painting by Miró – 'it was the first *free* painting that I saw & it made a deep impression – as I remember it a lovely rough circular white cloud on a deep blue background with an electric black line somewhere. One can only accept what one is ready for & *this* I was ready for.'[44] It showed Nicholson the way to free himself entirely from the restriction of copying appearances and instead to create purely in terms of colour and form.

The influence of Miró is evident in a number of works that Nicholson executed in 1933 – paintings, rug designs, painted boxes and linocuts – and briefly supplants the equally obvious debt to Picasso and Braque visible in the works of 1932–3. Take,
17 for instance, *1933 (still life, Mediterranean)*. On a small board Nicholson has first laid a gesso ground, then brushed over it a second ground of oil paint, which he has partially scraped down so as to simulate the weathered character of a natural object.

He has revealed the white jug by scraping back to the gesso ground, while indicating only the outline of its handle by drawing with a sharp point that pierces through the paint to the white gesso below. One might almost overlook the ghost of a mug, schematically outlined in the same way, to the right of the jug. The surface of the painting is enlivened by a network of calligraphic lines, some incised as far as the gesso, and so white, others drawn into the paint, and so black. Beyond the horizontal window-ledge, towards the top of the painting, an outline of hills is scratched in. The technique of incising the paint surface to produce outlines in gesso was learnt from Braque, but the main influence here is Miró, apparent in the 'automatic', space-creating lines and, more especially, in the black 'eye' on the spout of the jug (palely echoed by the white 'eye' on the mug) – elements which prompted Nicholson later to refer to the jug as 'surrealist'.

18 The Miróesque circles recur in *1934 (still life, birdie)* where a sculptural goblet, with a beak and an eye, takes on the personality of a bird. Here Nicholson has scraped down the paint surface on the canvas so that it looks like a peeling fresco, and used the still life as a springboard for a free exploration of colour and shape, line and plane. We are witnessing that shift from the particular to the universal which, taken a stage further, resulted in the white reliefs of the same year.

Miró's free-floating forms had had an influence on Alexander Calder's invention of the free-moving mobile in the previous year, 1932. When, at the end of 1933, Nicholson first saw a Calder mobile, he was entranced by its playful, poetic, seemingly free movement, and just such a movement can be felt in some of his best drawings made at a later date. Similarly, the moving shadows cast by the swing and swerve of the mobile were soon to find their counterpart in the effect of changing light over the shallow recesses of Nicholson's carved reliefs. He must also have felt in close sympathy with Calder's practical approach – his complete mastery of his materials and imaginative understanding of their potential.

A further influence (also noticeable in Hepworth's work) in that year of transition, 1933, was Arp. Not his reliefs, as one might hastily conclude in view of Nicholson's imminent discovery of that medium, but the sculpture in the round which Arp had only begun to make in 1930. Nicholson made this clear in a letter he wrote to Herbert Read in 1962:

> I don't think Arp's reliefs had any influence on mine – mine came about by accident & bec. of Barbara's sculptor's tools lying around. But Arp's *free sculptural forms* did have an indirect influence – there was a free poetry in these which H[enry] M[oore]'s & B[arbara] H[epworth]'s work lacked at that time – the same freedom was in Paris in Calder's earlier mobiles & Miró's of about '24–26 work – but *direct* influence came only from these [latter]. Arp's reliefs come from some almost literary poetic idea & for this reason he could conceive them & then have someone else carving them out? Mine come about bec. of a passion for working with my hands. It's an exact opposite approach I suppose.'[45]

There is indeed a radical difference between Arp's reliefs, which are assemblages made up of biomorphic shapes superimposed on a base, and Nicholson's, whose geometrical shapes are carved out of the base. But when, in December 1933,

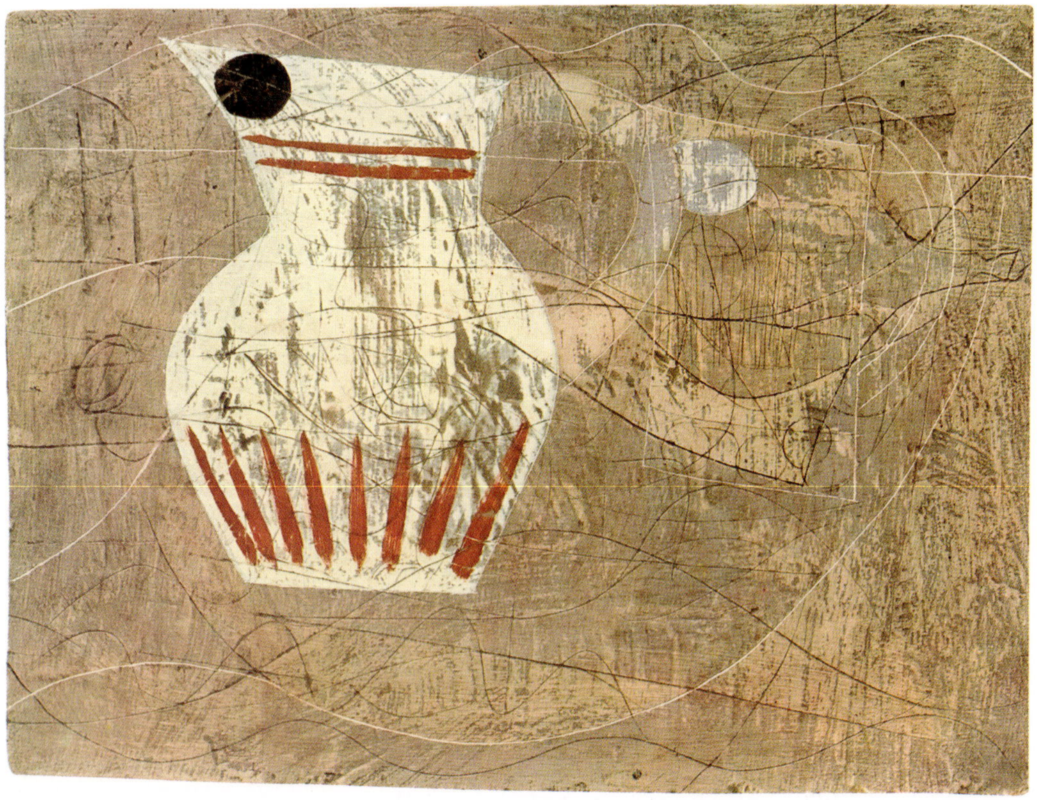

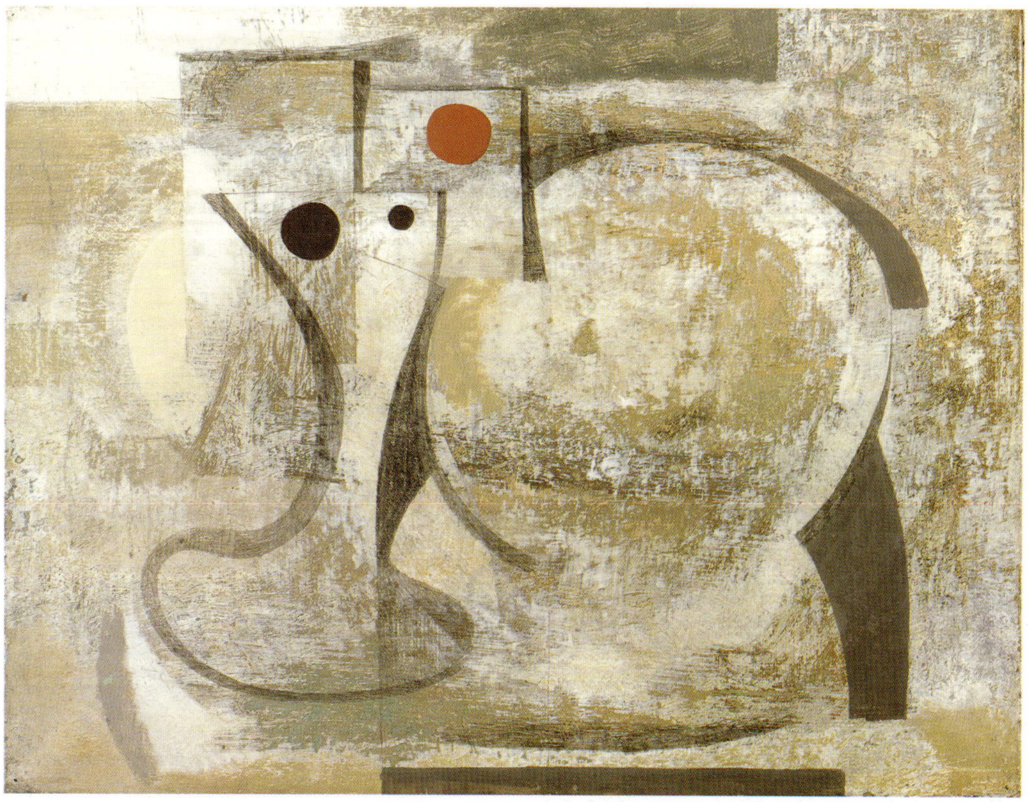

17 *1933 (still life, Mediterranean)*
oil and gesso on board
28 × 39.5 cm (11 × 15½ in)

18 *1934 (still life, birdie)*
oil and pencil on canvas
46 × 61 cm (18 × 24 in)

→ 19 *December 1933 (first completed relief)*
oil on carved board
54.5 × 25.5 cm (21½ × 10 in)

→ 20 *1934 (relief)*
oil on carved board
10 × 10 cm (4 × 4 in)

Nicholson first cut rough circles within rough rectangles, he may have had at the back of his mind Arp's *Constellation*, a *papier collé* of egg shapes within quadrilaterals, dating from 1922/3. It had been illustrated in *Cahiers d'Art*, 1931, and he had cut it out and pasted it into a scrapbook.

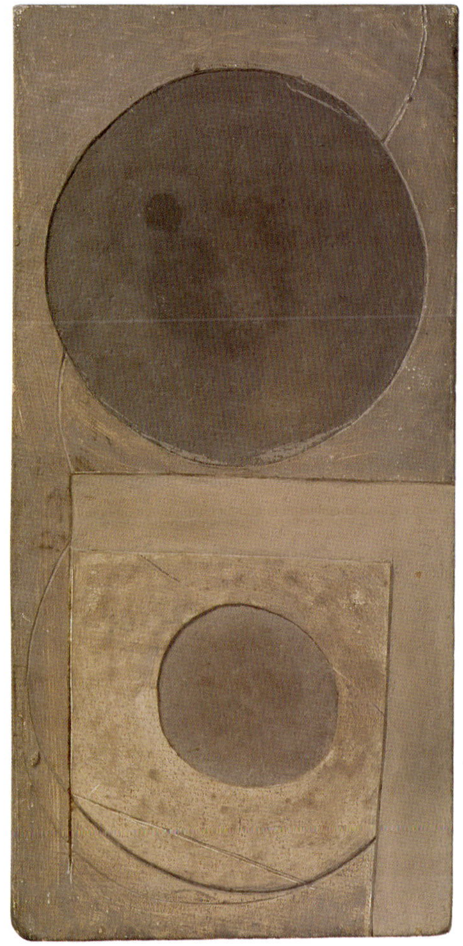

19 It was in Paris that he carved this first relief, out of a thin board which he had brought with him from London. He later claimed that this had come about by chance, when a small chip of gesso between two incised lines fell off,[46] but it would be truer to see in this 'accident' the natural outcome of several tendencies combined. First, there was his practice of scraping the paint and incising the gesso ground on his canvases and boards, from which it was a short step to carving the board itself.[47] Then there was his passion for working with his hands (he had often made, and sometimes carved, his own frames) and the inspiration he got from working the material. His turning to the carved relief was also a logical development from the painting of overlapping planes in shallow space which he had adopted from Cubism. And not least of the influences was the presence, often in the same studio, of Barbara Hepworth and, more generally, her way of seeing things in terms of sculptural form. As with Winifred in the 1920s the mutual give and take between him and Barbara was as enriching as it is impossible to analyse.

In a broader perspective Nicholson's painted reliefs can be seen as part of the interesting interplay between sculpture and painting engendered by Cubism. But his move towards carving emphatically did not come from a desire for greater immediacy than a two-dimensional surface could offer: he was always more interested in two-dimensional space relations with shallow recession. The act of carving helped him to create something alive, giving a direct experience of reality and existing in its own right, but he had no wish to exchange the conventions of painting for those of sculpture.[48]

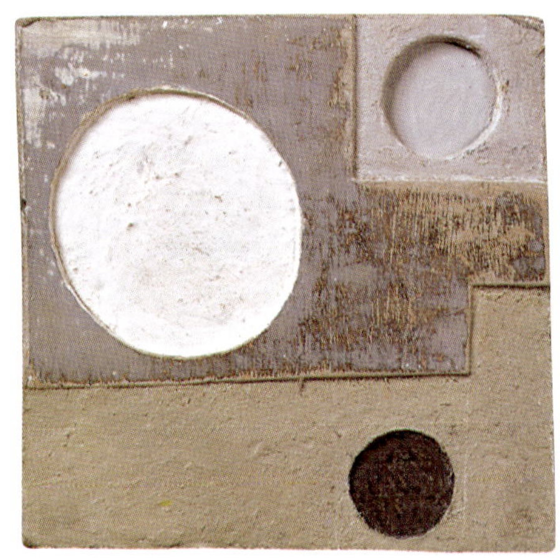

By February 1934 Nicholson had made his first white relief. The freely drawn circles, earthy colours and rough-textured surfaces of his previous experiments in carving now gave place to truer circles and rectangles, saturated in white, so as to make an altogether more powerful impact. Miró's freely floating, anarchic circle had been only a starting-point: it was now transformed into something serene, subtle and severe, with a transcendent dimension that brings to mind not Miró but Malevich. To the Russian Naum Gabo this connexion seemed obvious – the all-white painting,
22 the circle in the square – and if one looks at Nicholson's *1935 (painting)*, it is hard not to think of Malevich's *Fundamental Suprematist Element* of 1913. Yet, at the time, Nicholson, though he acknowledged Malevich as 'a considerable force', had never actually seen one of his paintings and denied any but the most indirect influence.[49] In fact it was to Winifred that he expressed a debt in developing his idea of the circle,[50] and though he did not particularize, he almost certainly meant her intuitive understanding of the poetic and spiritual connotations of the timeless circle, suggesting calm, wholeness and unity. She would also have been in sympathy with his use of white to convey a sense of the universal, the infinite – of purity, silence, serenity – as well as to harmonize the dynamic tension between circle and square or

rectangle.[51] Here again the original influence may have been the white of Arp's sculpture and reliefs, which Nicholson then turned to his own expressive ends.

An indication of the imaginative context of the white reliefs may be found in the statement Nicholson provided for the book that accompanied the group exhibition *Unit One* in 1934.[52] He begins by quoting the opinion of the Cambridge astrophysicist, A. S. Eddington, that scientific investigation is inadequate for explaining the nature of the universe we live in and that our only means to do so must be something like religious experience.[53] He then continues: 'As I see it, painting and religious experience are the same thing, and what we are all searching for is the understanding and realisation of infinity – an idea which is complete, with no beginning, no end, and therefore giving to all things for all time. . . . Painting and carving is one means of searching after this reality.'[54] One might object that, though the artist's imaginative, aesthetic experience is akin to the participative basis of religious experience, the two cannot simply be equated, religious experience being altogether a more complex thing. But one should not expect from Nicholson a rigorous philosophical statement. He was content to find his intuitions confirmed, whether by Eddy or by Eddington, and at no time felt the need for metaphysical theory to underpin his practice. What is important is his belief that the principal aim of the artist is to discover and somehow communicate a part of that reality which lies beyond the phenomenal world.[55] Given the immaterial nature of reality, it was a logical consequence that some of his works should dispense with any reference to the material world. Inspired by Miró, he had made non-referential paintings in 1933. The white reliefs were a further, purer development of these. As Herbert Read wrote at the time, 'Ben Nicholson . . . who is something of a mystic, believes that there is a reality underlying appearances, and that it is his business, by giving material form to his intuition of it, to express the essential nature of this reality.'[56] This might be said of all good painters, but in Nicholson's work the degree to which the inner reality effaces the outer is extreme, and raises the question of how far the art of painting can afford to dispense with the particular appearance of things. Is there not a danger in wanting to include so much that one may seem to include too little? Such fundamental questions about abstract art continue to be asked, even by those who admire individual examples of it, and we shall have to address them later.

Predictably, the first reaction to the white reliefs was bafflement, if not worse (and, to be fair, a white relief in a mixed exhibition of paintings must have given quite a shock). Geoffrey Grigson, later a friend of Nicholson and admirer of his work, voiced the opinion of the more moderate critics when he described the reliefs as 'admirable in technical qualities, in taste, in severe self-expurgation, but too much "art itself", floating and disinfected'.[57] In calling for 'a more varied affective and intellective content', he was making a general criticism of abstract art (one we have just touched on), but also surely missing the positive qualities of the reliefs – purity, vitality, order, contemplative calm, luminosity, and the sense of infinity. Familiarity with Nicholson's previous work should have made such misapprehension impossible. Besides, at no time did he abandon figurative painting and the use of colour and texture, in order to concentrate solely on non-referential work. The white reliefs were not a break with what preceded them so much as an extreme development in one direction: the culmination of Nicholson's aim to make his works autonomous, without particular reference to anything outside themselves. Ivon Hitchens, on seeing *Two Circles*, the first white relief to be exhibited, at the thirteenth exhibition of the newly styled *7 & 5* in March 1934, had remarked that 'this was surely going *too* far' (an opinion he was soon to retract).[58] Certainly it was going further than any British painter had yet dared to go, and as far as Nicholson himself would ever go in terms of reduction and concentration.

Meanwhile a further evolution in Nicholson's ideas was set in train by the example of Piet Mondrian whom he met in Paris in December 1933. The decisive experience came early in the following April when he paid his first visit to Mondrian's studio, high above the railway tracks that converge on the Gare Montparnasse. By his own admission,

> the paintings were entirely new to me and I did not understand them on this first visit (and indeed only partially understood them on my second visit a year later). They were merely, for me, a part of the very lovely feeling generated by his thought in the room. I remember after this first visit sitting at a café table on the edge of a pavement almost touching all the traffic going in and out of the Gare Montparnasse, and sitting there for a very long time with an astonishing feeling of quiet and repose (!) – the thing I remembered most was the feeling of light in his room and the pauses and silences during and after he'd been talking. The feeling in his studio must have been not unlike the feeling in one of those hermits' caves where lions used to go to have thorns taken out of their paws.[59]

The atmosphere of contemplative calm and the special quality of light, which so impressed Nicholson in Mondrian's studio, was what he aspired to in creating his white reliefs – works, like Mondrian's, conceived not for the museum but for harmonizing and energizing daily life. Indeed a white relief can only be fully appreciated as part of the light and space and life of a room that is lived in, not in the bright, even light of a picture gallery. Ideally there should be a strong side-light to bring out the very subtly graded depths of carving and to set going the drama of light and shadow, which is essential to the relief's vitality and presence.

Though there was a profound difference between Mondrian, the abstract Symbolist, and Nicholson, the non-doctrinaire creator of a poetic reality, the two men did have in common a highly developed instinct for space proportion. Later, Mondrian came to have such faith in Nicholson's eye that he would consult him on the thickness of his black grid-lines. Nor was Nicholson slow to submit to the powerful combination of magisterial order and vibrant intensity in Mondrian's painting, since its influence can be seen, from about 1936, in those works of his in which he creates a harmony out of circles balanced against orthogonal lines, or constructs with precise areas of flat, unmodulated colour. But in such works Mondrian's vocabulary is so completely translated into his own, less severe idiom as to produce an altogether different effect.

From Picasso and Braque, from Miró and now Mondrian, Nicholson drew those

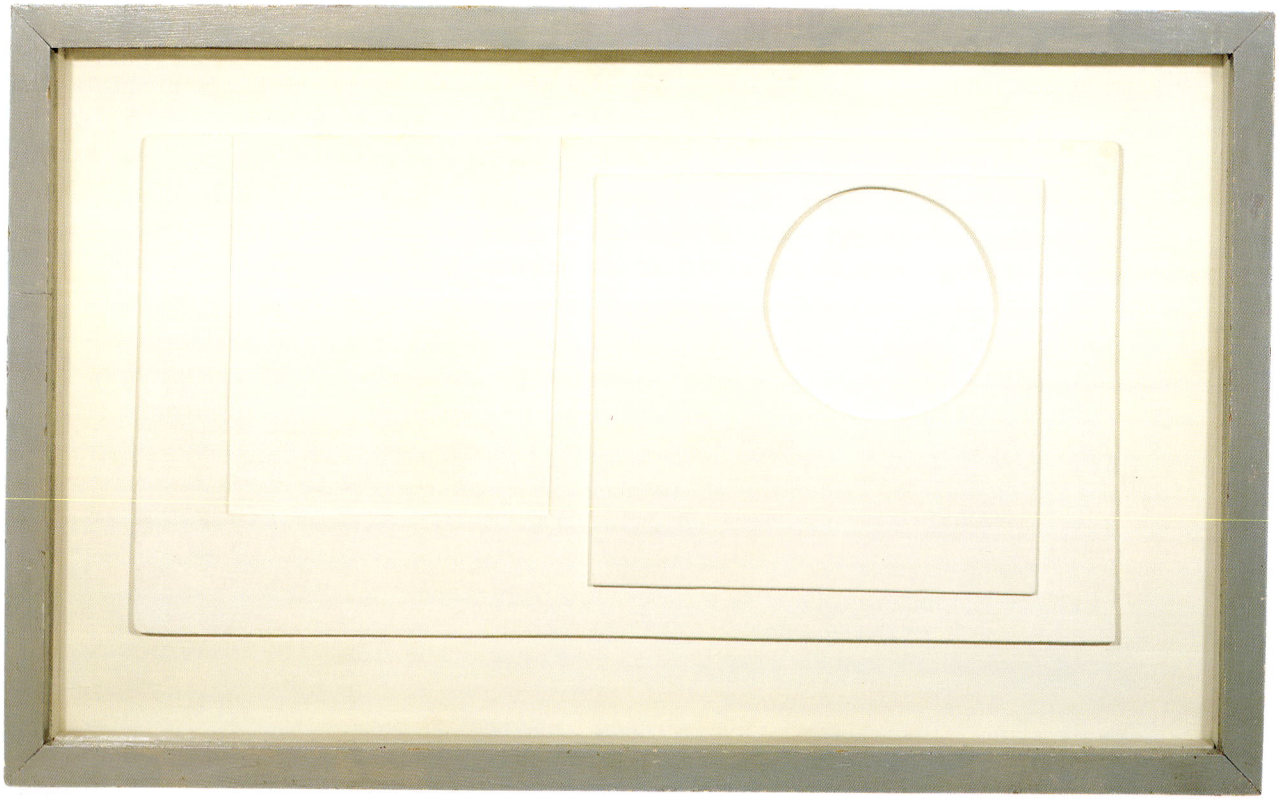

21 *1934 (white relief, circle and square)*
oil on carved board
35 × 61 cm (13¾ × 24 in)

22 *1935 (painting)*
oil on canvas
101.5 × 105.5 cm (40 × 41½ in)

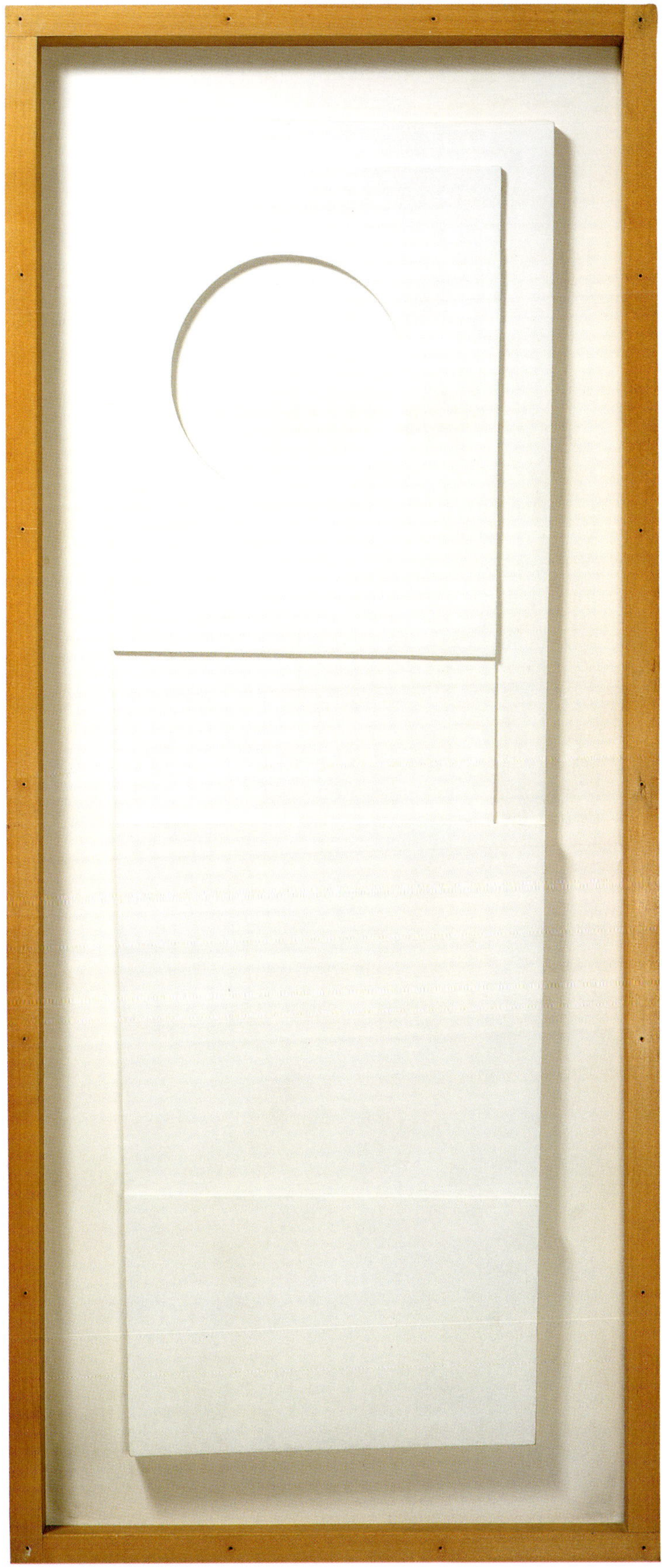

23 *1936 (white relief)*
oil on carved board
178 × 73.5 cm (70 × 29 in)

elements which answered his needs, combining and transmuting them so thoroughly that, although it is easy to point to this influence or that borrowed technique in many of his works in the years 1932–6, what one experiences is something unique to Nicholson. His approach to his work was both practical and intuitive. If he was influenced, it was by the paintings, never the writings, of an artist. He was sceptical about grandiose theories and shrill manifestos and though sympathetic in a general way to spiritual aspirations in art, would fight shy of any system or doctrine. Thus the experience of Mondrian's paintings was enough for him: why bother himself with his theories? He still remembered clearly his mother's reaction to 'art-talk' – 'it made her want to go *& scrub the kitchen table*'.[60]

Yet for all his indifference to theory, Nicholson did come to champion the so-called Modern Movement with something like a crusading spirit. Though no club-man, he was a natural leader, and tended to play a decisive role in any artistic grouping he chose to join. With Naum Gabo and the architect Leslie Martin he edited *CIRCLE: International Survey of Constructive Art* (1937), an anthology of abstract art and International Modern architecture and design, with an admixture of contemporary scientific and technological ideas. But each editor seems to have understood something different by the word 'constructive'. For Gabo it has a distinctly Utopian meaning: art hand-in-hand with science, building a Brave New World and reversing the cultural disintegration whose nadir he perceived in the Great War. Such an interpretation, with its echoes of earlier Russian Constructivism, was not shared by Nicholson, who was far too much of a romantic individualist to pay more than lip-service to such Dawnism. He was all for jettisoning every kind of outworn convention, was in tune with the purist aesthetic and the return to basic principles, and actively sympathized with progressive ideas. But he did not see art in terms of an overt social programme. Constructive, for him, was a temporarily useful label to denote the kind of non-representational work that is 'built up' in answer to its own demands, without conscious reference to anything outside itself. It was preferable to the horrible word 'abstract', with its suggestion of something cerebral, bloodless, lifeless, airless and rarefied out of existence. It also marked an antithesis to 'surrealism' and what might be thought to be its un-structured or destabilizing content – and *CIRCLE* was, in part, intended as a counterblast to Surrealism.[61]

The technocratic ideal and the belief in social programming expressed in its pages may tie *CIRCLE* to its epoch (and besides have scant relevance to the arts), but the section devoted to architecture, much the largest and most unified in the book, stands representative of aspirations that were soon to be quashed by the war. As for the artists and sculptors represented in it, their works are more eloquent than their words, which tend to be vague or meaningless. Nicholson's brief pronouncements noticeably lack the clarity and power which his white reliefs possess even in reproduction.

Yet there is a danger to these reliefs in the company they keep. Setting them in the context of Robert Maillart's bridges of reinforced concrete, Berthold Lubetkin's penguin pool at London Zoo, or, more invidiously, implying an affinity with the works of César Domela, László Moholy-Nagy, Sophie Täuber-Arp and Friedrich Vordemberge-Gildewart – all illustrated in this book – can be misleading. In the politicized 1930s it was tempting to annex the white reliefs to the 'new architecture', to ideals of hygiene and town-planning, to machine-age design. And such claims may have been made with the intention of shielding the reliefs from the charge of ivory-tower remoteness. But however much Nicholson himself may have welcomed the idea of being part of a progressive movement, there should be no doubt that in its purely intuitive conception, his work is always and fundamentally aesthetic. For him the poetic idea is more real than anything else. The white reliefs, because they are non-referential and constructed with geometrical forms, can be placed in the context of constructive art, but they have a poetic life which sets them apart from much abstract art which seems to proceed from theory not intuition.

In his earlier work Nicholson had involved the viewer by setting up several kinds of tension simultaneously – tension between forms in space, between planes that overlap ambiguously, between reference to the outer world and the material quality of the object itself. In his white reliefs, which make no reference to anything outside themselves, colour and texture are virtually abolished and though a confrontation between real space and illusory space contributes to the dynamic of the work, interest is mainly concentrated on the relative position of forms in that space. To achieve the dynamic equilibrium of forms, in which the material and the form become inseparably one, demanded many hours of mental and physical concentration: judgement of proportion, interval, and relative depth of carving had to remain completely coordinated with the laborious act of making – the whole process guided by intuition, not by premeditated mathematical calculation. This is why the reliefs, despite their geometrical form and their austerity, which seem to banish the lyrical qualities of the earlier work, retain a sense of mystery and a poetic aura.[62]

The compulsion to order, or re-order, things into a right relation was deep-seated in Nicholson. It is a dominant – if not the dominant – characteristic of his art, and showed itself equally in the careful carelessness with which he arranged his immediate surroundings. He would set out a simple picnic meal on a low table in the studio so that it looked like a still life. By the way he placed quite ordinary objects in a room he could make them seem intensely alive. And when staying as a guest with friends, he would not hesitate to rearrange the furniture in his bedroom.[63] In a similar way the abstract geometry of his reliefs and paintings comes alive because of the exact positioning of the forms.

I have not hesitated to describe the white reliefs as non-referential, bearing in mind the various influences that contributed to their development. Nicholson, however, in his desire to stress the non-metaphysical origin and intuitive process of his work, could at times misleadingly oversimplify. 'I have, I think, little intellect,' he once wrote, '– but not at all a bad INSTINCT. So that for example the circles which occur in my work originated with a plate on a table & not at all with say any idea of "infinity".'[64] Though we hardly need reminding about Nicholson's lifelong fascination with plates or bowls on tables (as already in *1919 (blue bowl in shadow)*), it

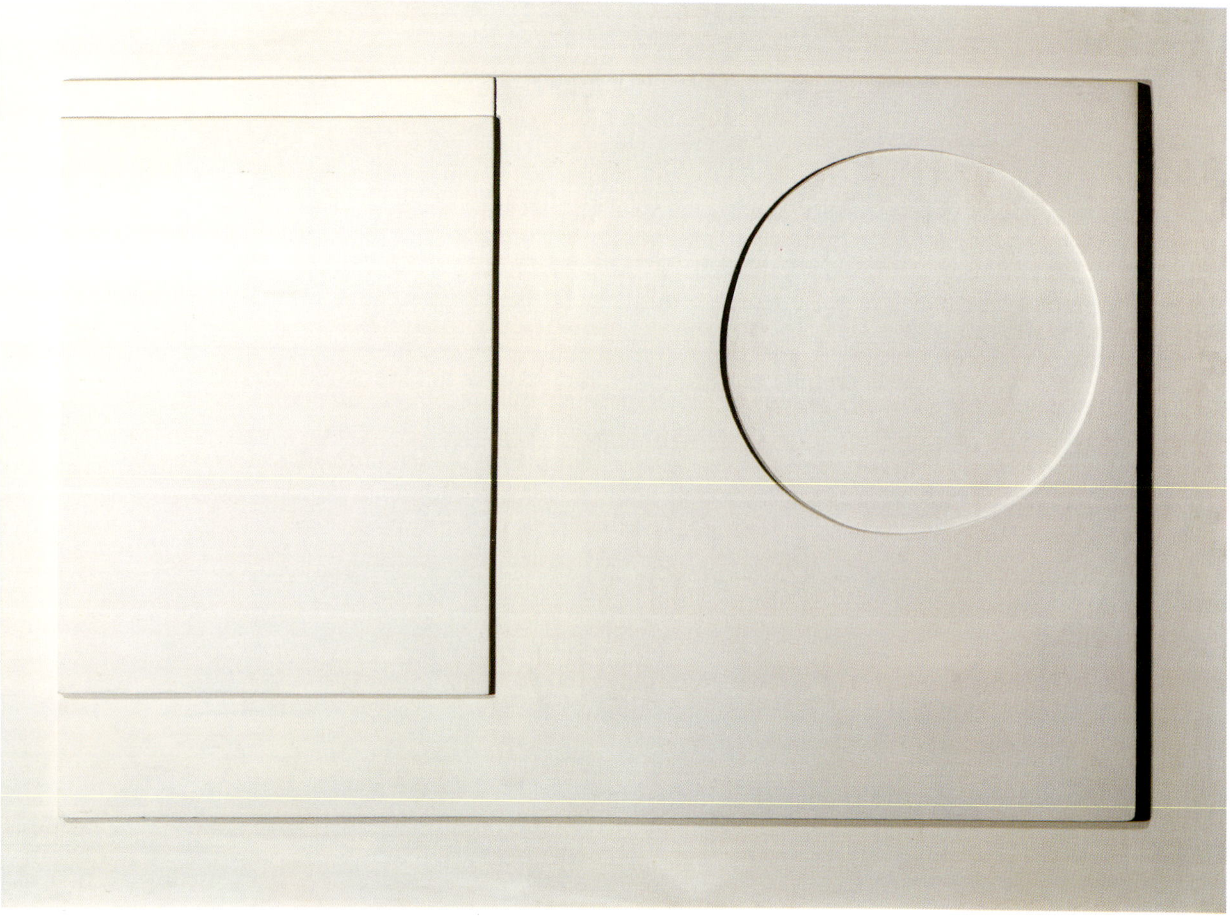

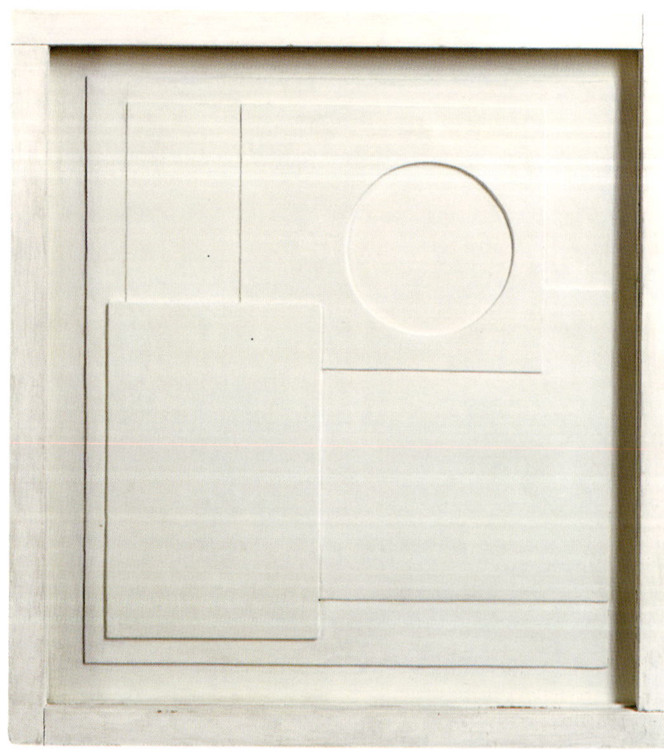

24 1935 *(white relief)*
oil on carved board
52 × 73.5 cm (20½ × 29 in)

25 1938 *(white relief)*
oil on carved board
26.5 × 28.5 cm (10½ × 11¼ in)

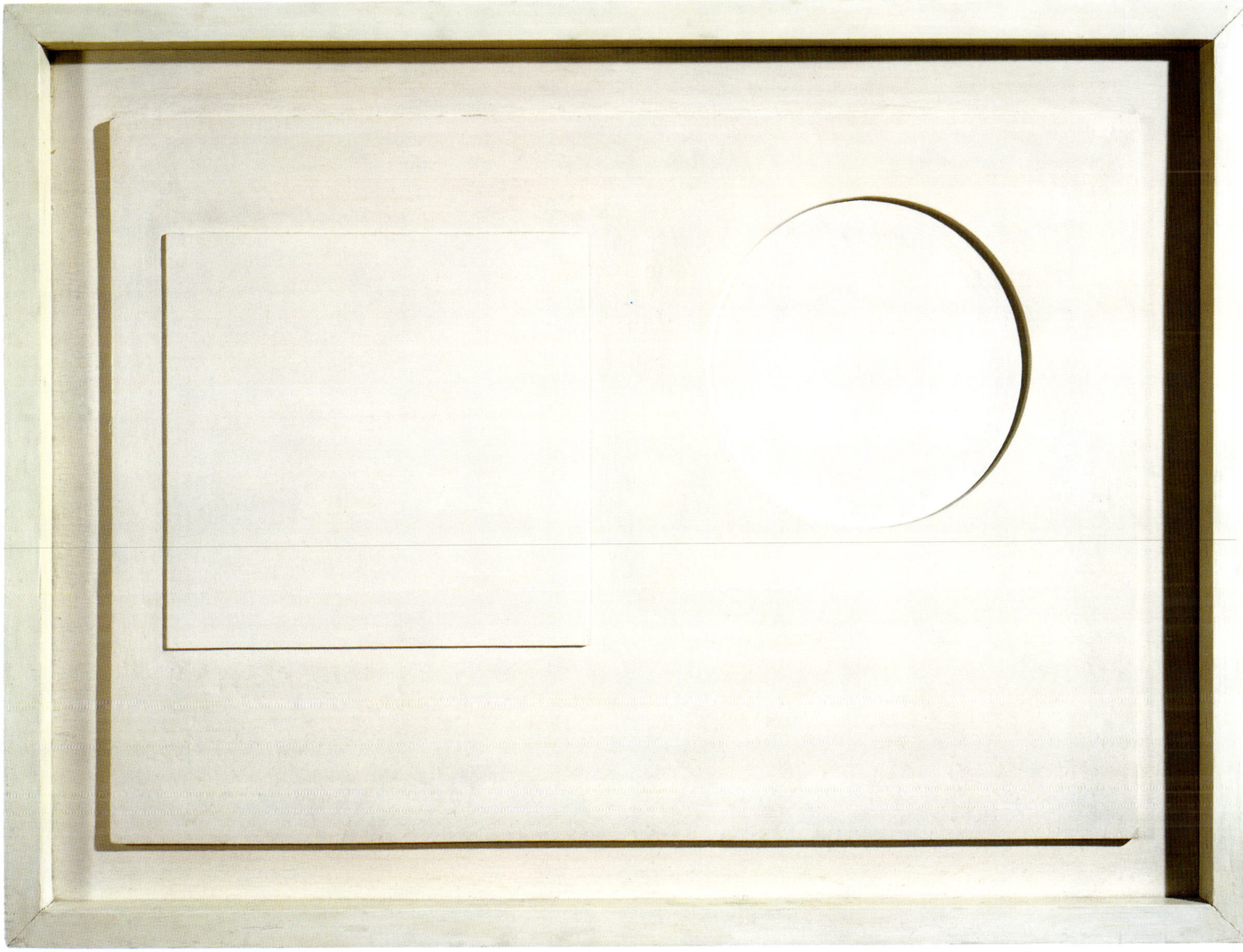

26 *1936 (white relief)*
oil on carved board
67.5 × 93 cm (26½ × 36½ in)

would be as true to say that his circles took their origin neither in a plate nor in a
symbol but, quite simply, as an archetypal form that required to be brought into rela-
26 tion with another archetypal form, a square or a rectangle opposed to it. And even if, in his handling of squares and circles, he was initially preoccupied with formal relationships, it by no means follows that the resulting work is merely the creation of a formal harmony and nothing more. As he himself stated, 'however "non-figurative" a painting may appear to be it has its source in nature'.[65] Which is to say that just as the artist, in organizing shapes and colours, inevitably draws on his experience of the physical world, so the viewer too is influenced by visual associations and memories, by the emotive power of particular shapes and colours. More importantly, though, it is Nicholson's passion that lifts his work above the tasteful arrangement of shapes and subtle interpenetration of surfaces and turns it into a living experience.

In truth the question of whether or not the circle originated in a cup or saucer, or the moon in the sky, is academic, since the power of the reliefs comes not from a reductive simplification but from an intensification which has burnt out all accidents of the phenomenal world so as to allow our awareness to expand to the universal. One is reminded of the circle (*ensō*) brushed in ink on paper by the Zen monk-calligraphers of Japan, for whom it is the fundamental subject.[66] As mysterious and universal as Nicholson's circle, it may represent the void or the totality of the universe, or both. To emphasize that it has no fixed or finite meaning, the monks often add teasing captions such as 'Eat this and drink a cup of tea' or 'Is this a rice cake? A dumpling? The rim of a bucket?' This, surely, is in the spirit of Ben Nicholson and the white reliefs mark his fullest emancipation from copying the world of appearances.

By contrast his paintings, with their concern for texture and tone, as well as the relationship of forms in space, make constant reference to the physical world. Gradually these two tendencies would merge, reaching their greatest expressive power in the late reliefs of the 1960s and 1970s. Meanwhile there was an equally important parallel development in Nicholson's drawing.

1939–58 the new scope of drawing

When Nicholson moved to Cornwall just before the beginning of war, in August 1939, he could hardly have guessed that it would be his home for the next nineteen years. He and Hepworth were now the parents of four-year-old triplets, and it was to rescue them from the supposed threat of enemy bombs on London that Adrian Stokes had offered refuge in the comparative safety of Cornwall. Earlier that year Stokes and his wife, Margaret Mellis, had moved into Little Park Owles which stood a little way out of St Ives, overlooking Carbis Bay. With the new arrivals the house was filled to capacity.

Nicholson immediately took to his new surroundings. 'Little P.O. is a stone house with a grey, small-tiled Cornish roof – long ago a stables & a very nice shape & nicely set into the ground – a wide, terraced garden & lovely dark pine trees through which one sees an incredibly blue sea below & a white lighthouse on the horizon . . . inland between here & Penzance – really most magnificent, primitive country with stone everywhere.'[67] After eight years during which London had been the centre of his activities, this complete change of environment, its geographical isolation increased by wartime conditions, meant also a complete change of life, while the impact of the landscape and the powerful presence of the Atlantic immediately affected his work. Colours of the natural world – green, grey, pale blue, russet – had appeared in his geometric paintings from their beginning in 1934. Now the colours, textures and light of Cornwall found their way into both paintings and reliefs. In
28 *1941 (composition)* the way Nicholson flecks and pits the surface of the board, then rubs colour into it to suggest the texture of rock or stone or whitewashed walls, harks back to the patinated, time-worn appearance he aimed at in earlier paintings, and points forward to the colours and textures of many of the reliefs he made in the 1950s and 1960s.

How his painting developed in depth and richness during the next few years can
33 be seen in the beautifully toned and textured *1946 (still life, winter landscape)*. As its title indicates, it is as much about the colours of Cornwall in winter – dead bracken, gorse, moor grass, rock, lichen, sand dune, sky – as an arrangement of mug, cup and goblet. Pencil and oil paint on canvas collude to suggest several interpenetrating planes in low relief with teasingly shifting perspective, all in accordance with Cubist precept. In still lifes such as this, and even in the abstract painted reliefs made at the same time, a lyrical, poetic quality resurfaces which, if never entirely banished, was submerged in the more rigorous abstraction of the 1930s. Both paintings and reliefs are quite small – 21 × 21 in or less, and rarely larger than 33 × 40 in – but at no stage of Nicholson's career does small necessarily imply minor: some of the reliefs, or
32 midget projects for reliefs, though less than a foot square, give an impression of monumentality because of the scale on which they are conceived. But even had he wished

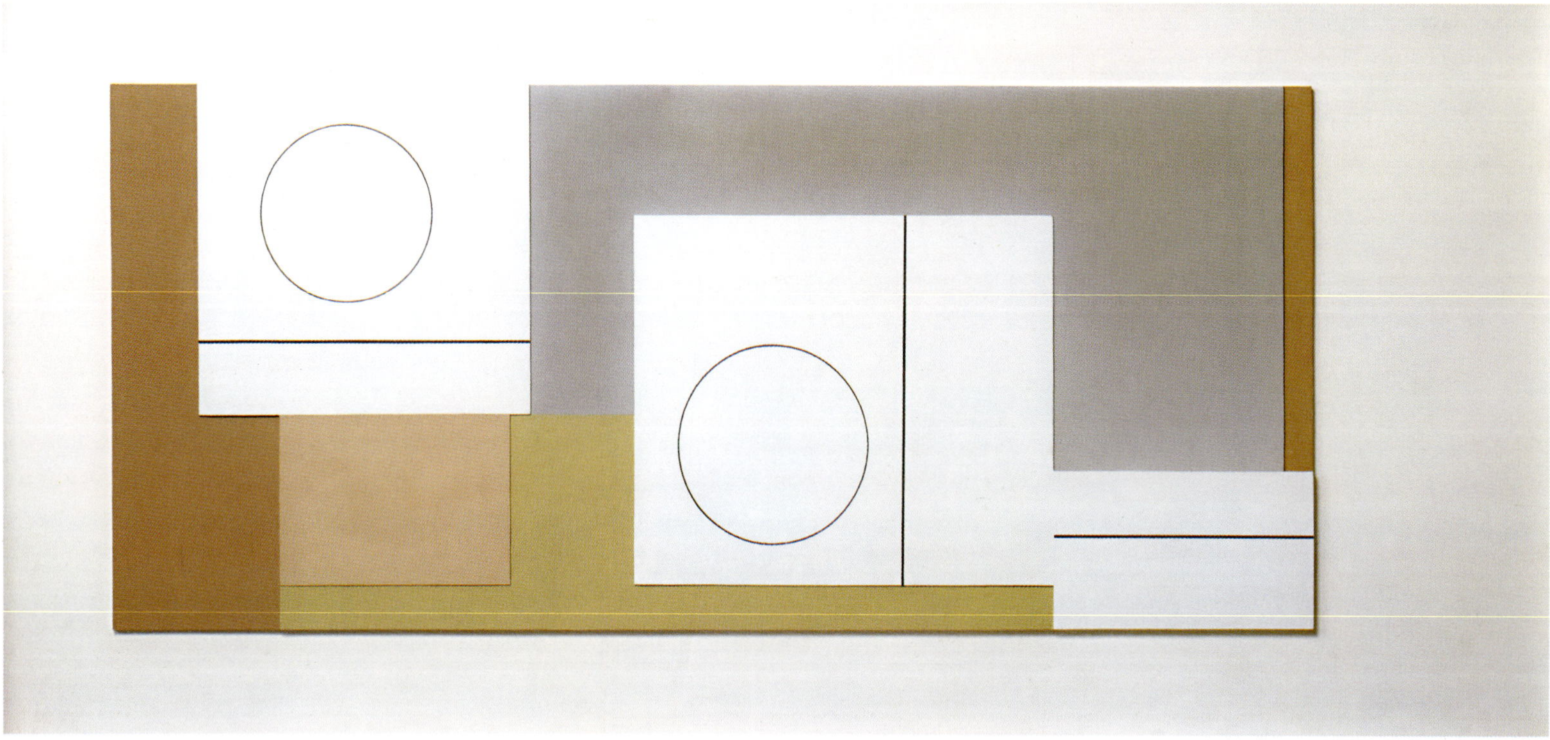

27 *1941 (painted relief, version 1)*
oil and pencil on carved board
66 × 140 cm (26 × 55¼ in)

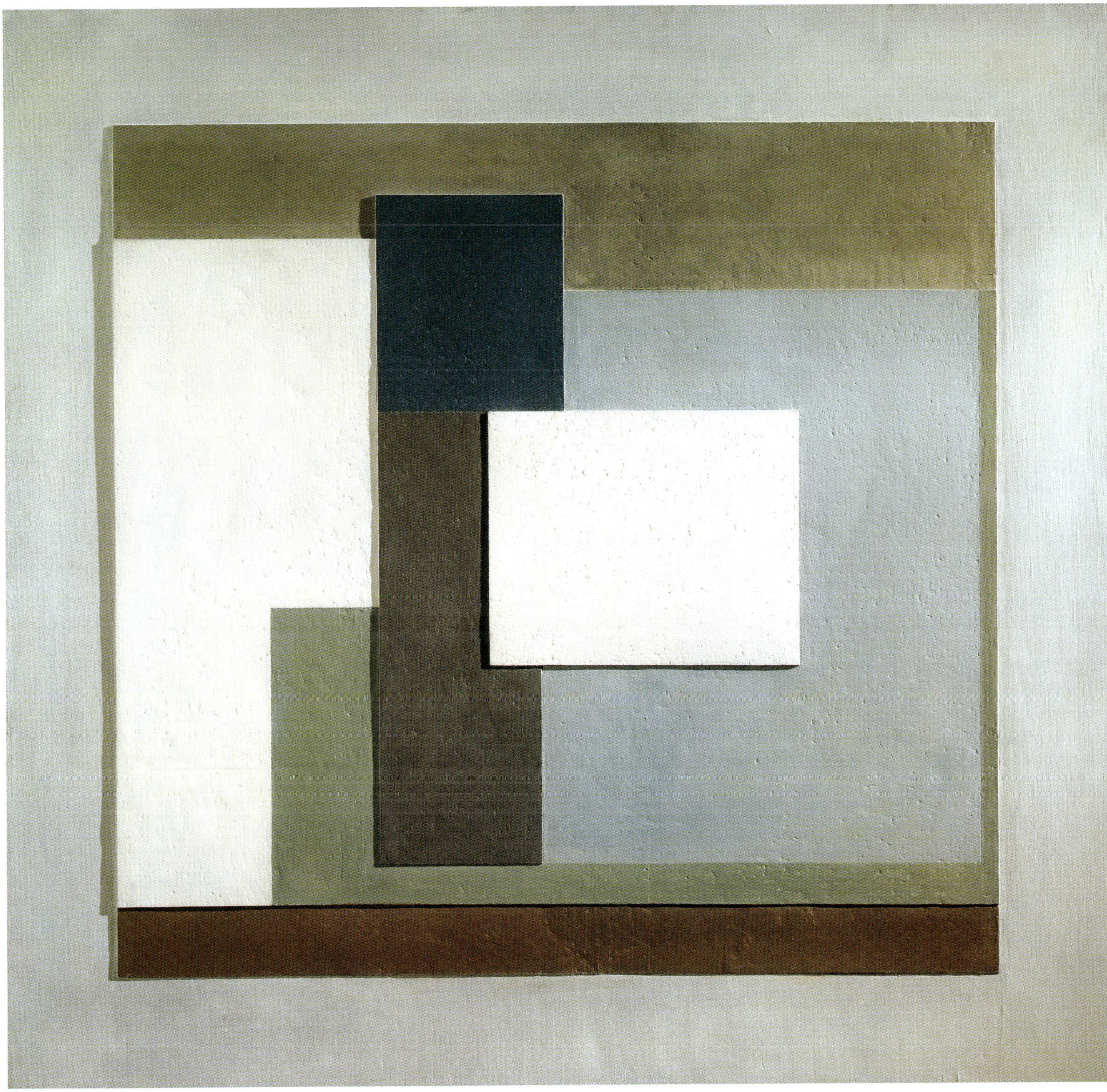

28 *1941 (composition)*
oil on carved board
95 × 90.5 cm (37½ × 35¾ in)

to do so, Nicholson was prevented from making any really large-scale works during the 1940s for want of a studio that was big enough.

After four months at Little Park Owles, the family, having decided to stay in Cornwall, moved to a house of their own called Dunluce, a quarter of a mile away. This 'wretched little villa', as Nicholson called it, was too cramped for him even to contemplate making large works, and Hepworth still had no space in which to resume sculpting. But things improved when, in August 1942, they moved to a larger house, Chy-an-Kerris, at the further end of Carbis Bay. Here, at last, they could each have a studio of their own and Nicholson's description of his new home, in a letter, is written in buoyant mood. It is worth quoting at length as it reveals his keen visual appetite and the power of his imagination to charge his surroundings with colour and vitality.

29 *1948 (three pears)*
pencil on paper
25.5 × 35.5 cm (10 × 14 in)

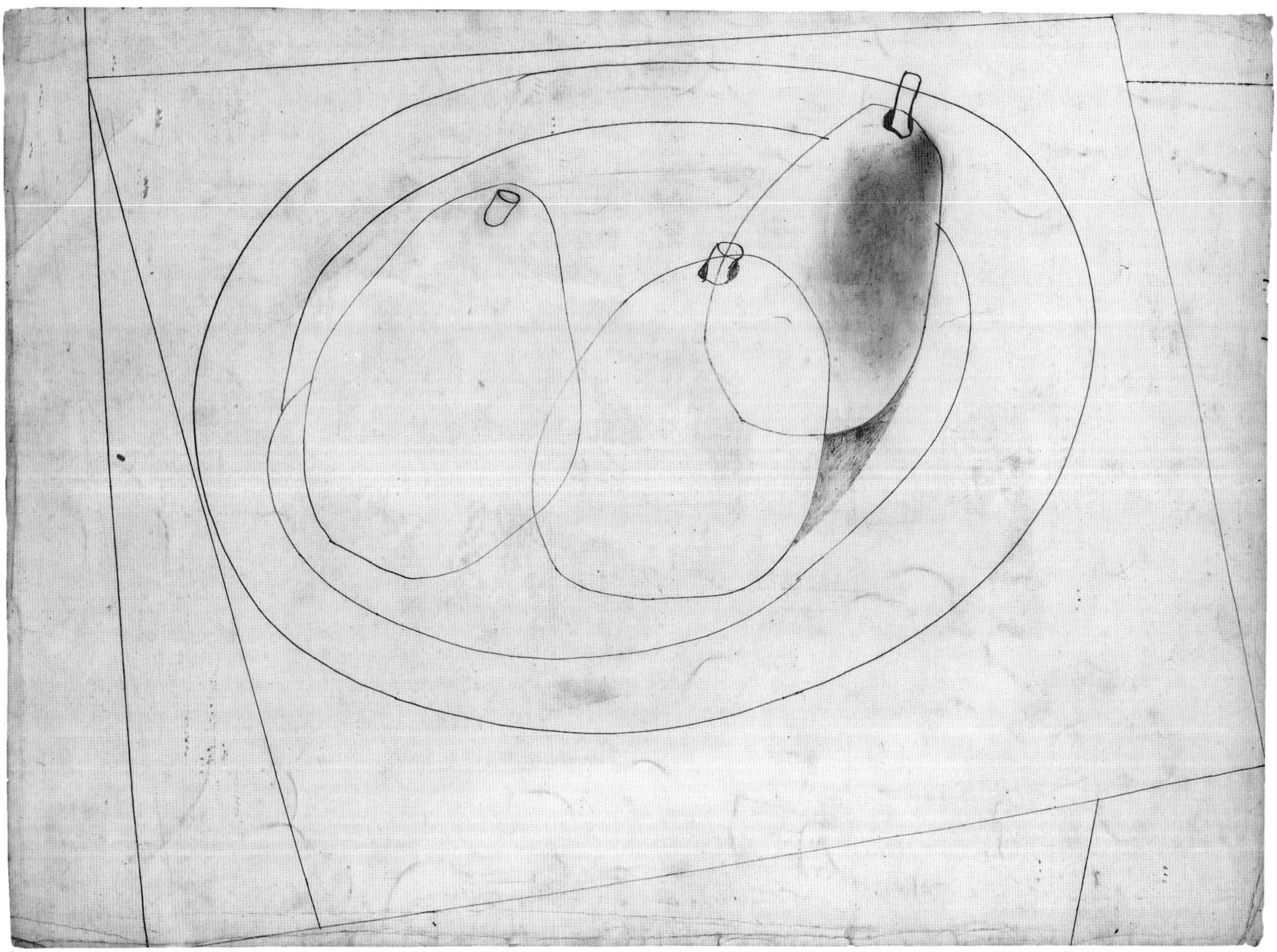

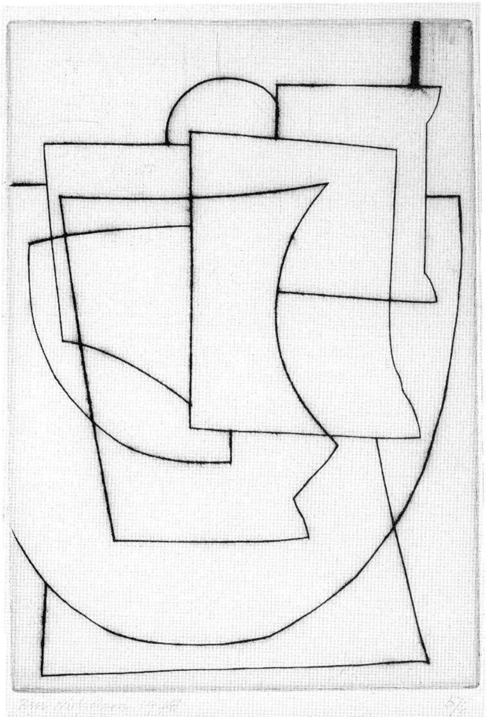

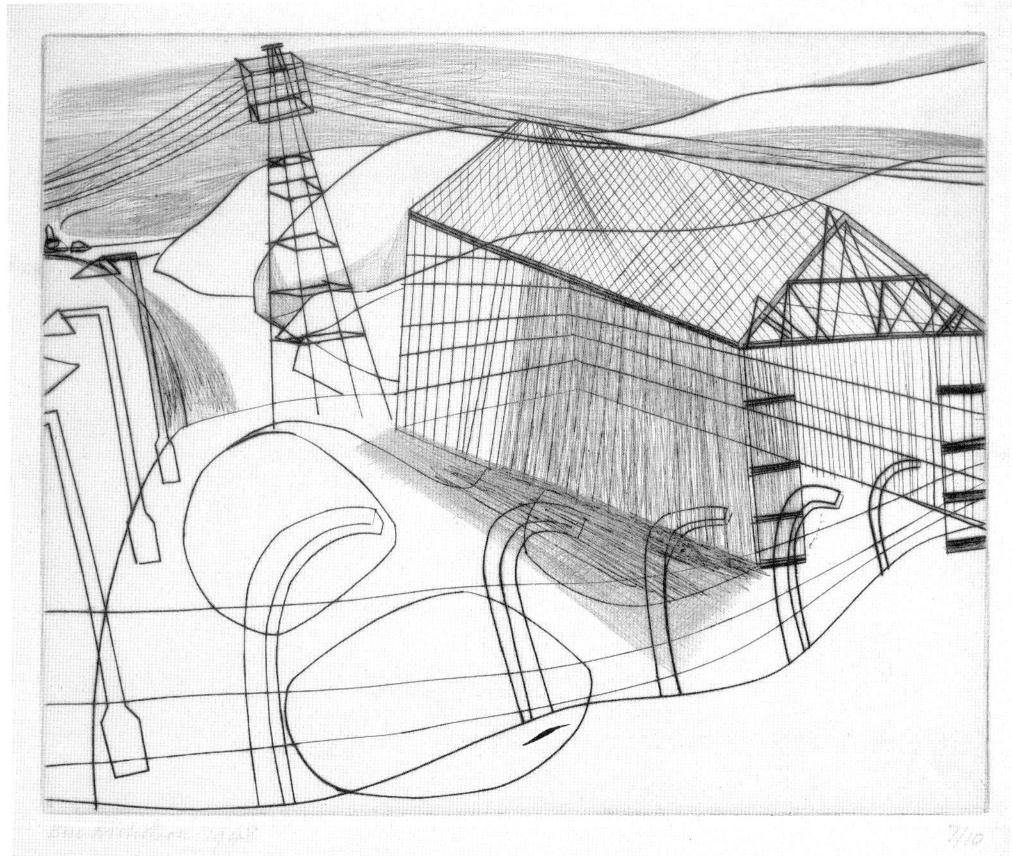

30 *1948 (drypoint)*
drypoint, 5/6
17 × 12 cm (6¾ × 4¾ in)

31 *1948 (ICI shed)*
drypoint, 7/10
20 × 25 cm (8 × 10 in)

It faces due N. – looking out to the Atlantic horizon with St Ives, like Greece, coming out into the bay on one side & Godrevy lighthouse & its rocks & N. Cornwall on the other – the sea as I write is blue beyond belief & small white yachts & an occasional brown fishing boat are here & there radiating from St Ives, a mysterious cloud bank on the horizon fades in a haze into a pale blue sky – but I like even better the due S. view which is as close & personal & warm as the N. one is cold & remote – there my bedroom I thought at first was a rather terrible Victorian pagoda but it turns out whitewashed, to be an exceptionally lovely little DUCCIO or Fra Angelico cell with two fragile white pillars & strange & rather lovely shaped ceiling & casement windows with the hot sun which comes in all day & changes to bright moonlight at night. I see a lovely old Cornish roof with a palm tree & pines & nice pale coloured & flowering shrubs & next door but one a snow-white walled garden with bright green leaves & red flowers & black cats in it & rather like a Paris suburb or the S. of France in feeling. Barbara for the first time since the war has a room for a studio & has been able to get her blocks of stone & wood, & her large sculptures out – the room is absurd because it really might be 7 Mall Studios only with the blue sea outside.[68]

But Nicholson did not experience Cornwall only from his bedroom window. He liked nothing better than to escape for a day's sketching to Halsetown, Towednack, Trendrine or Zennor – names associated with so many of his works, whether drawings, paintings or reliefs, in the following years. At first his range of motifs was limited by wartime restrictions on access to the coastline and by how far he could go on

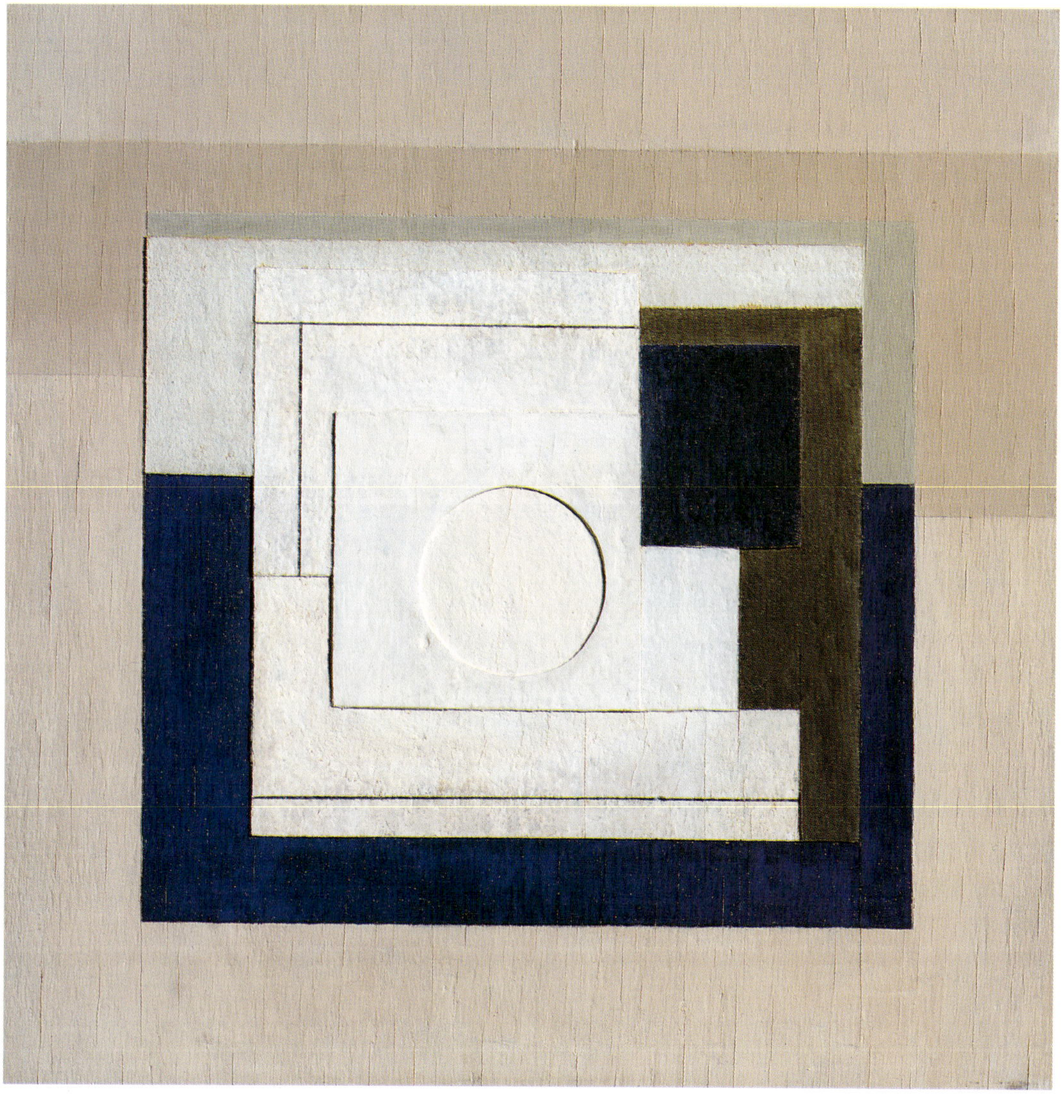

32 *1944 (relief project)*
oil and pencil on paper and carved board
20 × 20 cm (8 × 8 in)

→ 33 *1946 (still life, winter landscape)*
oil and pencil on canvas
59.5 × 56.5 cm (23½ × 22¼ in)

a bicycle. But by the end of 1948 he could afford a small motor-cycle and, three years later, a 1929 MG Midget (which he hand-painted a pale dove-grey). Now he could go further and faster and explore the westernmost coast of the Penwith peninsula – Pendean, St Just, Porthcurno and, by boat, the Scillies.

He did not like the word 'sketch', perhaps because it evoked the amateurish pastime of Victorian ladies. But like it or not, most of the landscape drawings he made at this time have the swift, unselfconscious notation of sketches. They were a means to absorb the look and feel of a place, not deliberate works of art, and his attitude to them was correspondingly relaxed: he would give them away or, if they failed to satisfy him, scrunch them up and throw them away without hesitation. Earlier, in Cumberland and Ticino, drawing *sur le motif* had, likewise, been a means of exploration, a vital preliminary to painting in the studio, but no more than that. He had
11 made drawings of St Ives on his first visit there in 1928, and of Paris and Provence
16 in 1932/3, the best of them lively, economical and clearly displaying a relish for his

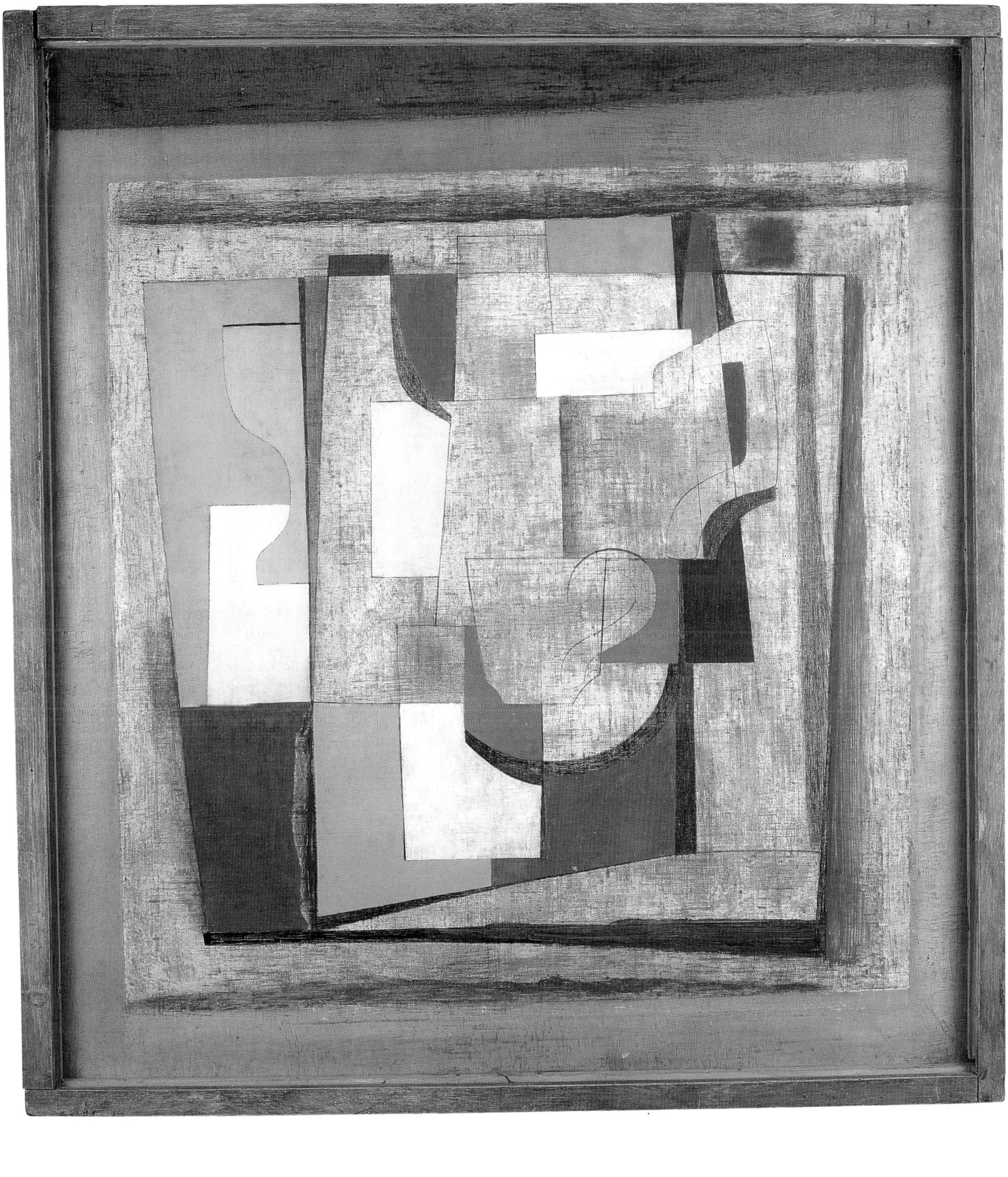

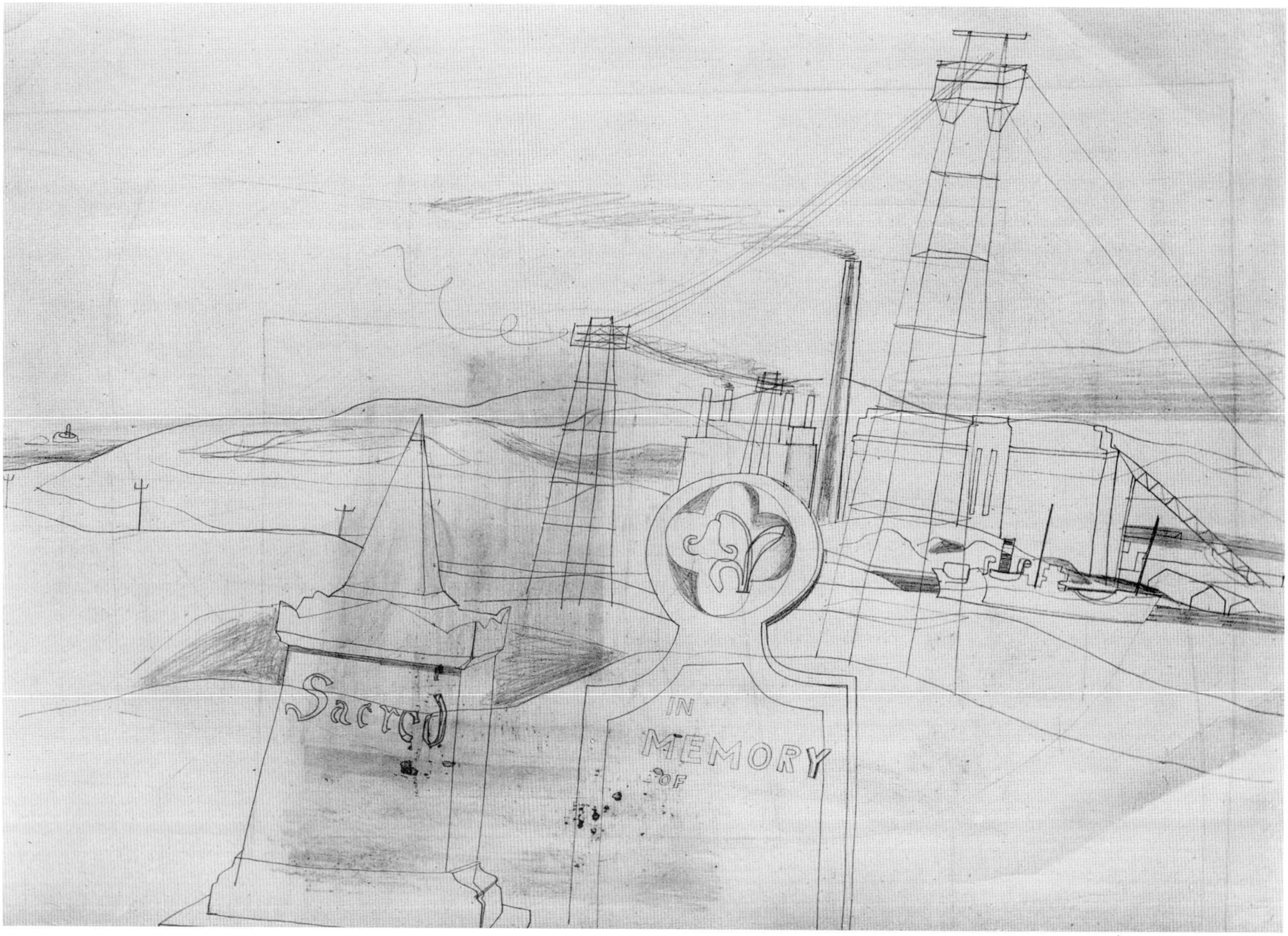

chosen subject. The drawings of Cornwall were made with the same unassuming
spontaneity. Sometimes, when his subject is solely the landscape – the plateau of
fields overspread with a net of stone walls, stretching away to a low horizon, or a
bird's-eye view of hills, dotted with farm-buildings, encircling a bay – the drawing
can seem a bit off-hand or non-committal, as if he felt uneasy about merely describ-
ing. But if he places a roofscape in the foreground or a telegraph pole so that its wires
35 swerve across the page – if he focuses on a church tower or some chimney stacks,
cunningly tilted, of a derelict tin mine – the drawing is suddenly transformed: the
pencil lines tauten and seem to quiver with energy. Because a tension is set up
between geometrical, man-made forms and the organic forms of nature, the design
takes on a life of its own, still anchored in a particular place, but also obeying an
internal logic. Among the best of Nicholson's landscape drawings few are without
some architectural element, and later on architecture will often squeeze out land-
scape altogether.

34 *March 1948 (two gravestones, Hayle estuary)*
pencil on paper
32 × 45.5 cm (12½ × 17¾ in)

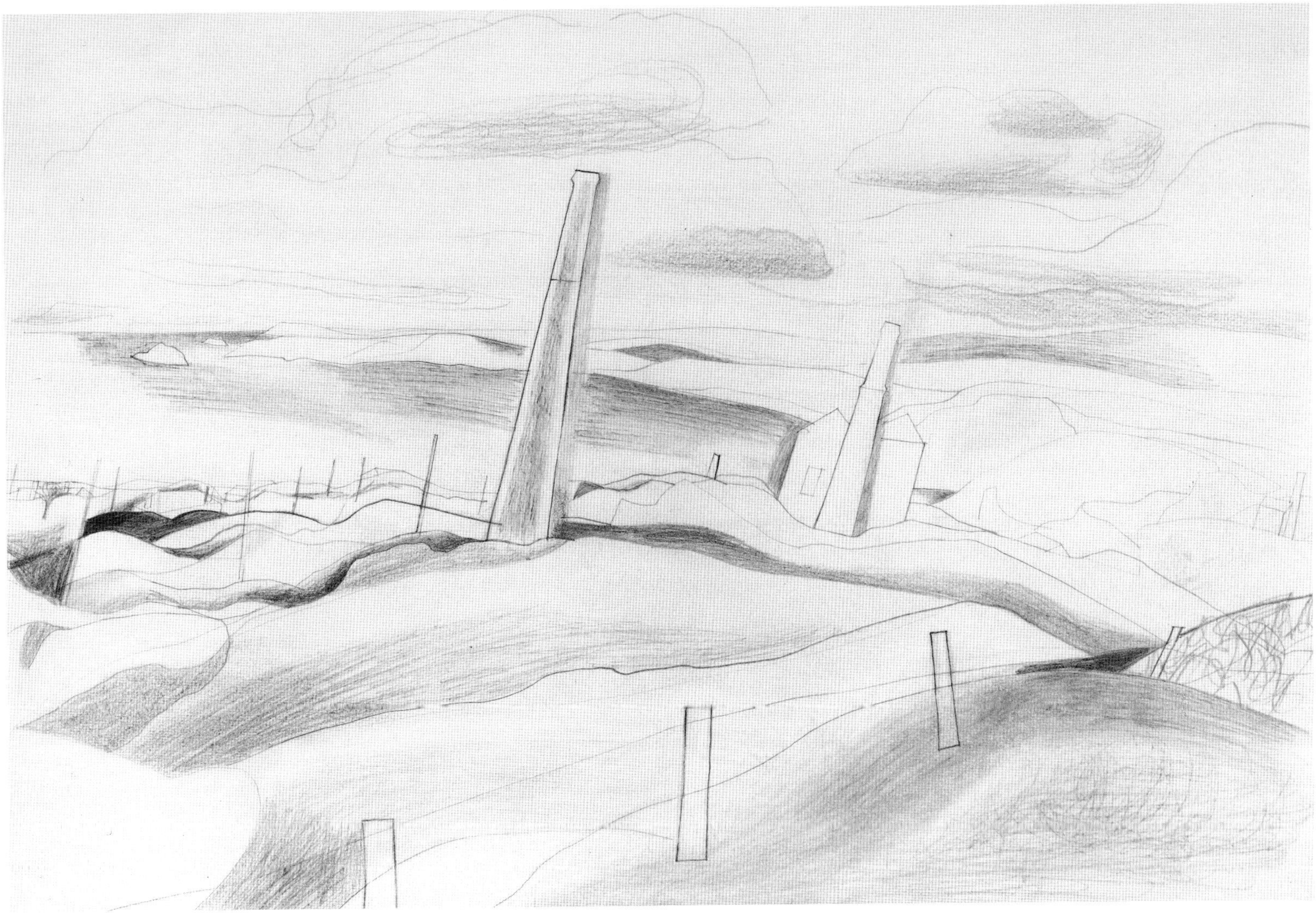

35 *August 13 1954 (St Agnes, Cornwall)*
oil wash and pencil on paper
39 × 56.5 cm (15¼ × 22¼ in)

In April 1949 Nicholson visited Brittany for the first time and was captivated by the landscape, the architecture and the people of this other Celtic realm, which twenty years earlier had inspired his friend Kit Wood and was now made poignant by his memory. In the train to the fishing port of Tréboul, subject of some of Wood's finest paintings, Nicholson wrote:

No one told me quite how beautiful this Breton architecture is, though one sensed it in Kit's ptgs – the beauty of some of these peasant cottages, their form down to the smallest detail & their colour – so lovely I cried at first sight of them! & the churches with these superb spires which pierce the sky. I had a room at Locmariaquer next to a XII cent. church (with a miraculous spire) & last night at Carnac ville – also a lovely little square with a small mairie & two small grey-shuttered houses opposite my hotel & a vast church with deep throbbing bells. I went off on a v. ancient blue bicycle with pedals that touched the ground & looked at those *mégalithes*. It is impressive the way there seems no reason why they should ever end & I feel they must continue right across France.[69]

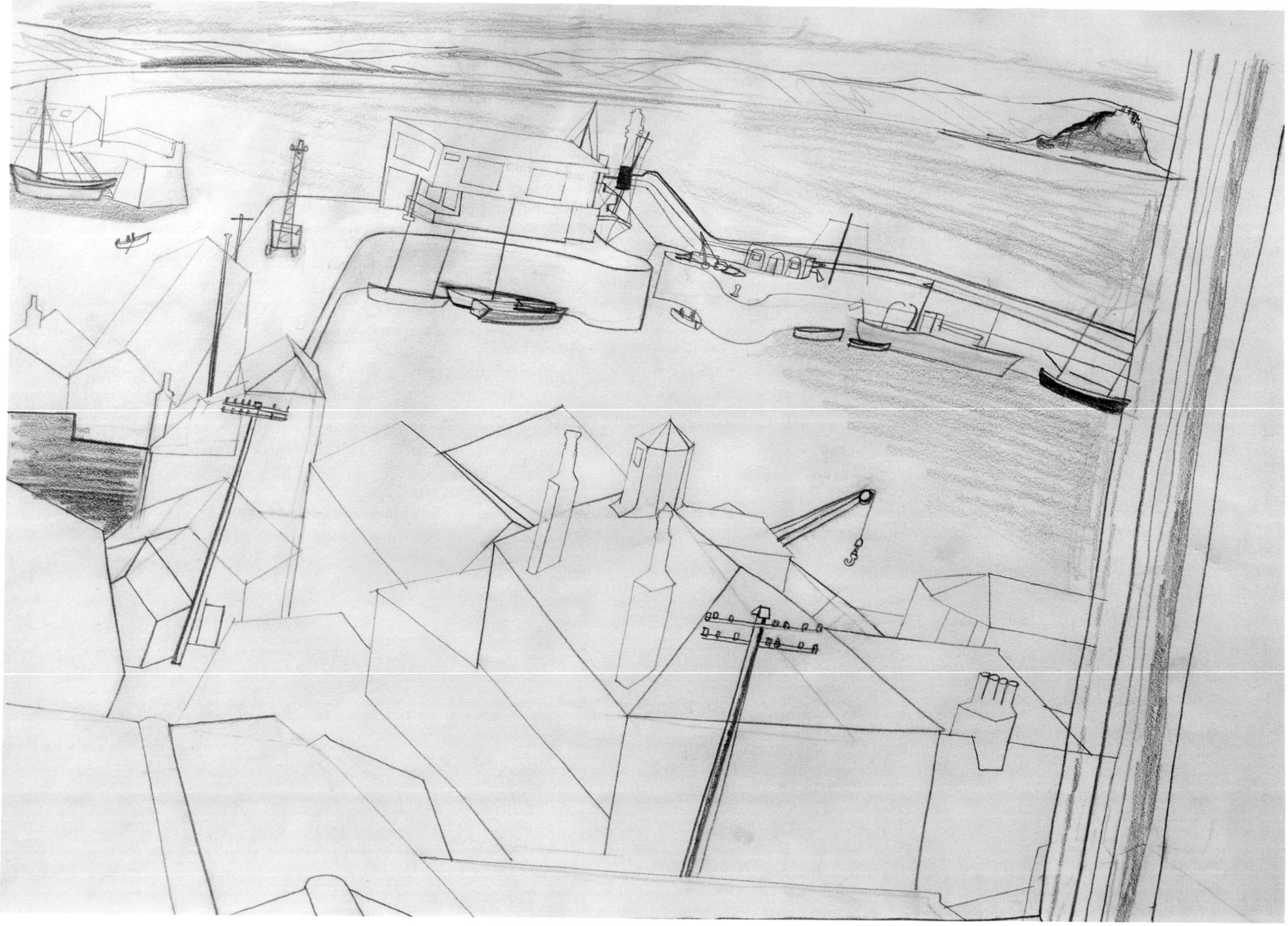

The sculptural form and the blotched and pitted surface of the ancient menhirs made a deep impression on him, renewed on subsequent visits, and eventually translated into what he called his 'primitive' reliefs.

Very few drawings survive as a record of this first visit. Yet, on his return, Nicholson reported to Helen Sutherland: 'It was tremendously hard work – & v. intense this searching for one's "motif". I think one's real "motif" is *where one lives* & all the rest is merely an added experience & an enrichment of this? But around 37 Huelgoat the most ravishingly lovely country, such beautiful *trees* – many Rafael-like ones in new leaf & the dark ones & the megaliths & the lovely unspoilt Breton people . . . & I like the language.'[70]

A real commitment to drawing landscape was clinched the following spring, 1950, when Nicholson went on the first of many drawing trips to Italy. After years of wartime isolation and post-war deprivation, the impulse to go south was widely

36 *June 16 1948 (Penzance, inner harbour)*
pencil on paper
35 × 50 cm (13¾ × 19¾ in)

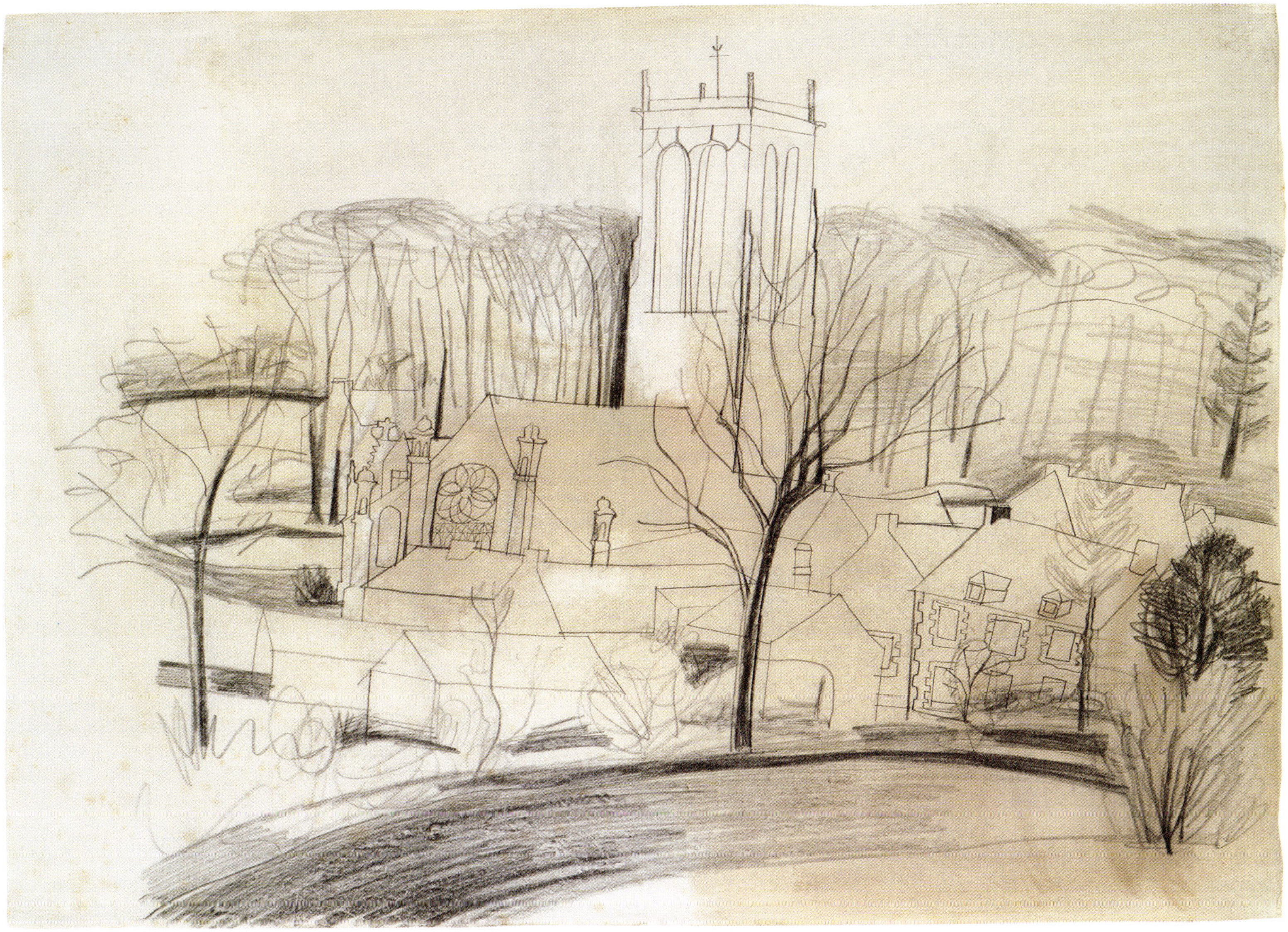

37 *April 19 1949 (St Herbot, Huelgoat, no.2)*
oil wash and pencil on paper
33.5 × 51 cm (13¼ × 20 in)

felt among the English, who yearned for the warmth and sunlight of the Mediterranean. But Nicholson's journey was at least as much due to the urging of his friend, Cyril Reddihough, who arranged it all. Reddihough had met Nicholson at Banks Head in 1927 and soon became one of his most important patrons, together with Helen Sutherland and Leslie Martin. He had quickly discerned the special qualities of Nicholson's drawing – his sense of space-proportion, his ability to suggest solid form by the most exactly inflected line, his ruthless omission of some details and often humorous emphasis of others – and felt that it showed sides of his temperament – perky humour, spontaneity, fantasy, a sense of drama – that were less evident in his paintings and reliefs.

And so together they set off from London on 11 May, crossing over to Dunkirk and then heading south, through France and Switzerland, to Italy. They decided they would explore the towns of Tuscany – Pisa, Lucca, Volterra, Siena and Arezzo –

38 *May 22 1950 (cloisters, San Gimignano)*
oil wash and pencil on paper
38 × 51 cm (15 × 20 in)

39 *May 24 1950 (single tower, San Gimignano)*
pencil on paper
39 × 58 cm (15¼ × 22¾ in)

→ **40** *May 22 1950 (early morning from San Gimignano)*
oil wash and pencil on paper
37 × 54 cm (14½ × 21¼ in)

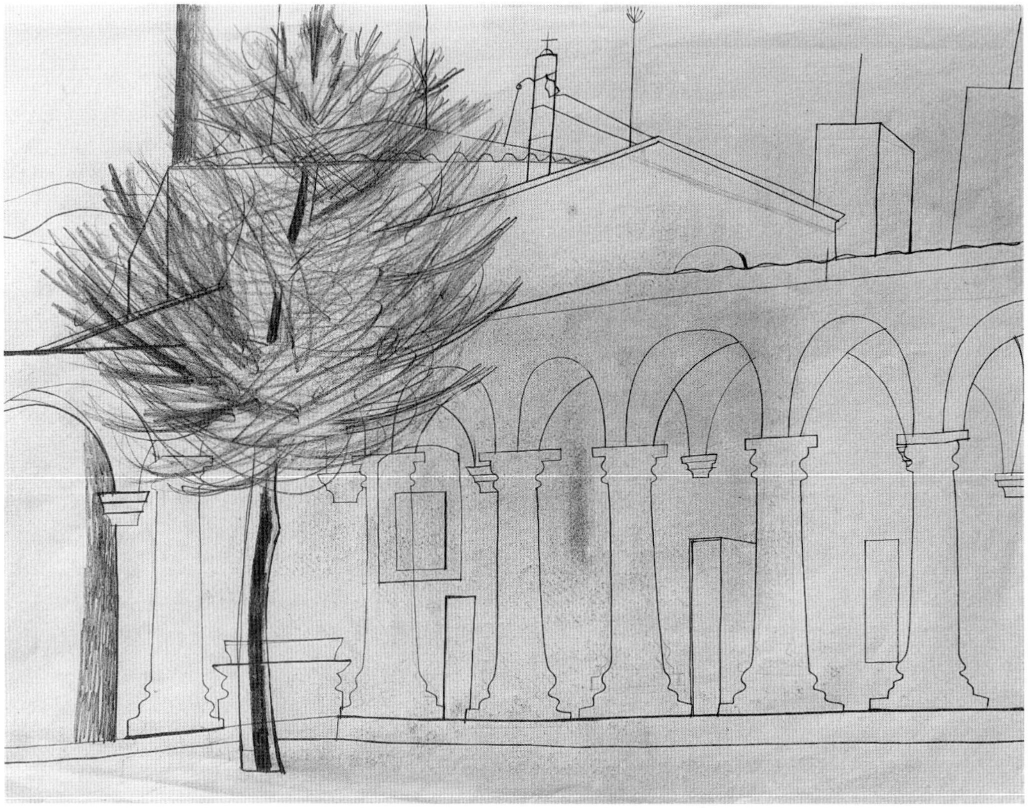

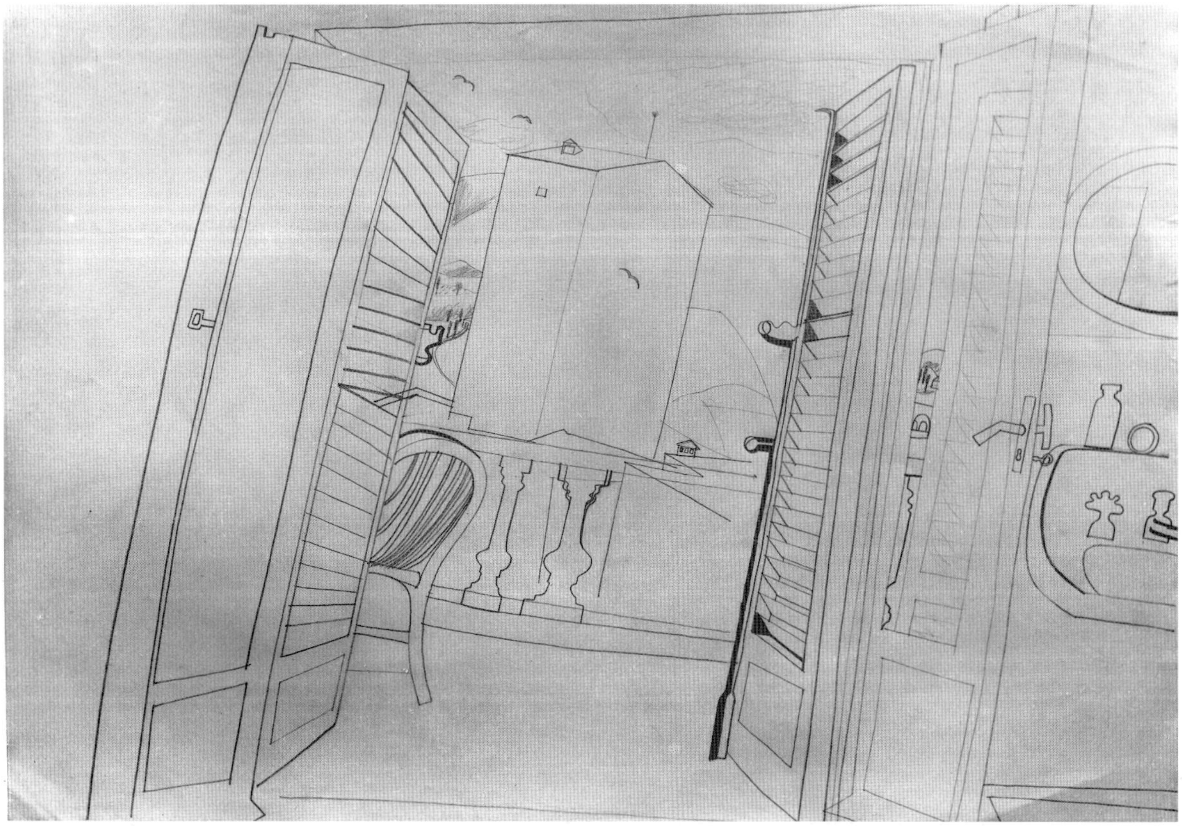

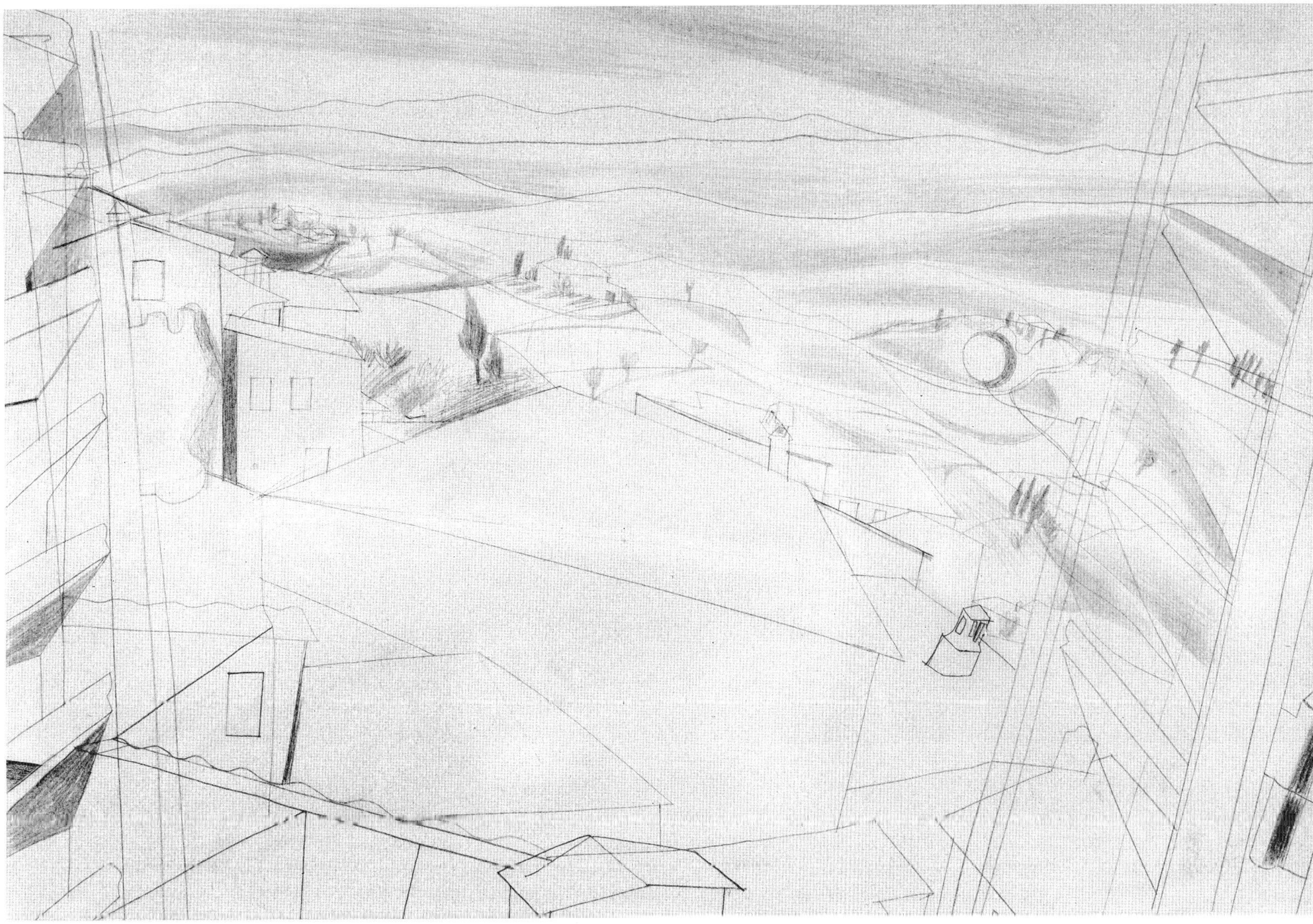

making San Gimignano their base. Here, in the Hotel La Cisterna, Nicholson found an attic whose window was on a level with one of the mediaeval towers for which the town is famous, and from it made a drawing. He had once told Paul Nash that he judged paintings by the quality of light they gave off,[71] and he might well have
40 applied the same criterion to his own drawings. In *May 22 1950 (early morning from San Gimignano)*, for instance, he captures the effect of dawn in springtime by the subtle placing of white highlights in the overall tonality of pale grey. The shifting perspective of taut lines in the foreground roofscape, played off, as usual, against the free-flowing lines of the landscape background, produces a feeling of movement – smooth, yet changing in speed – like that of a Calder mobile. Looking through the open shutters of Nicholson's bedroom window, across to the wide horizon, one has the sensation of being aboard ship. The same effect of movement is produced in *May
39 24 1950 (single tower, San Gimignano)* by the simple device of tilting the bedroom interior at an angle to the symmetrical rectangle of the sheet of paper. (With what

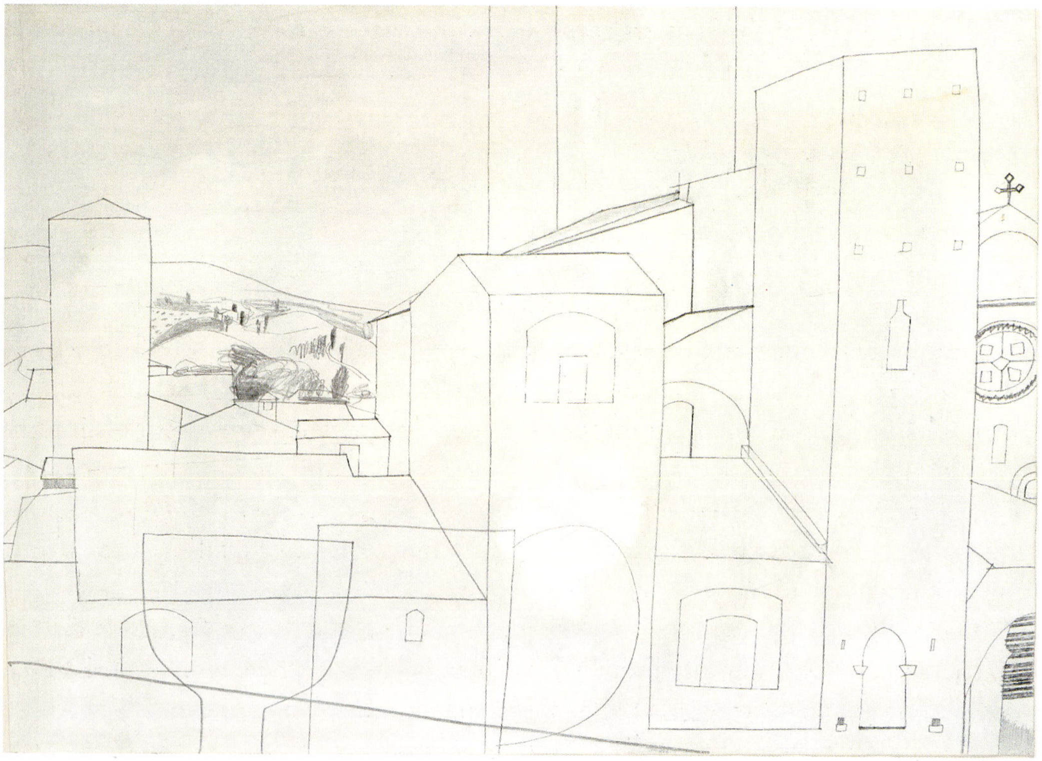

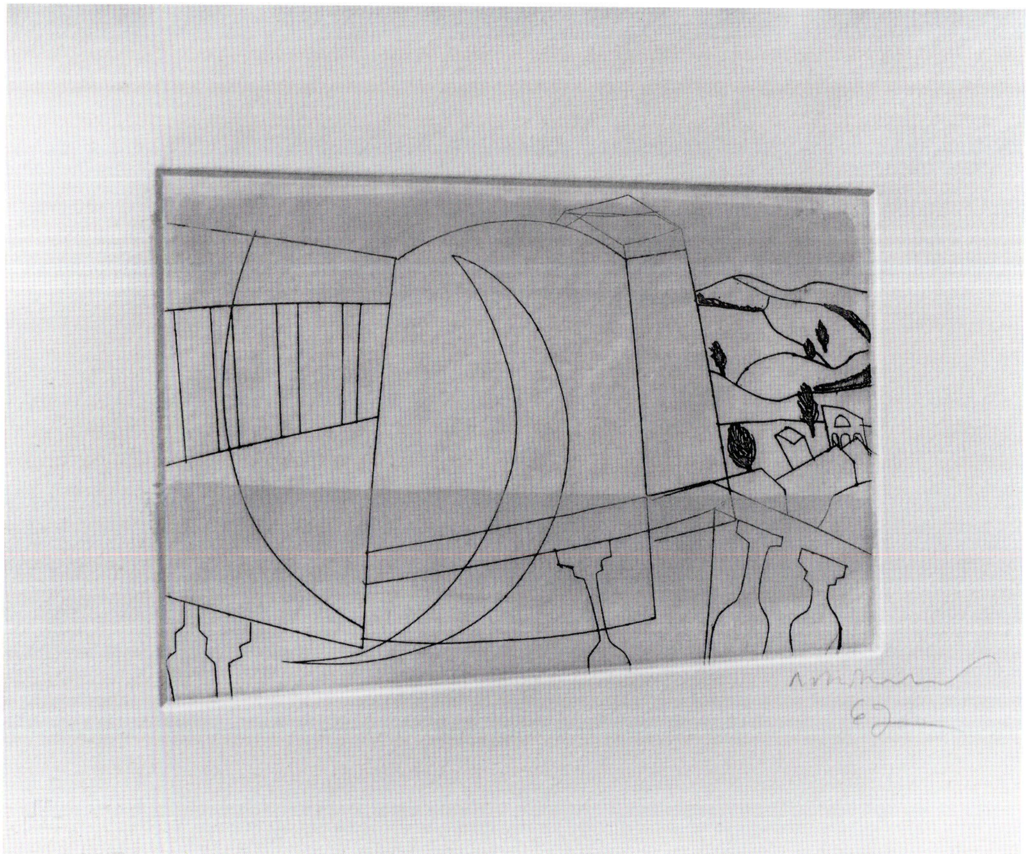

41 *May 21 1950 (San Gimignano)*
pencil on paper
35.5 × 51 cm (14 × 20 in)

42 *1967 (San Gimignano)*
etching with wash
17 × 24 cm (6¾ × 9¼ in), paper 27.5 × 34.5 cm
(10¾ × 13½ in)

relish is each slat of the shutters recorded, with what assurance each string of the
41 back of the chair and each detail of door and basin!) In *May 21 1950 (San
Gimignano)* the geometry of architecture and still life crowds out the landscape,
38 while in *May 22 1950 (cloisters, San Gimignano)* nature fights back in the wildness of
the tree contrasted with the still perfection of the cloister arcade. Another drawing
of a view from a balcony, this time Reddihough's, inspired a romantic little painting,
made some months after Nicholson returned from Italy. Measuring only 16.5 × 31 cm
43 ($6\frac{1}{2} \times 12\frac{1}{4}$ in), this densely packed composition of close-up still life ambiguously
merging into architecture, of mediaeval tower and distant landscape, all under the
sign of a crescent moon, might almost bring to mind a painting by Samuel Palmer,
such is its richness of colour, its mottled texture and, above all, its intensity – in complete contrast with the spacious rhythm and linearity of the drawing that is its basis.
This painting was in turn the basis for an etching Nicholson made in 1967 within
42 whose small compass of 17 × 24 cm ($6\frac{3}{4} \times 9\frac{1}{4}$ in) the gemlike quality of the painting is combined with the crisp clarity of the original drawing.

In that group of drawings made in San Gimignano Nicholson's draughtsmanship reached a new high-point. But they were only a beginning: there would hardly be a day without some drawing. He might spend the morning wandering around a town, then be struck by some architectural feature or grouping and feel moved to draw it. Laying no claim to a technical or historical knowledge of architecture, what

43 *February 14 1951 (San Gimignano, crescent moon)*
oil and pencil on board
16.5 × 31 cm ($6\frac{1}{2} \times 12\frac{1}{4}$ in)

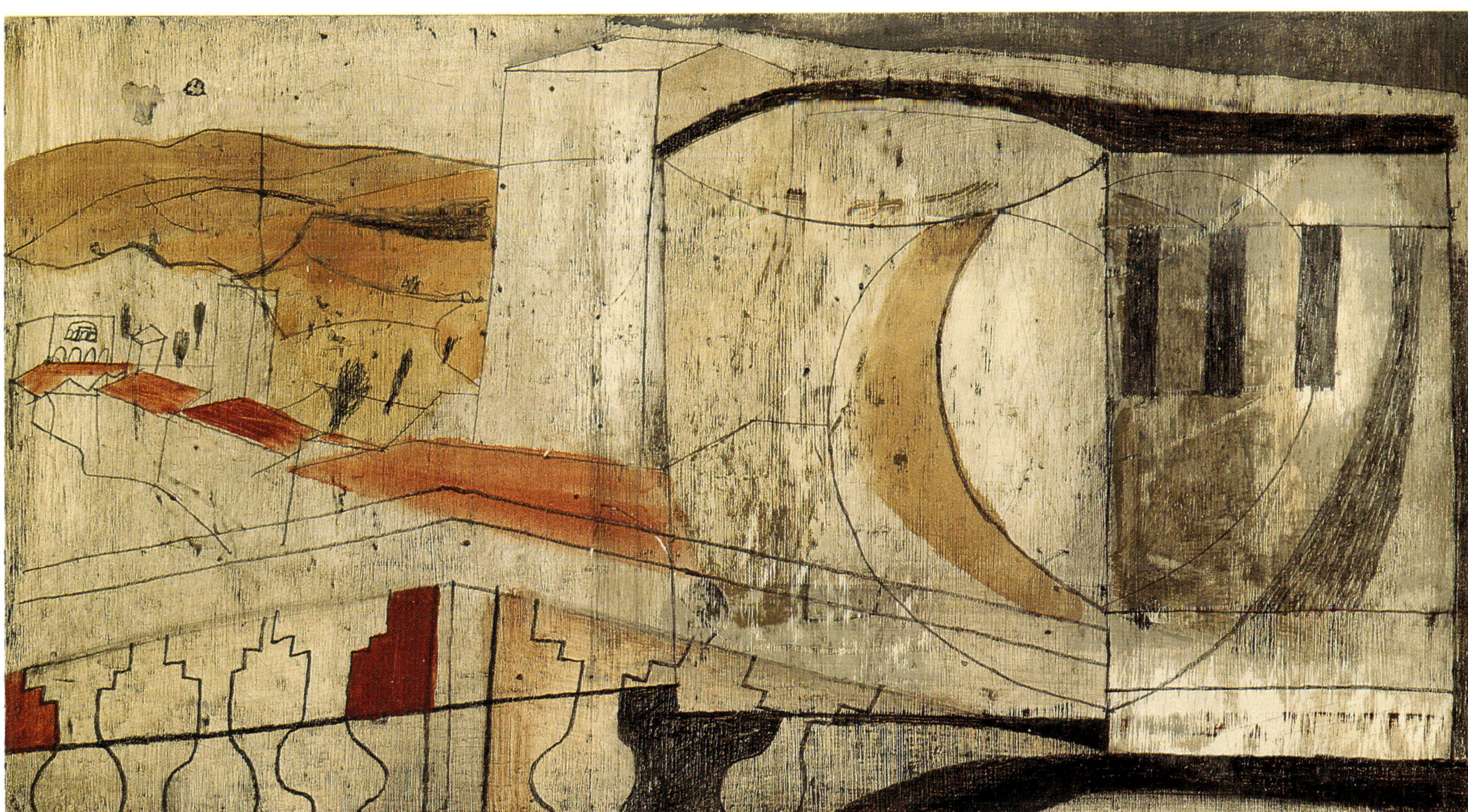

interested him was the shape, the proportion, the lie of a building – its inner essence or personality would spark off an idea for a free variation based upon it. Buildings, like still-life objects, were a starting point only: naturally there was no point in mere imitation. On the contrary, Nicholson realized that he had to dare to be free when creating one work of art out of another. Architecture in landscape offered an opportunity to combine his love of precise structure with his feeling for poetry and acute sensitivity to the spirit of place.

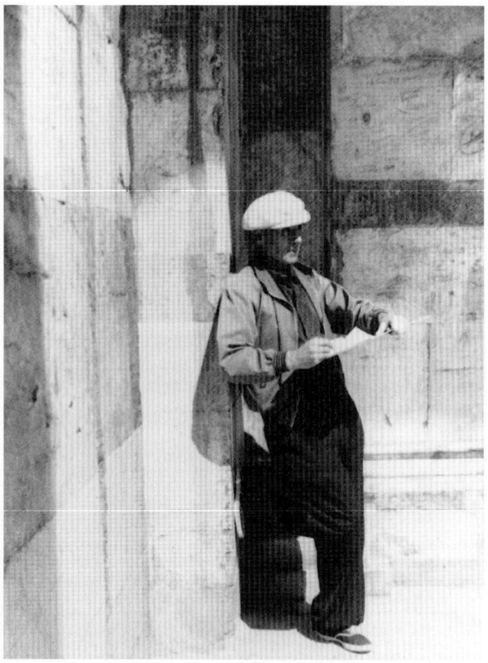

44 BN drawing in Pisa, June 1950 (photo: Cyril Reddihough)

Having exhausted one motif, he would get into the car and go in search of another. Reddihough would do the driving, while Nicholson, through a windscreen kept immaculately clean, would look out for a likely motif. Something in a landscape or townscape would interest his eye and he would then settle down and try to isolate the thing that excited him, while leaving out the rest. This would usually take between one and two hours. What may seem surprising, in view of the strength and absolute control of his sweeping lines, is that Nicholson frequently stood up to draw, holding the drawing-board steady against his body – a practice he kept up well into his sixties.

In the evening, after dinner, he would take a fresh look at the drawing he had made that day and consider its formal design without reference to the motif. He might then alter an emphasis or rub out and reposition a line (often deliberately leaving traces of the original still visible), but none of the changes would be very great.[72]

After almost three weeks in Tuscany, they returned north, via Ferrara, Ravenna and Padua, to Venice, where Barbara Hepworth was exhibiting at the *Biennale* – an honour accorded to Nicholson four years later. Looking back on this first Italian trip, Nicholson called it 'easily the most exciting holiday I've ever had . . . I think by car rather than by train or 'plane is the ONLY way in which to *experience* a country – to travel freely through the countryside & come to one superb architectural village or town after another'.[73] It was natural that he should wish to repeat such an experience, and inevitable that it should prove unrepeatable.

On their second trip, in October 1955, Reddihough and Nicholson worked south from Tuscany, through Umbria to Rome. They stopped off mainly in hill villages, not in towns, and this gave the expedition quite a different feel from their earlier one, as did the very cold weather (in May 1950 it had been superb). But by the time he reached Rome, where his niece, Jenny Nicholson, lived in the Piazza del Grillo, he had a sheaf of drawings, mostly architectural, gathered from various motifs discovered on the way: Buonconvento, Chiusure, San Quirico d'Orcia, Pienza, Radicofani, Spello and others.

One sign of the enhanced status of drawing within Nicholson's work as a whole was his practice, from the late 1940s, of applying a thin wash of oil paint to part of each sheet of paper on which he intended to draw. This he did well in advance, without any idea as yet of the subjects he would choose to draw. Raw umber, raw sienna, turquoise or blue would be diluted with a varying proportion of turps, allowing the white ground of the paper to shine through. Like the prepared ground for a relief or painting, the colour, shape and position of the oil wash provided a starting-point for

work as well as giving the finished drawing more body and individuality. From a sheaf of these prepared sheets he would select whichever seemed appropriate to his idea of the landscape, architecture or still life he was about to draw. We have already noticed how, in *May 22 1950 (early morning from San Gimignano)*, the thinnest of pale grey-blue washes is offset by the white gleam of untreated paper to evoke the
46 unearthly light of dawn, while in *October 3 1955 (Chiusure, Tuscany)* the dark umber wash reinforces the urgent scribble and widely varying tonality of Nicholson's pencil marks to register the drama of the ravine. Even in the medium of pencil on paper
47 he can make telling use of a change of texture, a good example being *October 2 1955 (metallic landscape, Buonconvento)*. Here, to achieve the silvery 'metallic' effect on the trunks of the olive trees, Nicholson has scraped away part of his thick pencilling back to the white paper, leaving a very slightly roughened surface that eerily illuminates the whole drawing.

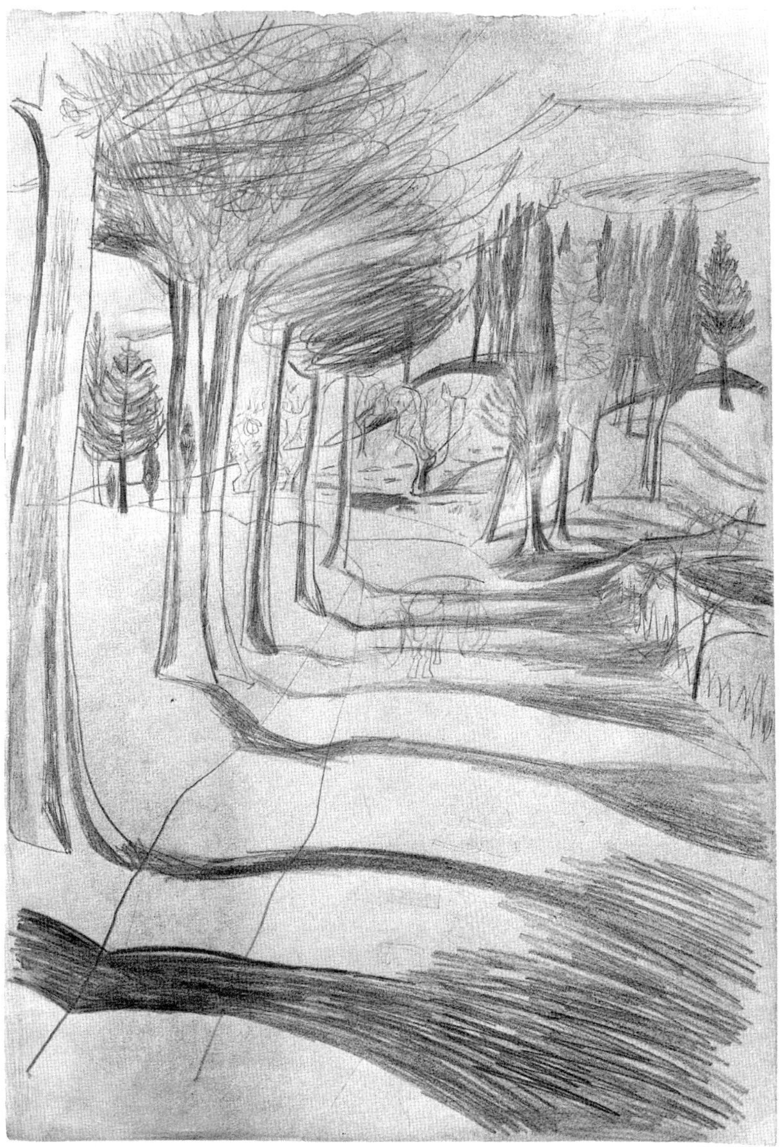

45 *October 3 1955 (road to Monte Oliveto)*
pencil on paper
51 × 35.5 cm (20 × 14 in)

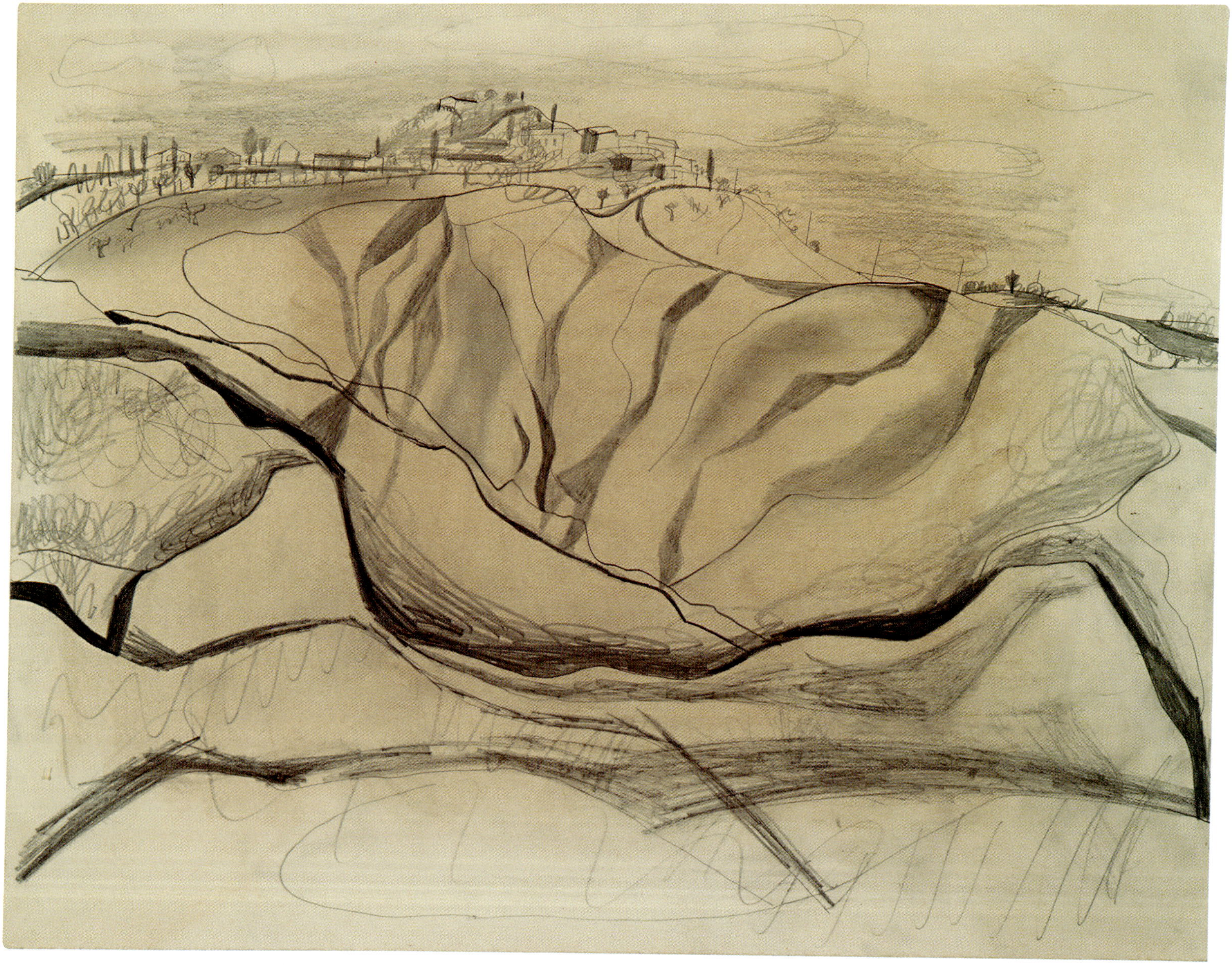

46 *October 3 1955 (Chiusure, Tuscany)*
oil wash and pencil on paper
38 × 50 cm (15 × 19¾ in)

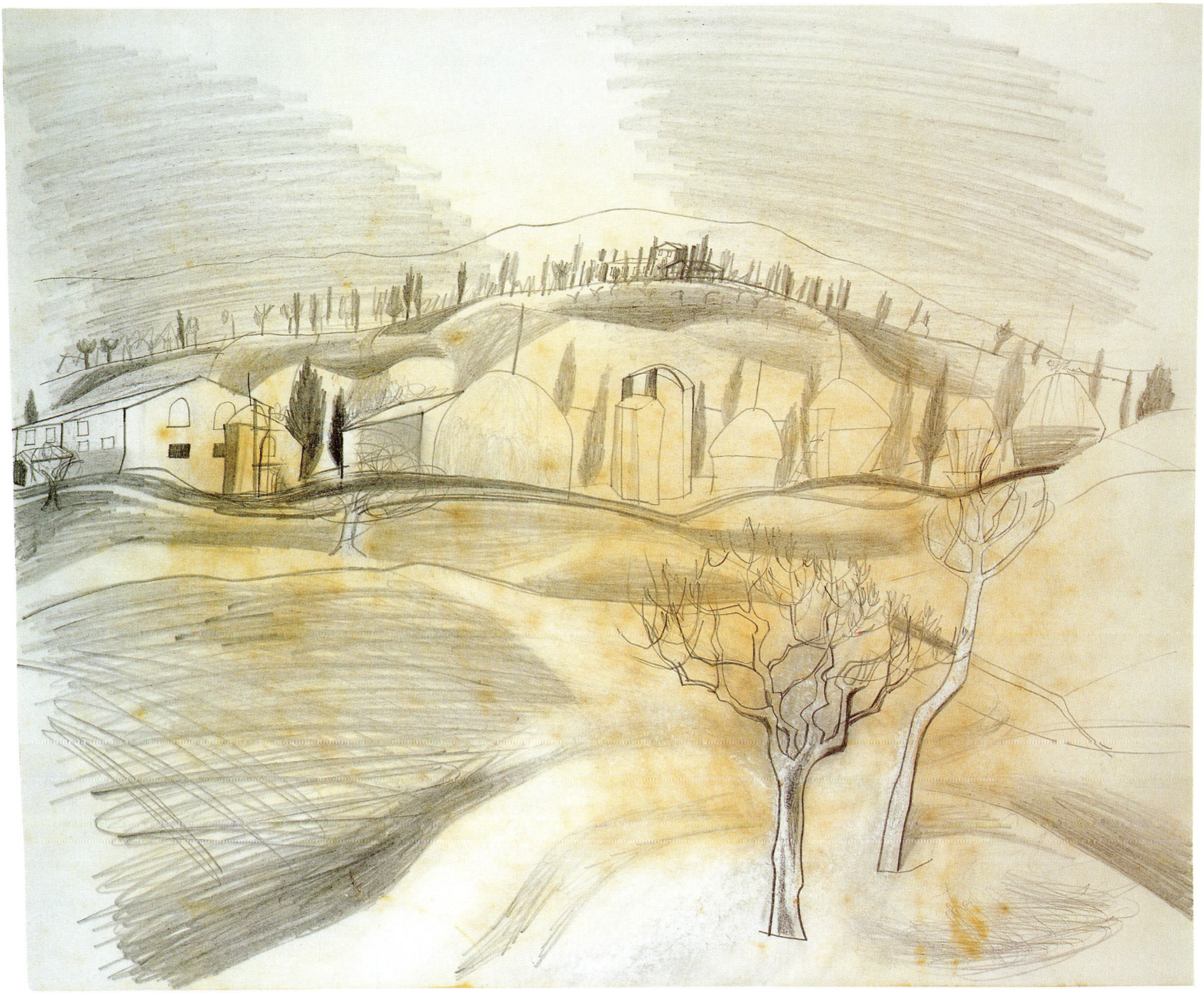

47 *October 2 1955 (metallic landscape, Buonconvento)*
oil wash and pencil on paper
36 × 44 cm (14¼ × 17¼ in)

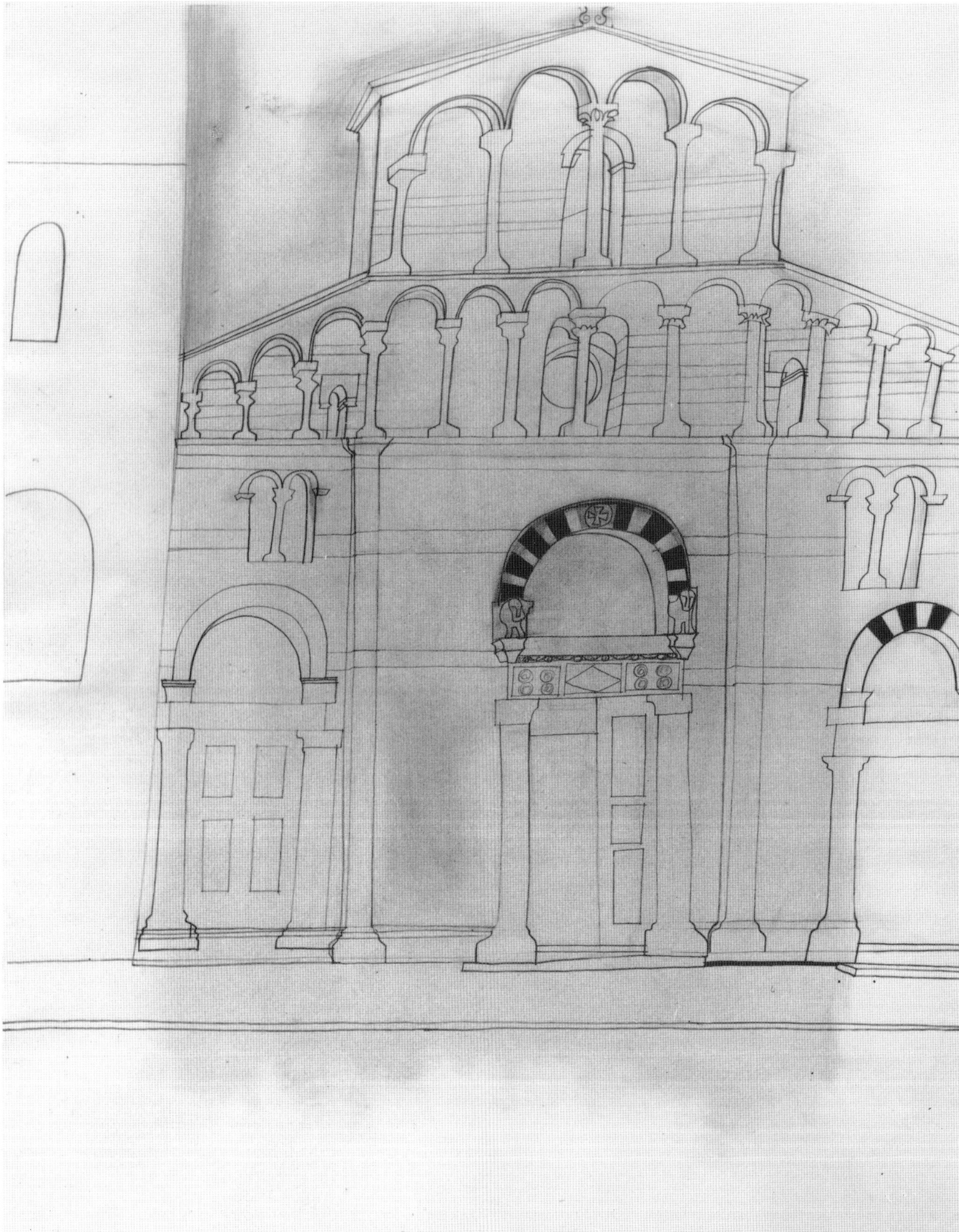

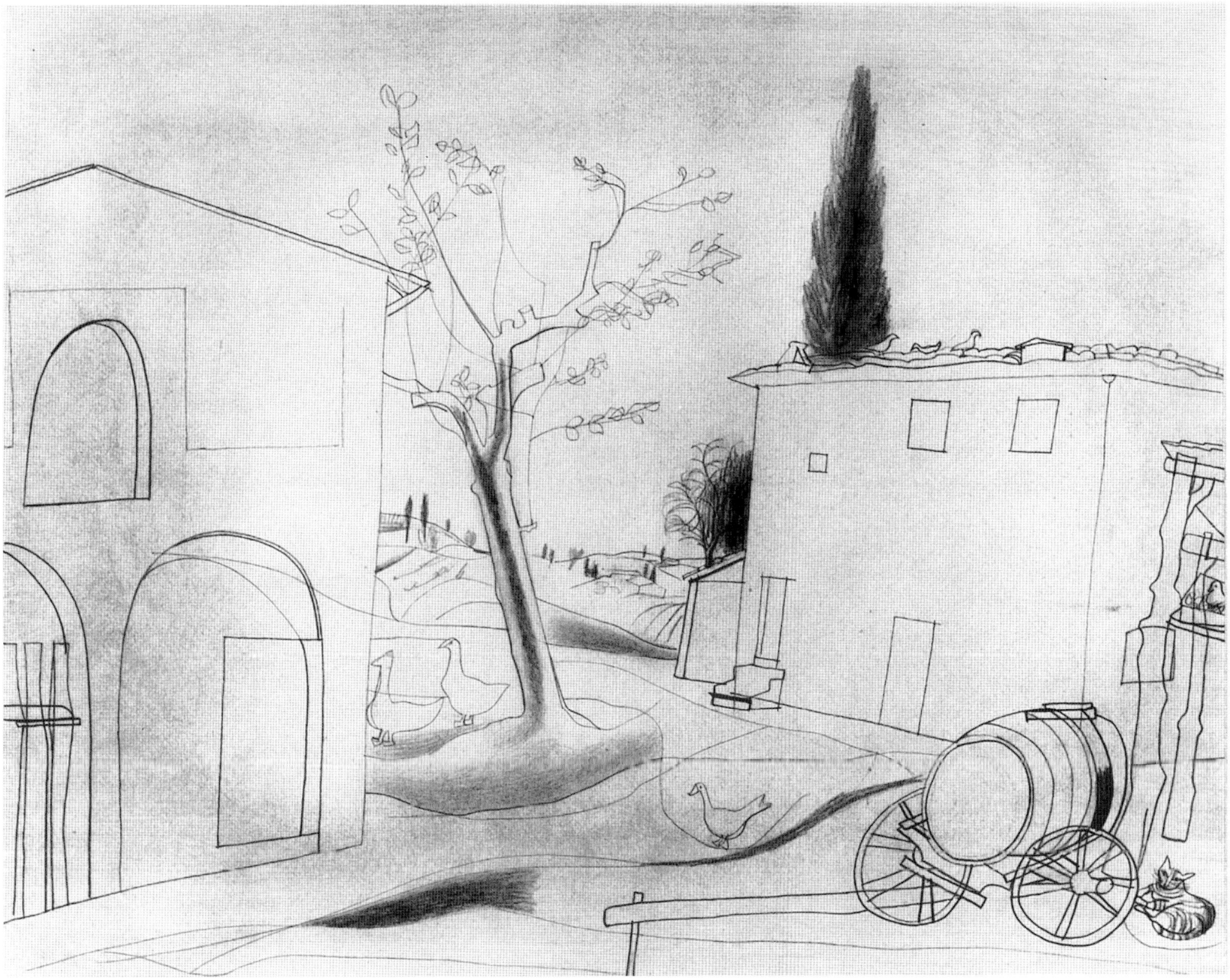

← 48 *1956 (San Pietro, Lucca)*
oil wash and pencil on paper
dimensions unknown

49 *September 1956 (La Buca, Tuscany)*
oil wash and pencil on paper
35 × 51 cm (13¾ × 20 in)

Though he made five separate visits to Italy between 1950 and 1957, on all of which he made drawings, Nicholson was not dependent on the *mezzogiorno* for inspiration. In the same period he visited Yorkshire equally often, and not only because two of his oldest friends lived there – Cyril Reddihough at Ilkley and Herbert Read at Stonegrave. He loved the drama and severity of the moors: the dry-stone walls emphasizing the form of the bare hills, their lines playing against one another and creating a two-dimensional pattern over the hillsides; the smooth outlines of the ridges against the sky; the rock so close to the surface of the land, and the clints breaking through it; the timelessness of the landscape, its roughness and wildness, and, not least, the stone-built barns and cottages, the ruined abbeys and ancient, rock-solid bridges – all appealed to him greatly and made him want to draw.

To these years belong drawings of a Wharfedale hamlet under snow and of the
50 ruined nave of Rievaulx Abbey. In the first, snow-light radiates from the pure white patches of untouched paper, in strong contrast to the two evergreens in the centre; the stone walls sweep around and across the hill in a springy rhythm; and the two milk churns set against a wall, big and blank except for the empty square of a window, invite a quite separate contemplation of pure forms in space. The omission, the selective emphasis, the touch of humour, the reordering of the motif into a rhythmic whole, the play of geometric roofs against organic trees and hillside, the unconcern with illusionistic accuracy, are by now the recognizable hallmarks of Nicholson's
51 coolly romantic draughtsmanship. In the Rievaulx drawing the same omission and selection of detail are evident in the arches on the right, whose rhythms mount up to the one big arch that frames the rainy landscape. Trees and foliage and the outlines of the hills that rise in the background are indicated with summary freedom since the music of space and form has already established the imaginative truth of the scene.

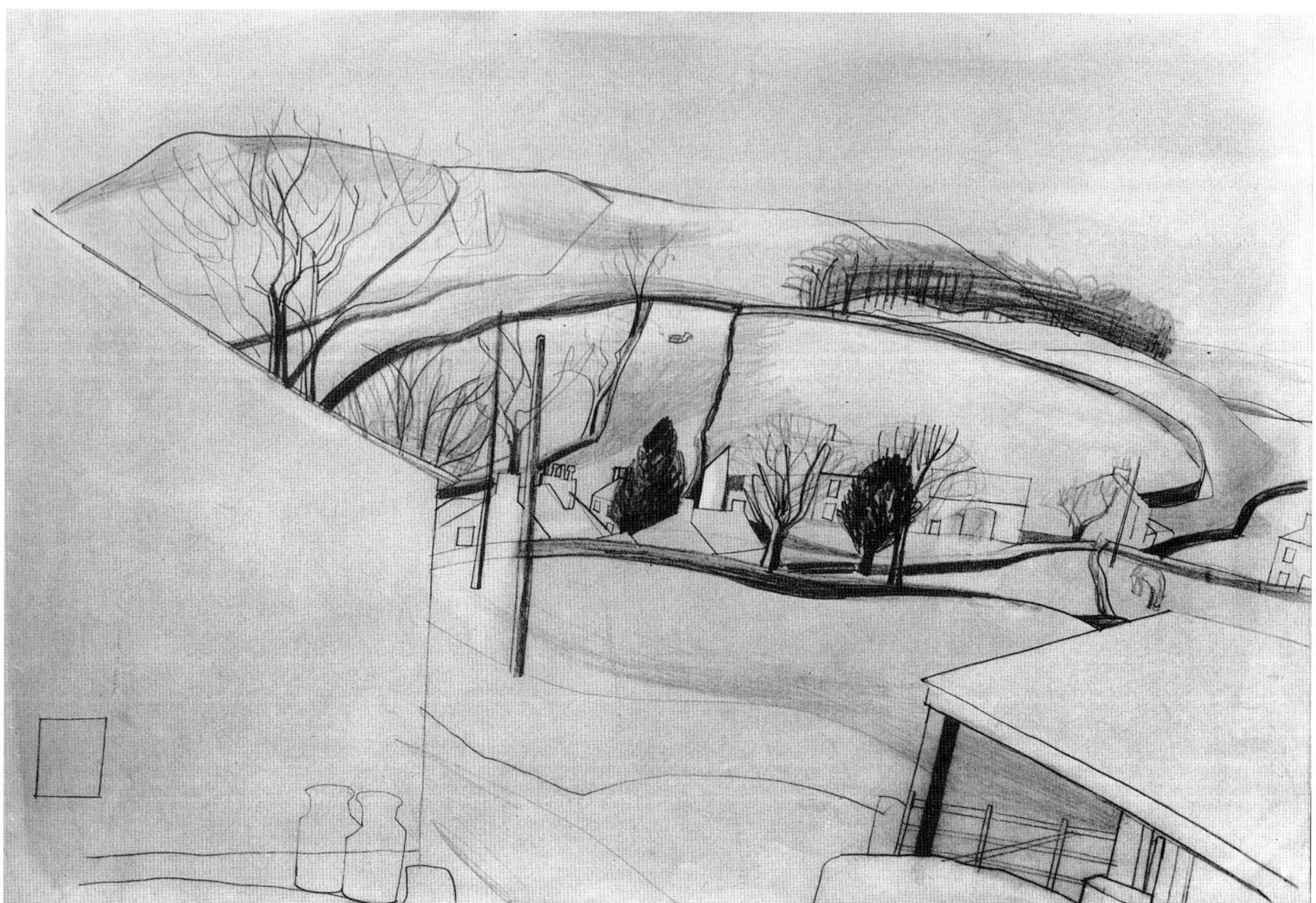

50 *January 4 1953 (Thorpe, Wharfedale in snow)*
oil wash and pencil on paper
38 × 56 cm (15 × 22 in)

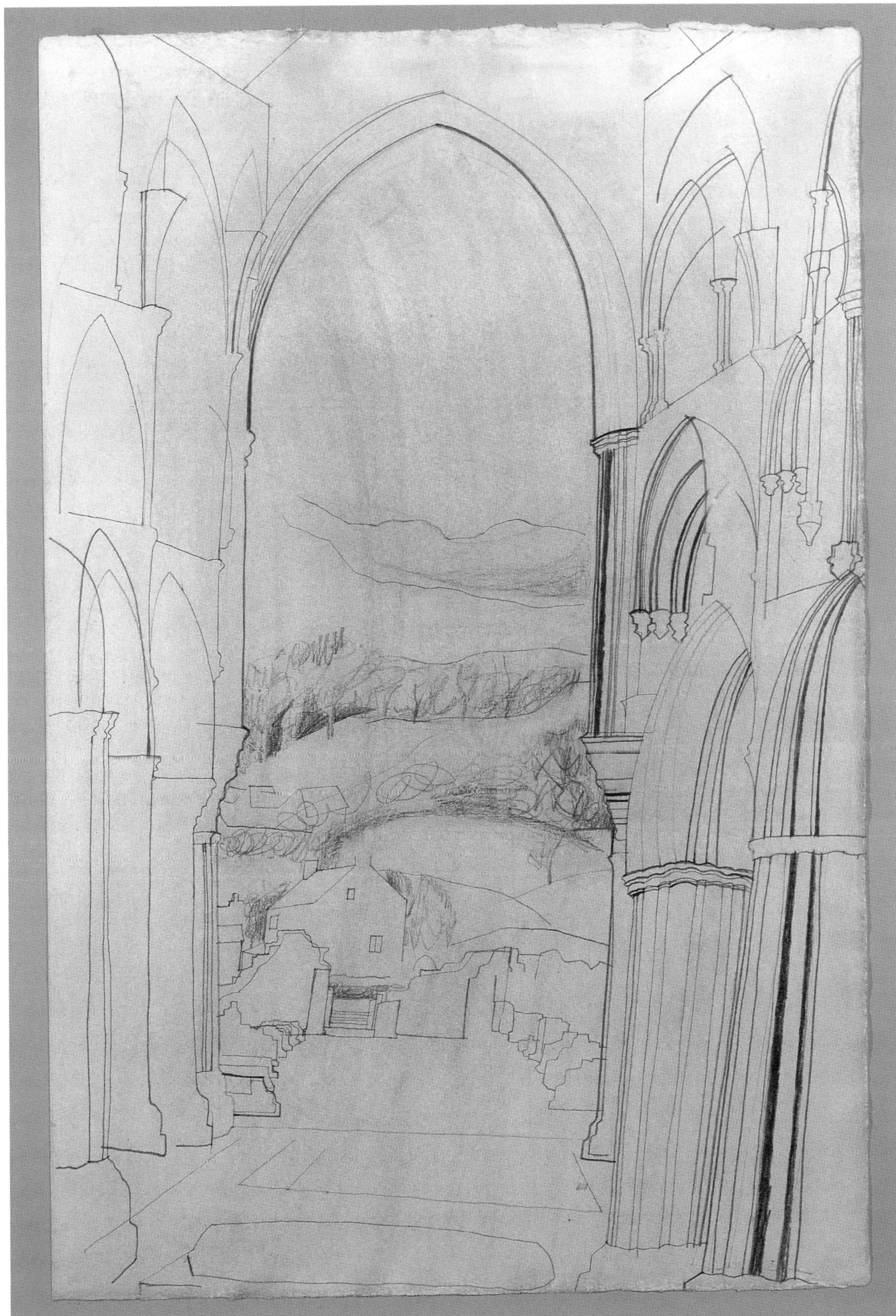

51 *October 1954 (Rievaulx)*
oil wash and pencil on paper
57 × 39 cm (22½ × 15¼ in)

We have now traced the evolution of Nicholson's landscape drawing from its renewal, as a result of his move to Cornwall, to its first full flowering, stimulated by his travels abroad. From the early 1950s his drawing becomes more assured, achieves an ever greater clarity and *élan*, and moves from a subordinate to a privileged place in his work. Drawing and the linear element also begin to play a dominant part in Nicholson's paintings from the late 1940s. Over the next few years the still-life group on a table-top remains the constant theme for a series of variations, inventive and virtuosic, in which the by now familiar outlines of jug, goblet, cup and carafe are presented in multiple perspective, then echoed, counterpointed, fragmented, reconstituted and playfully transformed in free but perfectly controlled fantasias of line and precisely demarcated areas of colour.[74]

When, in October 1949, he took over one of the Porthmeor Studios in St Ives, these still lifes immediately grew in size and also in assurance. After ten years of cramped working space, it was 'like being able to breathe deeply again to be able to work on this scale – to walk about and paint at arm's length'.[75] The contained
53 rhythms in the monumental *1950 (still life)* and the sweep, the energy and the beau-
54 tifully judged space proportion of *March 14 1952 (WBG)* bear witness to that exceptional hand–eye coordination which he inherited from his father and which showed itself in their shared passion for ball games: William enjoyed demonstrating his skill at bilboquet, while Ben, having won the Junior Diabolo Championship at the Crystal Palace in 1906, went on to become a redoubtable tennis player, and invented a special brand of ping-pong at which he was virtually unbeatable. In the autumn of 1947 he took up golf at the nearby links at Lelant and soon found it as much an aesthetic as a physical recreation: the change of texture from rough to fairway to green, the contrast between the curve of the ball rolling towards the hole and the straight lines of putter and flag were a pleasure in themselves. Striking the golf ball called for the same decisiveness and economy of gesture as driving a pencil in sweeping trajectory across canvas or paper (and, as if to demonstrate this equivalence, he was happy to swap a painting for a golf club he particularly liked, just as Haydn is said to have exchanged a string quartet for a pair of good English razors). The physical act of drawing was, for Nicholson, in large part a game of skill, a test of his dexterity in keeping the perfect balance between control and freedom of line. Often he seems to
55 delight in putting this balance at risk. For example, in *August 1956 (Val d'Orcia)* the outlines of the still-life objects break dangerously free into coiling arabesques, while the staccato punctuation of black and Venetian red produces a Miróesque effect of quick, darting movement. The table itself (or rather, table/animal, Nicholson being as fond of a visual pun as of a verbal one), with its thrusting diagonals and tautly bent right-hand edge, suggests power barely held in control. Not only does Nicholson's array of mug, jug, goblet and carafe dissolve in the rhythmic flow of line but it is simultaneously invaded by landscape memories: the umber of the Tuscan soil and the blue-grey of rock. As he put it in a letter to Helen Sutherland, just after finishing this monumental painting: 'These still lifes, so-called, always turn out to be *landscapes* for me – either Cornish or Tuscan . . . and this is Tuscan.'[76] This seeming

paradox he pushed a little further in a published statement of the same year: 'My "still life" paintings are closely identified with landscape, more closely than are my landscapes which perhaps relate more to "still life".'[77] And at this period, it is true, landscape and still life were particularly closely fused in his work. But throughout the sixty-year span of his productive life these two themes, always the main sources of his inspiration, overlap, mingle and interchange: already in 1925 an ostensibly still-life subject has a place-name for title. We know also that a long history lies behind the blotched and mottled surface of *Val d'Orcia*,[78] scraped back in places to show the white gesso ground: the suggestion of a natural weathered surface goes back at least as far as the rubbed and scraped surface of *1928 (Pill Creek)*.

Texture was always of prime importance to Nicholson, whatever the medium he was working in. It was in the search for a greater contrast of surface texture than the scraping and incising of his prepared canvas could give that he had first begun to carve and cut away wooden board to varying depths, each depth potentially differing in colour or texture. And now again, in the spring of 1953, after an interval of over six years in which he had made almost no reliefs, he must have felt this same urge actually to excavate an object.

At first he continued where he had left off: a circle, or two circles in asymmetrical balance, incised or drawn on a rectangle; the rectangle cut away so as partially to reveal other square or rectangular shapes overlapping each other in shallow and ambiguous recession; a contrast between smooth and rough surfaces; a narrow tonal range; a hint of luminosity seeming to come from behind a carved edge; a sparing use of colour, more often rubbed into the surface than painted onto it. One new element does, however, appear: some of the drawn lines or carved edges are tilted out of true,
58 almost imperceptibly at first, then at a bolder angle. This is no longer the subtle

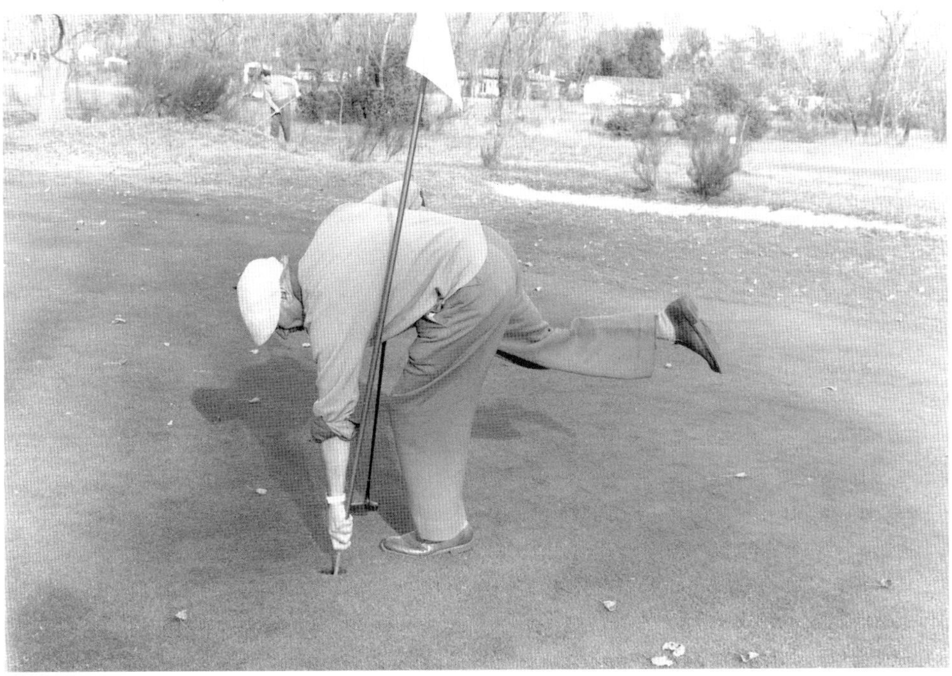

52 BN on Lelant golf course (photo: Charles Gimpel)

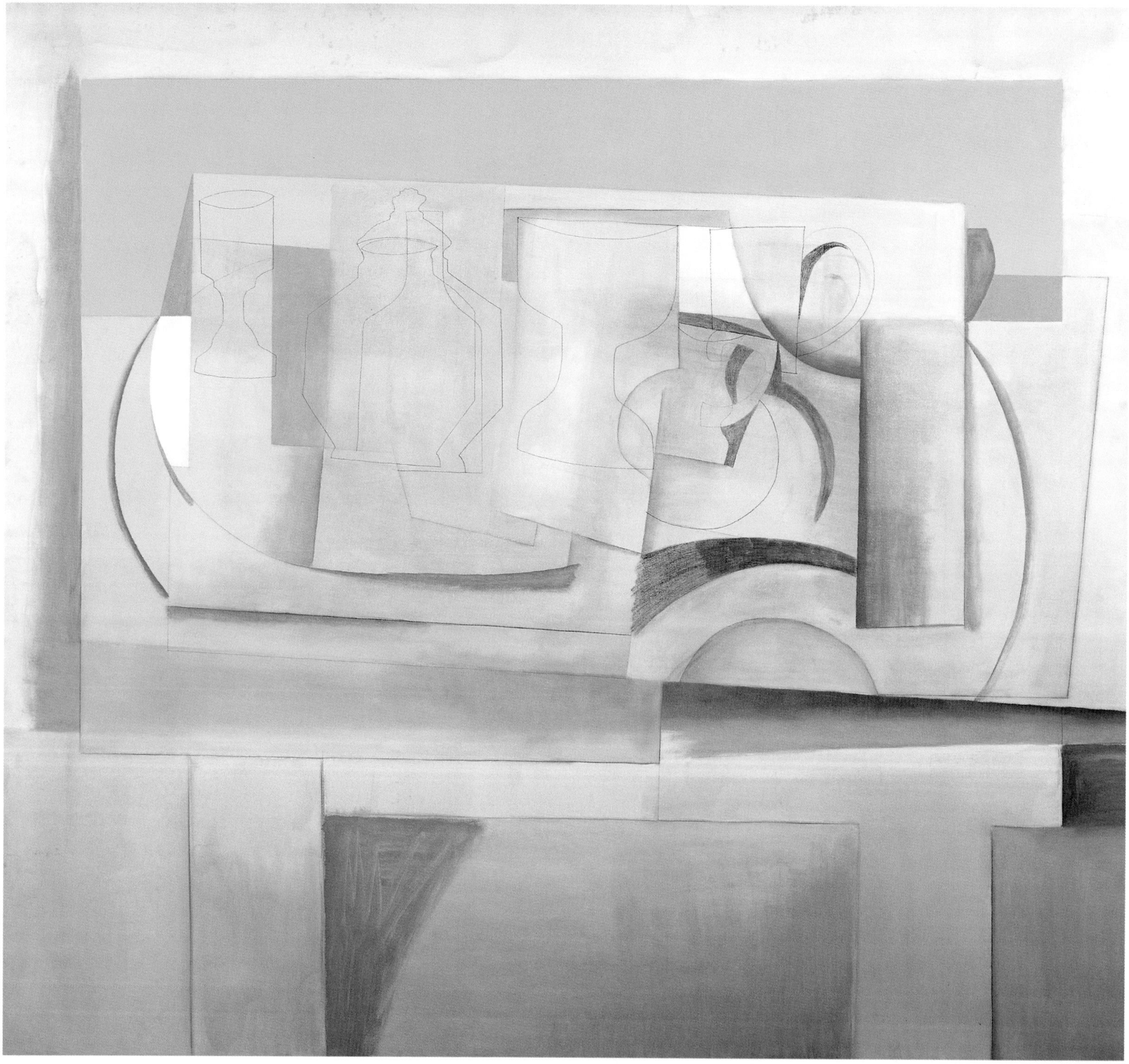

53 *1950 (still life)*
oil and pencil on canvas
203 × 228 cm (80 × 90 in)

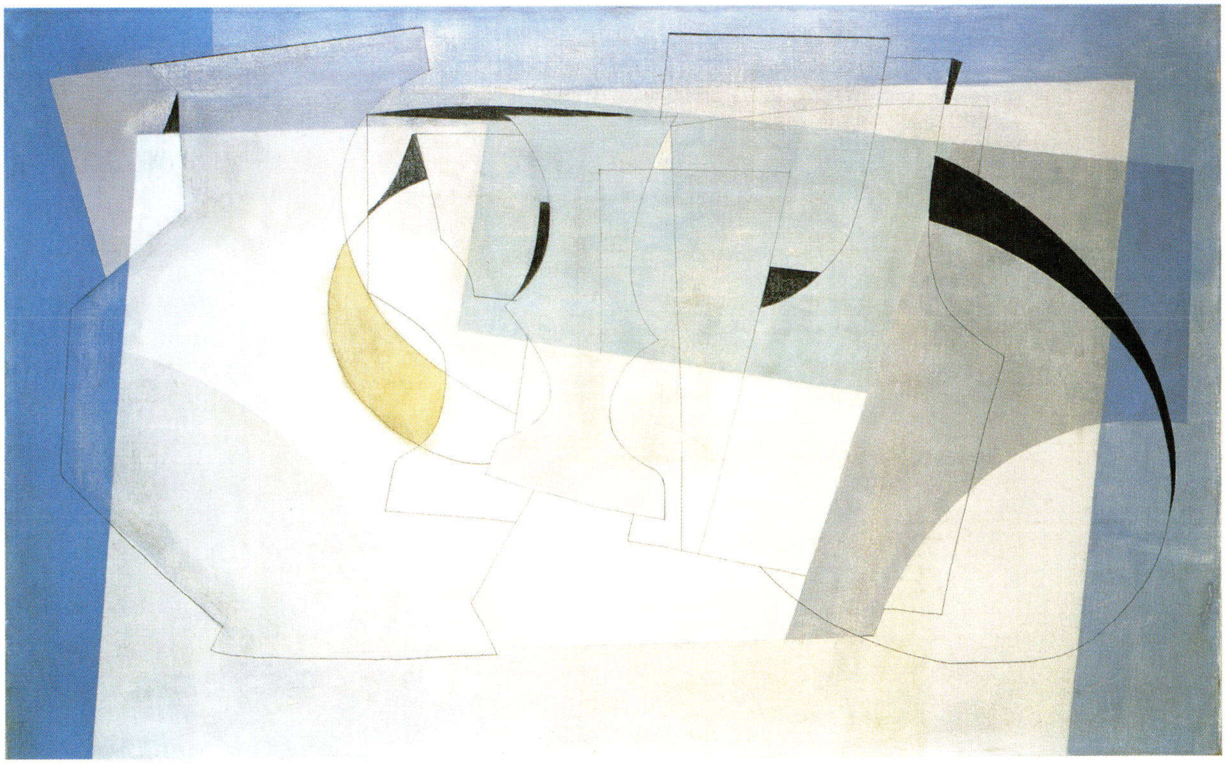

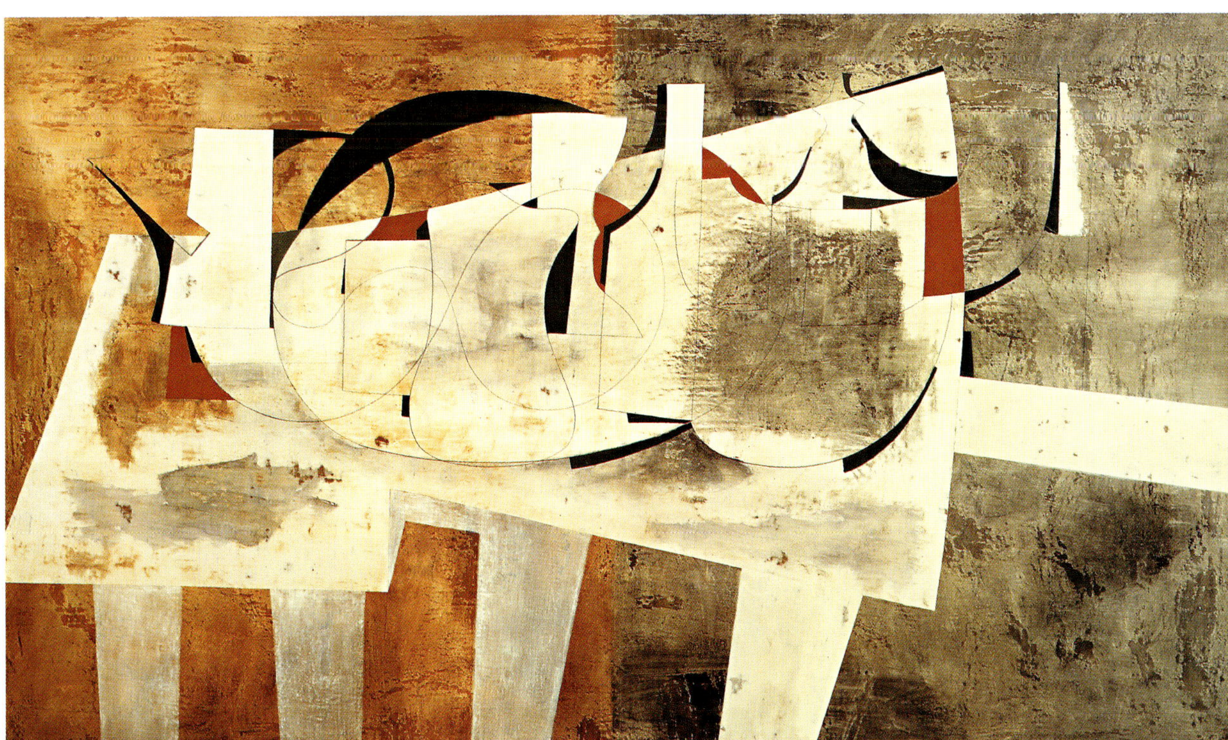

54 *March 14 1952 (WBG)*
oil and pencil on canvas
58.5 × 99 cm (23 × 39 in)

55 *August 1956 (Val d'Orcia)*
oil, gesso and pencil on board
122 × 213.5 cm (48 × 84 in)

imperfection that emphasizes the hand-worked quality of the carving in some of the early white reliefs, but a calculated destabilization for dramatic effect. Static orthogonals give way to a more organic, more dynamic slanting line, like that of the table's edge in *Val d'Orcia*. Movement is introduced, and the drama of converging lines of force. The relief is no longer self-contained, self-equilibrated, but moves beyond itself, is part of something larger. Simply by slanting or slightly curving a line, the vertical–horizontal balance is disturbed, and the whole character of a relief is altered, subtly but decisively. The reliefs Nicholson made in the next three or four years, however large-scale in conception, are most of them quite small in dimension, their surface often measuring no more than one square foot (by contrast with the large paintings made at the same time). Soon they were to expand to the truly monumental, and the implications of the tilted angle, curved line and trapezoid shape would be explored in a series of works that were the culmination of a long career.

The years 1950–7 were marked by new achievement and growing recognition, but were less happy in personal terms. Just as his relationship with Barbara Hepworth had begun by their working together with intense excitement in the same studio in Hampstead, so it ended when each found a studio of their own in St Ives. After some years of strain and increasing acrimony, they finally separated in 1950 and were divorced a year later. Nicholson stayed on by himself at Chy-an-Kerris until 1955, when he moved into St Ives so as to be closer to his studio. His new house, Trezion, looked out across the harbour to the Atlantic, with the rounded end of the Zion
57 Chapel roof immediately below – 'a playground for cats & birds, the birds teasing

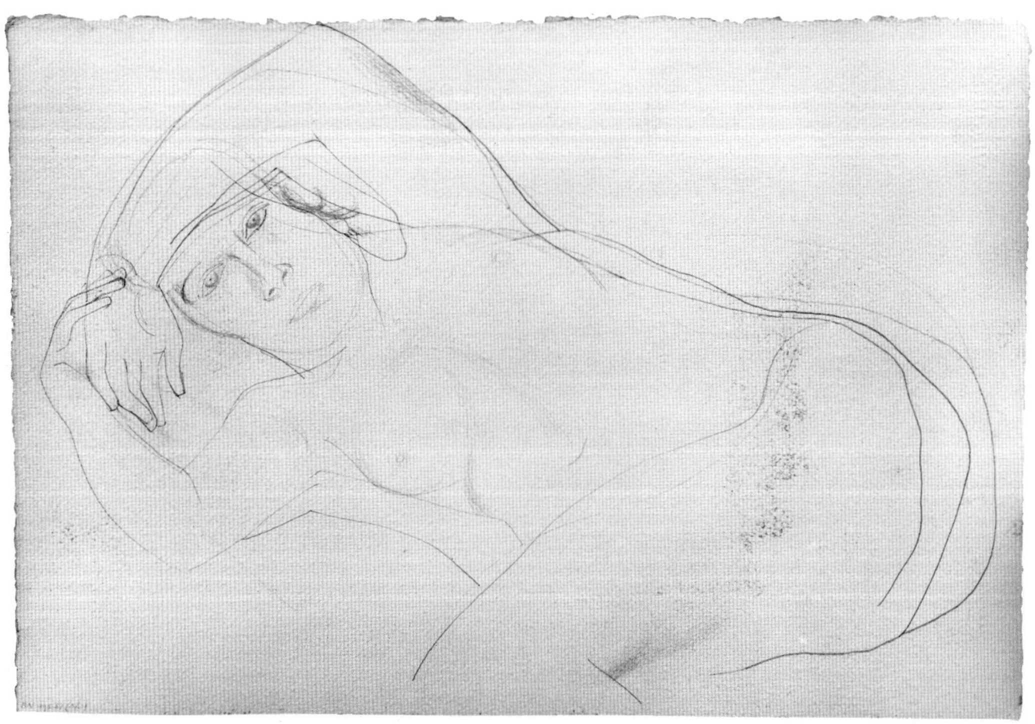

56 *August 1951 (nude, Copenhagen)*
pencil on paper
dimensions unknown

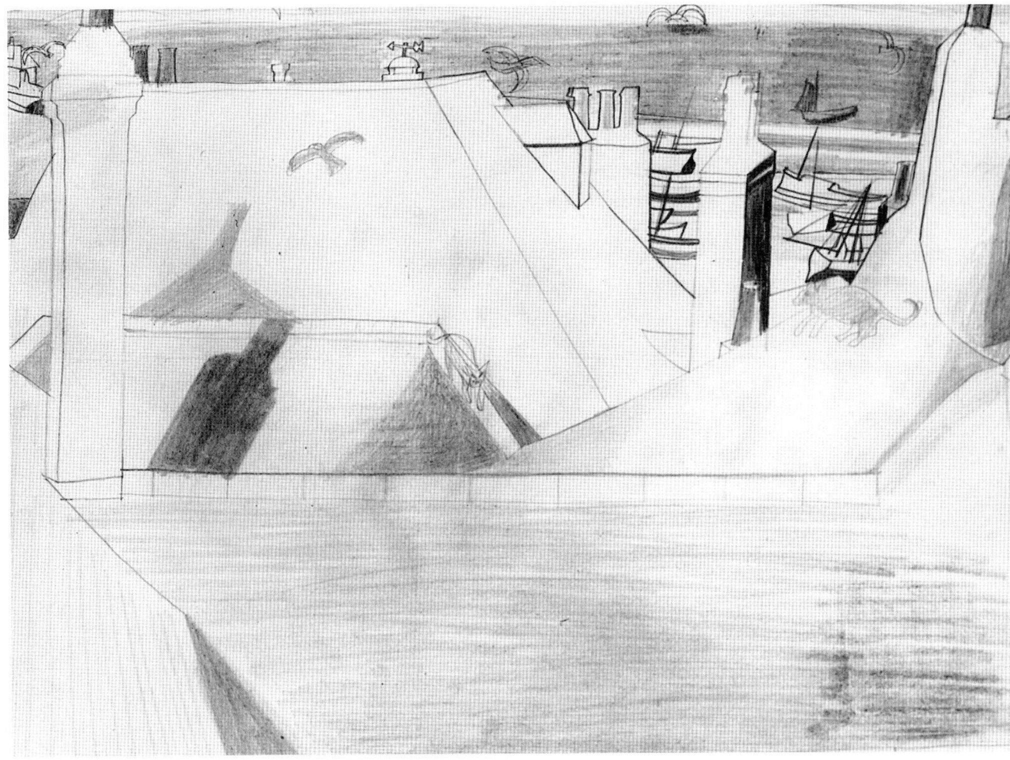

57 *1951[?] (rooftops, St Ives)*
oil wash and pencil on paper
27.5 × 37.5 cm (10¾ × 14¾ in)

the cats into thinking they can stalk them, or is it stork them?'[79] This had long been one of his favourite viewpoints, recorded in a number of drawings and paintings both before and after moving into the house.

In a letter he wrote on the eve of his sixtieth birthday, Nicholson told Jim Ede that he felt no older than twenty-four or twenty-five. No doubt the consciousness of being at the height of his powers and of at last receiving due recognition for his work helped to keep him youthful. Two months later, in June 1954, fifty-three of his paintings and reliefs (over half of them made in the previous four years) were exhibited at the *XXVII Venice Biennale*, and though he was unhappy about having to share the show with Francis Bacon, whose vast works dominated the British Pavilion, he nonetheless succeeded in carrying off the Ulisse acquisition prize. Another prize had come to him that May from the Belgian critics, who judged his exhibition at the Galerie Apollo in Brussels to be outstanding. Altogether, appreciation of his work was greater abroad than in England, and most of his income at this time was coming from America (and, to a lesser extent, from Canada and Japan).[80] In 1952 he had won first prize for his painting *1949 (poisonous yellow)* at the *39th International Exhibition* at the Carnegie Institute, Pittsburgh,[81] and in February 1957 he went to New York to receive the first $10,000 Guggenheim International Painting Award (for *August 1956 (Val d'Orcia)*) from President Eisenhower. Like all such awards, these prizes were absurdly dependent on the vagaries and machinations of international juries. But publicity did have the effect of stimulating demand for his work, and from now on he was free from worries about money. The publicity, it must be said, was confined entirely to Nicholson's work: he had a horror of the personality

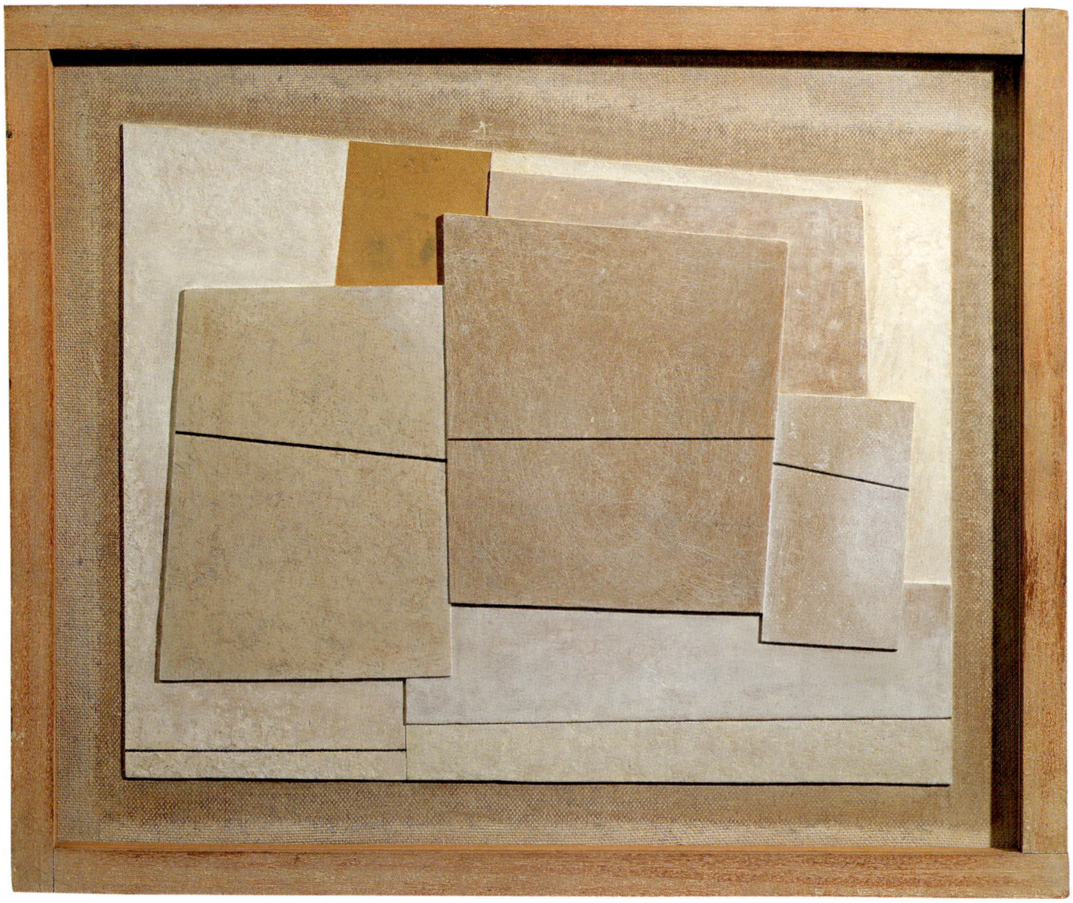

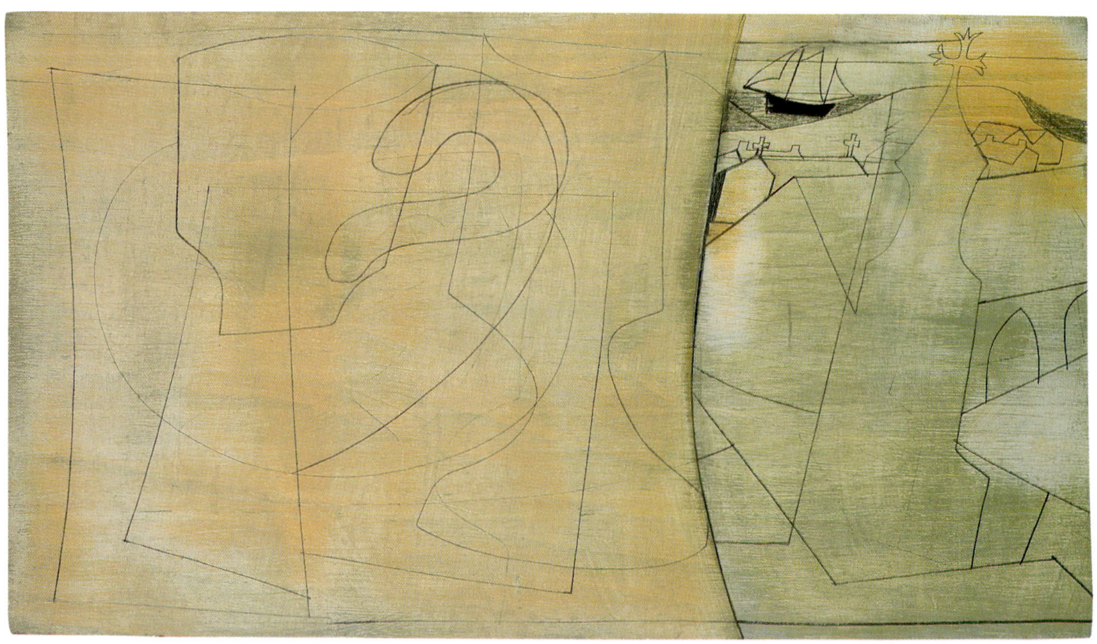

58 *February 1956 (granite)*
oil and pencil on carved board
50 × 62 cm (19½ × 24½ in)

59 *October 1951 (still life, steeple and ship)*
oil and pencil on board
20 × 35.5 cm (8 × 14 in)

→ 60 *May 1957 (Siena campanile)*
oil wash and pencil on paper
48 × 37 cm (19 × 14½ in)

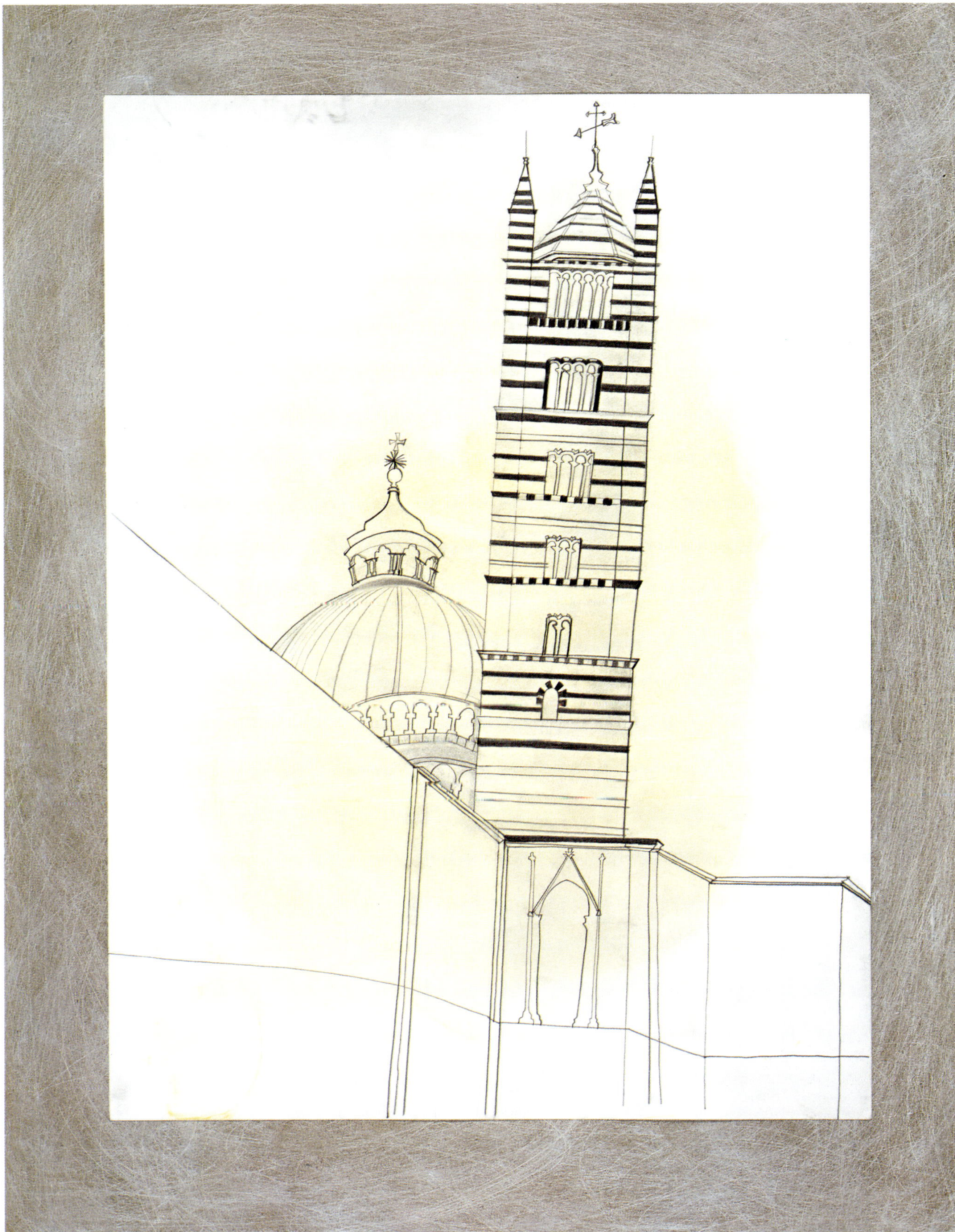

cult of the artist. And this is perhaps reflected in a self-portrait, commissioned as one of a series of artists' self-portraits published in *Art News and Review*, which he made at the time of his exhibition at the *Venice Biennale* (see *frontispiece*). Among the several portraits Nicholson made of himself with Barbara Hepworth in 1932/3 only one is naturalistic and a reasonable likeness. For the others he invented a teasingly abstract, linear style, partly echoing Picasso's 'Etruscan' profiles, partly Miró's anarchic line. In this new self-portrait, twenty years on, he understandably reverted to the playful freedom he had learnt from Miró (even borrowing Miró's favourite symbols of moon, star and maze-circle) so as not to tie the drawing down to a literally interpreted portrait. To speculate on the psychological motive behind this might be interesting, but the interpretations are likely to be as diverse as the interpreters and to shed more light on their own personalities than on Nicholson's.

For the new-found recognition and the steadily increasing sales of his work he owed a considerable debt to his old friend Herbert Read, who since the 1930s had held an unrivalled position as spokesman and interpreter of the various trends in contemporary art. In the face of philistine hostility he had shown courage, patience and never failing courtesy while advocating all that was new in art and vital to the society he dreamed of. His fair-mindedness and integrity had won him the respect of widely differing factions, so that now, in the 1950s, he enjoyed an international reputation. One consequence was that he was in great demand as a jury member for the growing number of international awards for painting and sculpture, a task which put a heavy strain on his sense of justice. Another was that he had great influence in selecting the exhibitions which the British Council sent abroad after the war as part of its cultural propaganda.[82] Impartial though he tried to be, Read persistently promoted Nicholson's work, with the result that he and Henry Moore together became Britain's most exported artists. As Nicholson wrote to Read, at the time of the *XXVII Venice Biennale*: 'I find my work in the difficult position of being more appreciated abroad than in England but of being dependent on the English assessment of it to exhibit it abroad.'[83] Since the British Council was virtual arbiter of which British artists were to be shown abroad, it was as well that Nicholson had Read to look after his interests.

Success at the *Venice Biennale* led to the exhibition being mounted in Amsterdam, Paris, Brussels and Zurich before coming to the Tate Gallery in June 1955. At these subsequent showings the number of works was increased from fifty-three to eighty-six, the main addition being twenty-three pencil drawings (nearly all made since 1950) – a clear sign of Nicholson's new valuation of drawing. He had hoped to make this retrospective 'something which will really show the process of *natural* development into "abstract" work as opposed to popping a few squares & triangles onto a canvas – so much of the abst. work being done today seems to me quite unreal'.[84] But even the appreciative critics tended to praise him for his craftsmanship, his concern for texture, his acute sense of formal relations and refinement of colour, and to omit to mention the all-important qualities of poetry and imagination which animate all these and distinguish his work from the 'unreal'. Beyond the circle of devoted followers, Nicholson's work, and especially the purely abstract part of it, met with more respect than understanding. The general lack of comprehension can be gauged by the elementary arguments he himself used on the rare occasions when he ventured into print. In attempting to allay the public's wariness of 'modern art', he was at pains to stress that his work was not about anything but itself – that it was to be approached directly, without preconceptions, and experienced in its own right. Less persuasively, he appealed to higher authority in the person of the Director of the National Gallery who had 'done a great deal to encourage modern art'.[85]

In May 1957 a freelance radio journalist came to St Ives to make a feature on the 'artists' colony' for Bavarian Radio. She had no previous knowledge of Nicholson and, by an irony of fate, was introduced to him by Barbara Hepworth. The enthusiasm and vivacity of the young woman immediately attracted him. Felicitas Vogler, then in her mid-thirties, had been born and brought up in Berlin. Already as a child she had inherited her father's passion for the camera and had since become a practised photographer of landscape and architecture. She was planning a long visit to India as soon as she had finished her present assignment in Cornwall. But Nicholson, who felt and behaved like a man half his age and who at this time very much needed the female companionship so essential to his work and well-being – who was, in fact, all ready to be swept off his feet – now exercised the full power of his charm. They were married that July and, while Reddihough and his family were on holiday abroad, borrowed his house for their honeymoon. From here they explored Wharfedale together, visited Fountains Abbey and Rievaulx, and called on the Reads at Stonegrave.

By now Nicholson had grown weary of the gossip, the backbiting and all the other drawbacks of the small, enclosed community – everyone too much on top of one another – in St Ives. He had already for some time been eager to move, but did not know where to go. It was 'Feli' who suggested Ticino, the Italian-speaking canton of southern Switzerland.[86] The mild climate and clear air, the beauty of its lakes and mountains strongly attracted him as did its strategic position, giving access to any part of Europe within a few hours. Most persuasive, though, were his memories of the past. His first glimpse of the Ticino had been from the window of a railway carriage by the light of a full moon in the winter of 1912/13. At that time he was staying with a family in Milan in order to learn Italian. Here he had met and fallen in love with a German girl, and it was with her and some friends that he went to spend a couple of days at Castagnola. No doubt her presence in the railway carriage made the moonlit Lake Lugano and the snow-covered mountains seem even more romantic and also coloured his memory of Castagnola, so that when he revisited it eight years later, at the end of his honeymoon with Winifred, he did not hesitate about buying a house that they found for sale there. Both Ben and Winifred looked back with nostalgia to the winters they spent at the Villa Capriccio. Winifred never returned to the Ticino, but in March 1958 Ben and his new wife left St Ives for good to spend the next thirteen years in Switzerland.

1958–71 drawings and painted reliefs

The new life began in the village of Ronco outside Ascona, where a temporary home was made in the two-room Casa Ticinella just below the church. From its balcony, suspended over Lake Maggiore, Nicholson found the view even more beautiful than that which he remembered from Castagnola. Eager to recapture the spirit and atmosphere of that earlier time in the Ticino, but also with a real sense of starting afresh, he adapted to the lack of space and set about making the first of a spate of drawings – some two hundred over the next two years – all of them variations on familiar still-life objects. He had grown up amongst the striped and spotted jugs and mugs, the glass goblets and faceted decanters which his father collected and painted, and had himself accumulated a collection that now proved an inexhaustible source of inspiration. Throughout the 1940s and 1950s still life was a major theme in his paintings. Now he would explore its latent possibilities purely in terms of line. Such voluntary restriction, like the rules of a game, acted like a spur. The line of a cup or beaker extends in an abstract rhythm and plays against the free-flowing lines of a jug or goblet in one, seemingly continuous, movement; or else the silhouette of a vase and its handle is conveyed by the irreducible minimum of subtly inflected line which by itself suggests mass: a likeness that is not a likeness, sometimes even verging on caricature. The shape of the spaces between objects is as important as the shape of the objects themselves, so that there is a teasing interchange between the two. Always Nicholson's drawings bear the marks of their physical making, nothing is fudged or concealed, each line is to be appreciated for its qualities as a line as well as for its function of delineating.

Until he moved to a larger house nearby, later in the summer of 1958, he was restricted to making small reliefs, but as soon as he was installed in his new garden-studio they grew bigger. Now that he was financially secure, he was free to work in whatever medium and on whatever scale he chose. And so, throughout his time in the Ticino, he concentrated on these complementary activities of drawing and carving, combining the two when he became absorbed with etching in the second half of the 1960s. By that time he no longer painted on canvas.

In 1960 the foundations were laid for a house of his own. The site was high up a wooded hillside above the village of Brissago, a few miles south of Ascona and just short of the Italian border. Below it the ground dropped so steeply that one looked straight out over the huge expanse of Lake Maggiore to the mountains rising up from its further shore. The grand scale and the constantly changing effects of light on the lake and mountains soon became a powerful influence on his work. Winter was his favourite season, with its clear skies, bright sunshine and crisp, invigorating air. The landscape too was then at its most beautiful: the bare trees outlined against the translucent waters of the lake; the moon rising in a pale-blue sky above the dark-brown,

→ 61 *December 1958 (tree at Sava, no.1)*
oil wash and pencil on paper
51 × 35.5 cm (20 × 14 in)

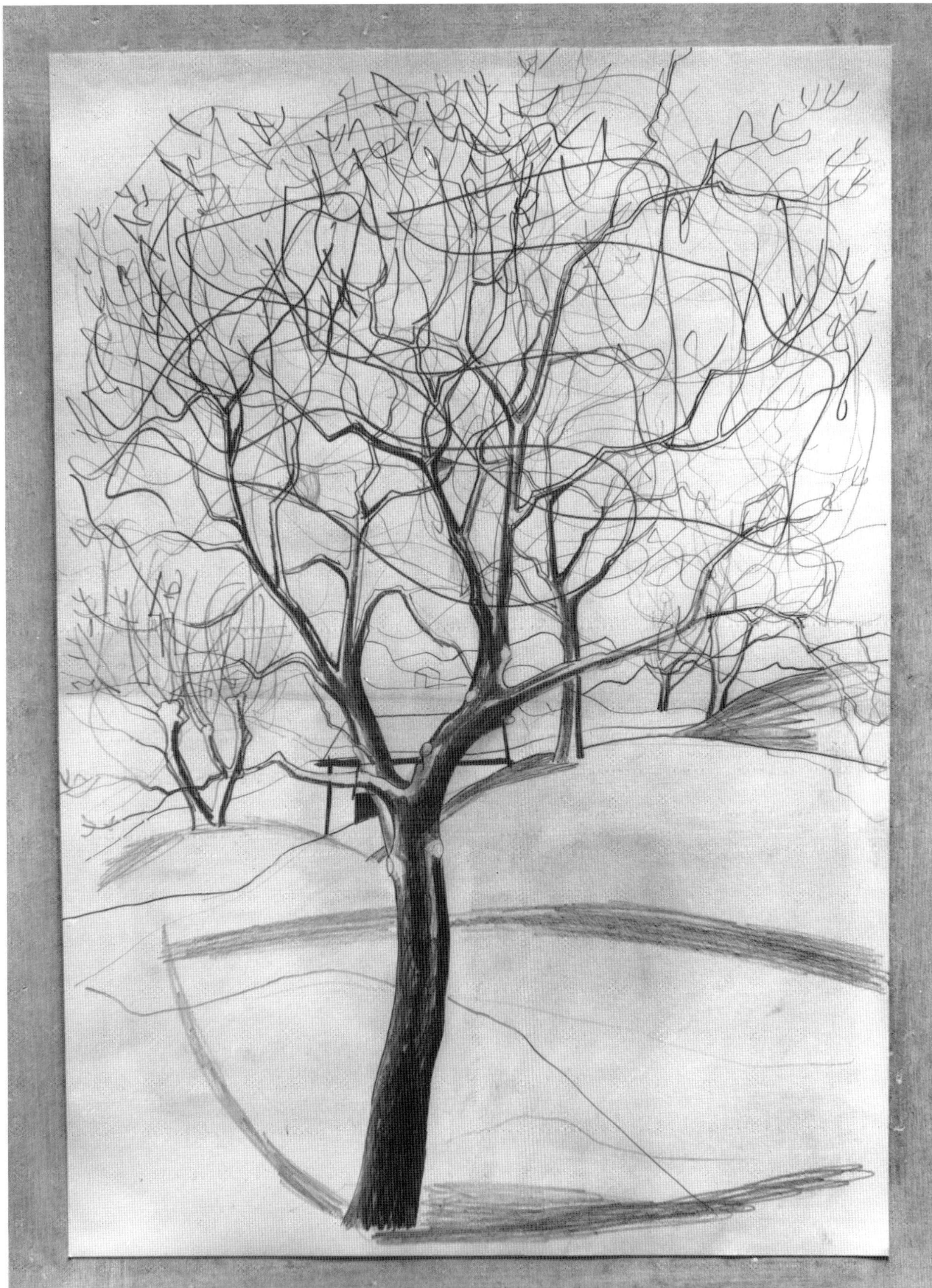

snow-capped mountains; and nights of hard frost when the lights along the shore ran up the hillsides and joined the stars.

The house itself, when finished, turned out to be adequate but unspecial (despite all Nicholson's attempts to inject some fantasy into the architect's functional design). There was compensation, though, in the small terraced garden. Over the next few years it was planted with birch, olive, purple magnolia, chestnut, oleander, cypress, a row of poplars (whose shimmering leaves Nicholson never tired of watching) and some pines, as well as a fifty-year-old palm tree. Grassy paths disappeared under tunnels of leaves, creating the illusion of space and a sense of mystery.

The studio was built at a short distance from the house. With its assortment of cutting tools and pencils invitingly laid out on a large worktable, it had the atmosphere of a carpenter's workshop. Here Nicholson liked to work for long hours at a stretch, often late into the night (with one pinkish and one bluish fluorescent light to approximate daylight). It was only after tirelessly 'pegging away' at a relief that he found it would suddenly come to life, often in an unexpected way, and then seem to take control of the creative process. Some of the larger reliefs required that he actually crawl over them as he worked – a test of his agility and of the power of his idea which he rather enjoyed.

62 *April 1958 (Prato)*
oil and pencil on paper
34 × 29.5 cm (13½ × 11½ in)

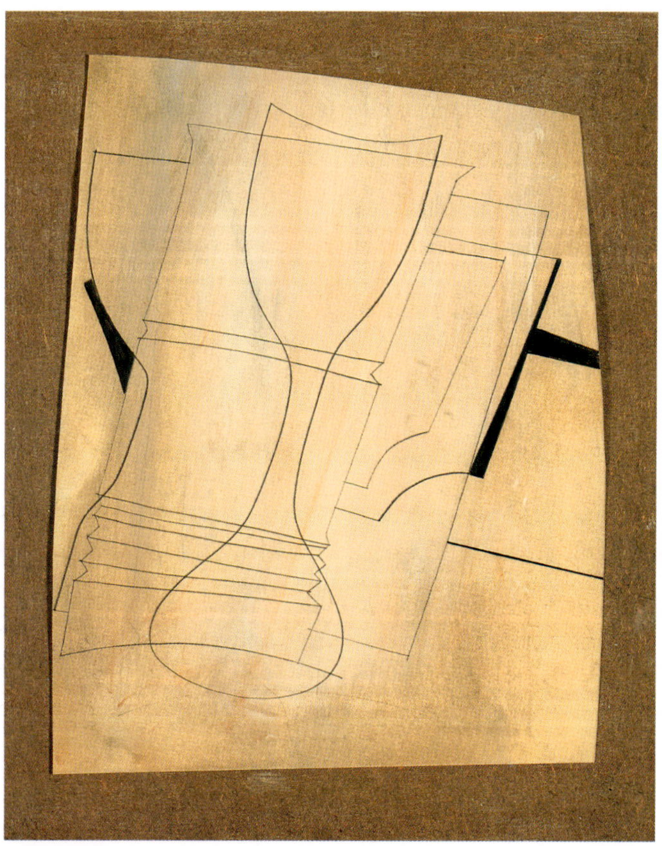

In the past he had carved out of natural wood such as mahogany, only sometimes using composite building board. Now he preferred to work on synthetic hardboard which has the advantage over natural wood that it expands and contracts less, and does not warp. However it is bone hard and extremely difficult to work with a chisel. For Nicholson this was a challenge. As he explained to Adrian Stokes: 'I *like* the *tough resistance* of material bec. it forces one into a feeling for it & for the "idea". A little bit like my poodle Black Billy who tugs at a paint rag & the more I pull the more he growls & harder he pulls, in fact rather a good description of making a relief?'[87] On one relief, *1960 (ice – off-blue)* (Tate Gallery), over which he struggled patiently during an especially cold winter, he used up over three hundred razor blades to achieve exactly the levels of depth and sharpness of edge he wanted. But it was not just patience that was needed to bring a work to completion – vision and passion were the essentials, as he insisted in a letter to Herbert Read:

> The danger even with intelligent people <is> that they think that beside tachism my kind of art is *precise & calculated*. I dislike any emphasis at all on these 2 qualities bec. so much dud art has in fact been based on this alone. In the end it is an artist's VISION & PASSION that count & whatever else I have or have not got, I *have* got *these* (I hope). The patience to use a razor blade is NOTHING, the passion to *achieve an end by whatever means* that is the point? I am sure you agree. My painting comes from a kind of inner driving force which at times is so strong that one is very conscious of it – & one switches off everything else at such moments in order to give it its maximum chance to function. I think by whatever means one has discovered some kind of a new (& enduring) world? This is particularly true of the reliefs it seems to me.[88]

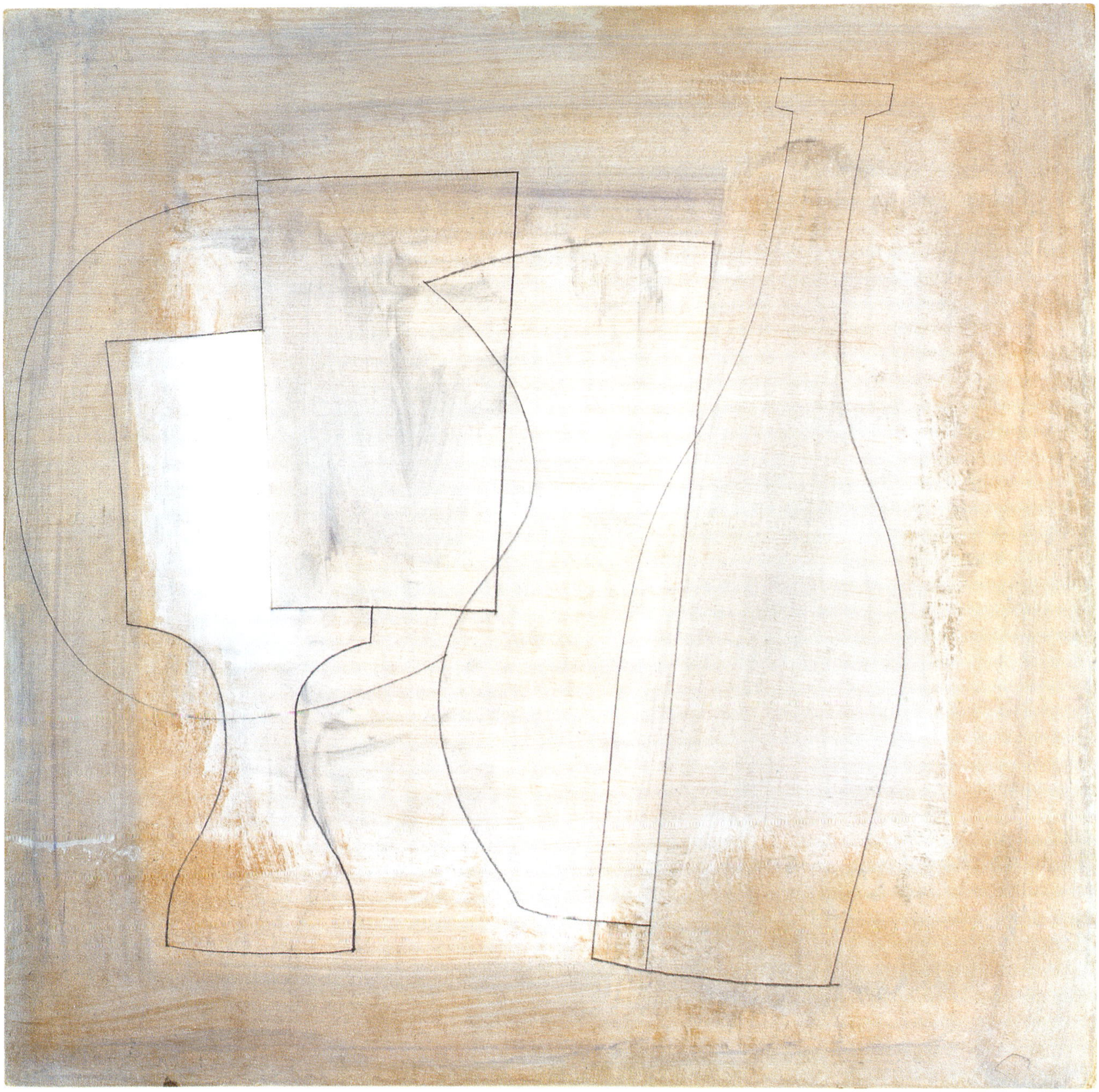

63 *June 1961 (Alnwick)*
oil and pencil on board
80 × 81 cm (31½ × 32 in)

What was this new world which Nicholson felt he had discovered in the making of his reliefs? It is clear that when he began work on a piece of hardboard he had no precise idea of what the final product would look like. His starting point was the material itself. Something in its shape, colour or texture would suggest his intervention. And that first imprint would begin a long process of adjustment in which he would follow his unconscious promptings until, at a relatively late stage, the idea became manifest in the material and the work took on a life of its own.

Nicholson often used the word 'idea' when referring to his own or other artists' work. 'A painting or a carving,' he said, 'is quite simply the expression of an idea.'[89]

Already in 1926 Helen Sutherland had noted: 'Ben says of his paintings "I don't want it to be like a painting but an idea".'[90] By which he meant that he wanted to paint the inner life he perceived in things and that this idea should so imbue the whole painting as to transcend its material actuality. Feeling and memory would act upon the outward visible form, penetrate, eliminate, concentrate, and so refashion it as to accord with his apprehension of an inner reality. This holds true for many good painters, but with Nicholson interiorization can be taken to such an extreme that at times it excludes almost all reference to the physical object. From the early 1920s, the jugs and jars in his paintings are never to be considered as mere objects, but as signs of an inwardly felt idea.[91] His aim was to express his sense of the reality which invests these objects – their 'aliveness', as he would have called it – a reality which transfigures them and touches on the universal, revealing the mystery of the everyday. In the expressive potential of the painted relief, which he was about to develop further than ever before, he would find a way of conveying the whole of his experience, not only that of his eyes but of all his senses.

The stone-like surface or patinated effect that we have noted already in works of the 1920s and 1930s is now used to greater effect. Neither is intended simply as an ingenious, but pointless, simulation of stone or of some time-battered, antique object. The range of reference is altogether more complex and subtle. A late relief by Ben Nicholson – one made at any time between the mid-1950s and the mid-1970s – is a self-existent object whose colour, form and texture are to be appreciated as one, indivisible whole – a concrete reality in its own right. Equally, it is a means of conveying his experience of living: not a representation of something seen but a re-creation of the experience of seeing it, tinged with other memories and emotions.

The range of feeling that these works arouse is hard to describe in conventional terms, but in the Zen-influenced Japanese aesthetic one finds terms appropriate to some at least of their qualities. Each of these expresses a constellation of meanings for which there is no one-word equivalent in English. Most familiar, even to the most obstinately Eurocentric, are *wabi* and *sabi*. *Wabi*, literally 'impoverishment', is associated in particular with the *raku* tea bowl. It suggests an aesthetic asceticism (but
67 with a deep, inner joy): asymmetry, calculated imperfection, weathered surfaces, faded colours – charcoal grey, grey-green, ash-brown. *Sabi*, literally 'loneliness', evokes the beauty of solitude with a similar range of drab colours and worn surfaces patinated with moss or lichen or rust. A fundamental quality of many of the late reliefs is also expressed by *yūgen*. *Yū*, by itself, suggests faintness, shadowiness, insubstantiality, rarefaction; *gen*, dimness, and the darkness of profundity. The combination *yūgen* denotes both mystery and profundity – the intangible that underlies the solid, empirical world, the invisible beyond the visible. It is 'what lies beneath the surface, the subtle as opposed to the obvious, the hint as opposed to the statement'.[92] In the *Nō* drama it is the suggestion of the eternal or absolute – of deep emotion or significance – by a single gesture. Finally, *shibui*, literally 'astringent', which qualifies the beauty of simplicity, depth, irregularity, subtlety, reticence, austerity.

Naturally these notions correspond only to some of the attributes of Nicholson's late reliefs: there is gaiety as well as severity to be found in them; luminosity and bright colour too. But intrinsic and vital to both the Zen aesthetic and Nicholson's is a moral dimension: the refinement of sensibility expressed in a tea-bowl or carved relief implies and inspires a correspondingly refined awareness.

The Far-Eastern affinity can even be taken a little further. Nicholson himself coupled the thirteenth-century Chinese monk–painter Mu-ch'i with Giorgione as the most poetic of all painters, though since he can only have seen Mu-ch'i's work in reproduction, it would be foolish to make too much of this statement.[93] Nevertheless there is an undoubted affinity between some of Nicholson's late reliefs and Mu-ch'i's paintings, whether of fruit, flowers or animals in nature: they suggest limitless space and a reality beyond outer appearances (*yūgen*). Nicholson, we may be sure, would have understood and thoroughly approved the belief held by Mu-ch'i and his followers that it was only by 'opening the third eye' – by awakening his faculty of intuition – that a painter could hope to convey the universal dimension of some particular landscape.[94]

64 *June 1958 (nude, Venezia)*
oil wash and pencil on paper
48 × 34.5 cm (18¾ × 13½ in)

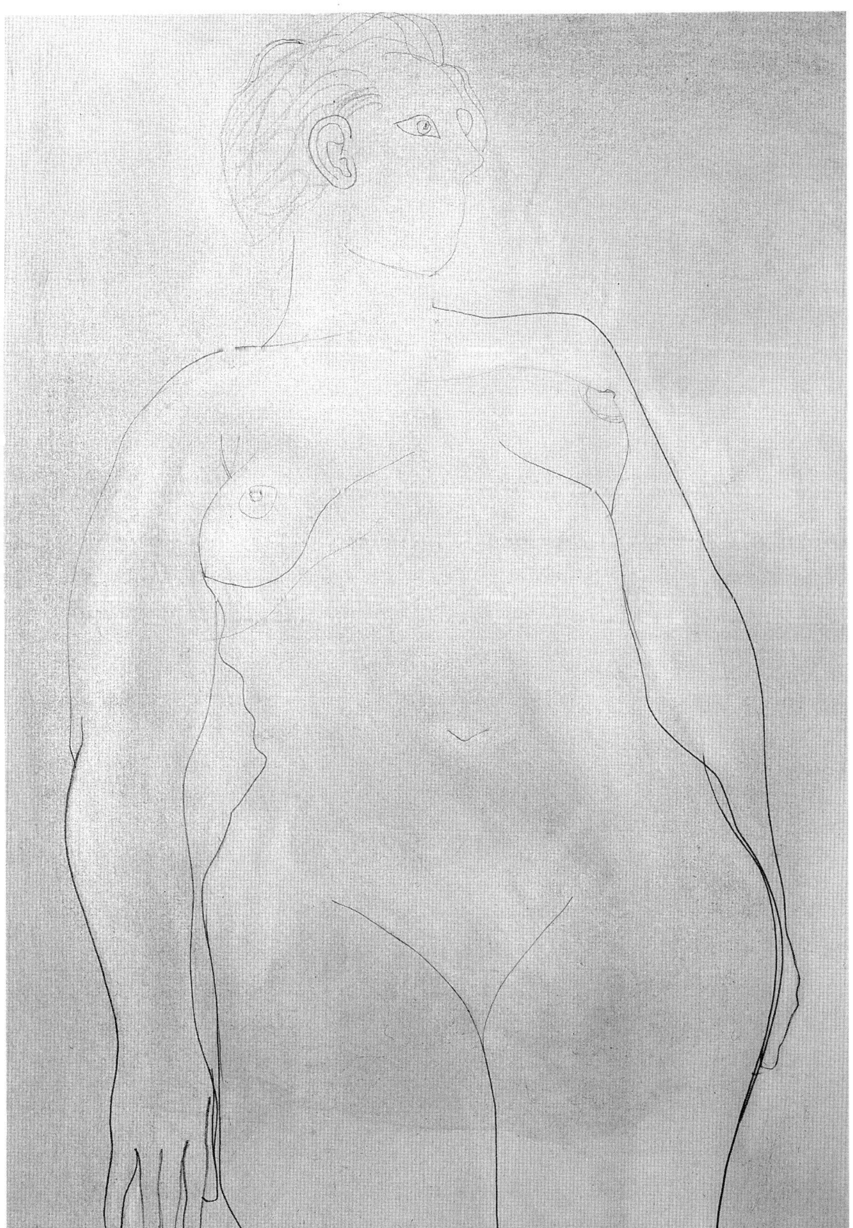

But now we are bound to ask: in what sense can these late reliefs be considered as landscapes? Granted that when Nicholson began work on a sheet of hardboard he had no clear idea of where 'the magic hand of chance' might lead him, when its character did emerge, and bore some relation to landscape, how specific was this?

One indication can be found in the style of title he adopted for his works from 1950 (and which it is now usual to apply to them all). The title was, in effect, the date of the work's completion. After it he added a name-tag in brackets. The order of the two, with lower-case type except for proper names, shows their relative importance and Nicholson's desire to avoid any literal, literary or over-precise association that might interfere with the experience of simply looking at the work. Yet he did invent titles which, at the very least, hint obliquely at the mood if not the 'subject' of the work – the subject being the work itself. (Debussy likewise gave evocative titles to his *Préludes* after completing them, but directed that they be printed at the end of each piece.)

Take a random sample of landscape titles belonging to reliefs made in the 1960s: *Aegean Landscape*, *Lindos*, *Patmos*, *Altamira*, *Dordogne*, *Amboise*, *Tuscan Relief*, *Valley between Rimini and Urbino*, *Zennor Quoit*, *Carnac – red and brown*. Now look at

65 *July 1960 (back to back)*
oil on carved board
43 × 43 cm (17 × 17 in)

66 *January 1964 (Menalon off-green)*
oil on carved board
50 × 88 cm (19¾ × 34¾ in)

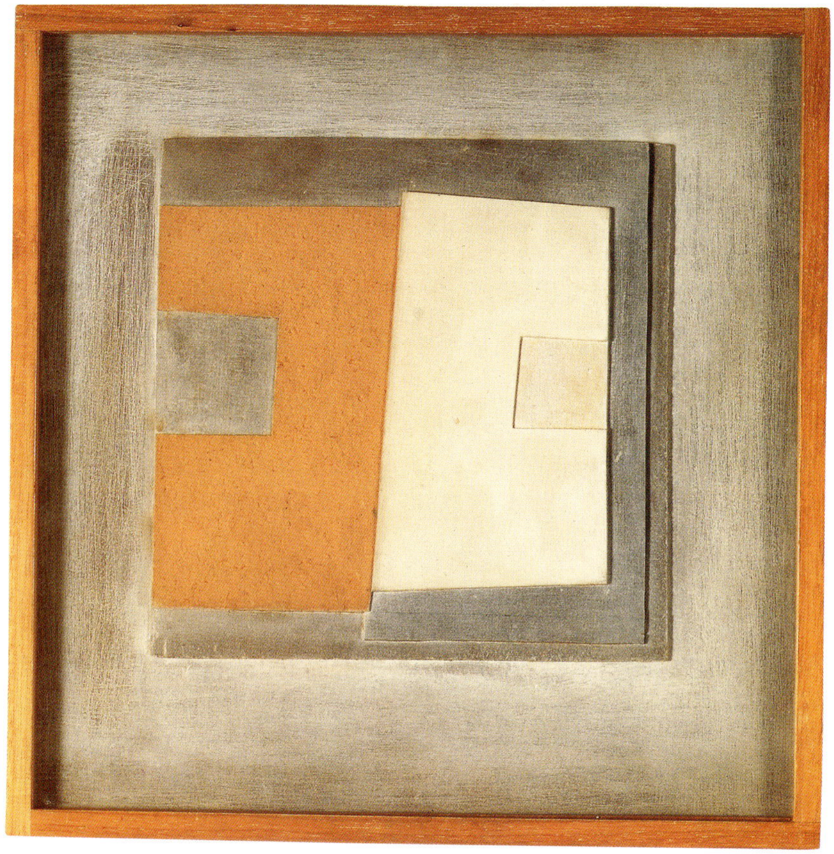

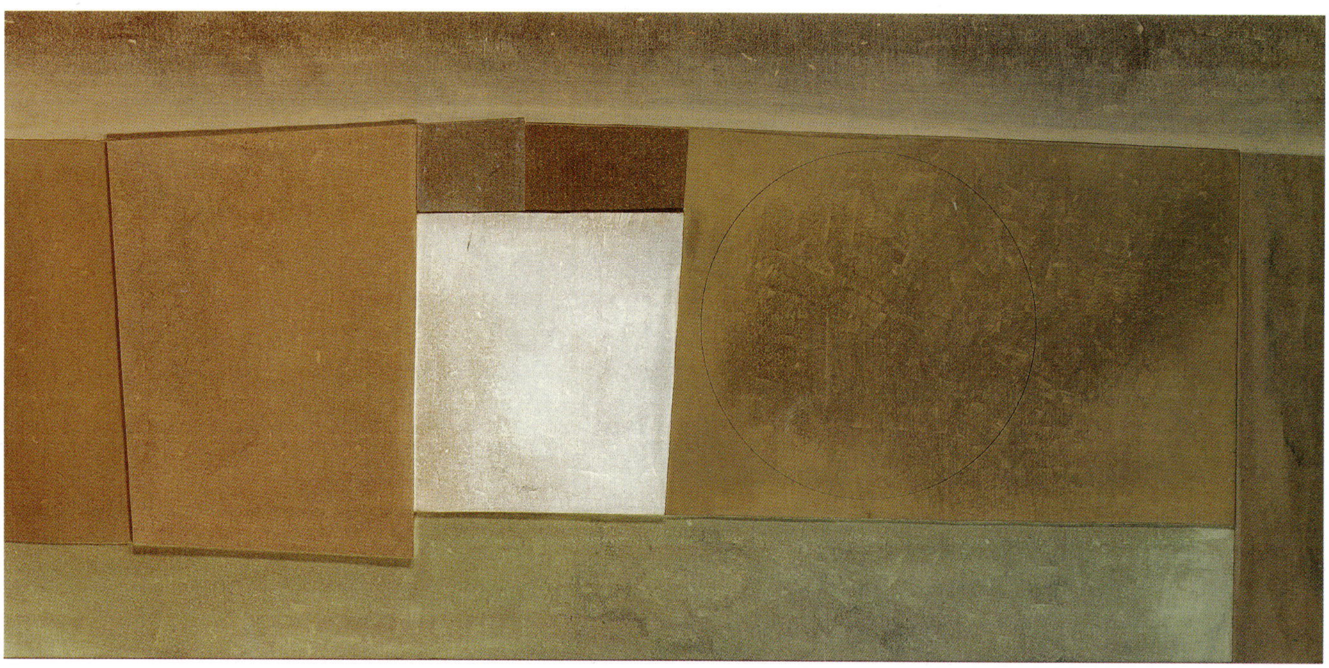

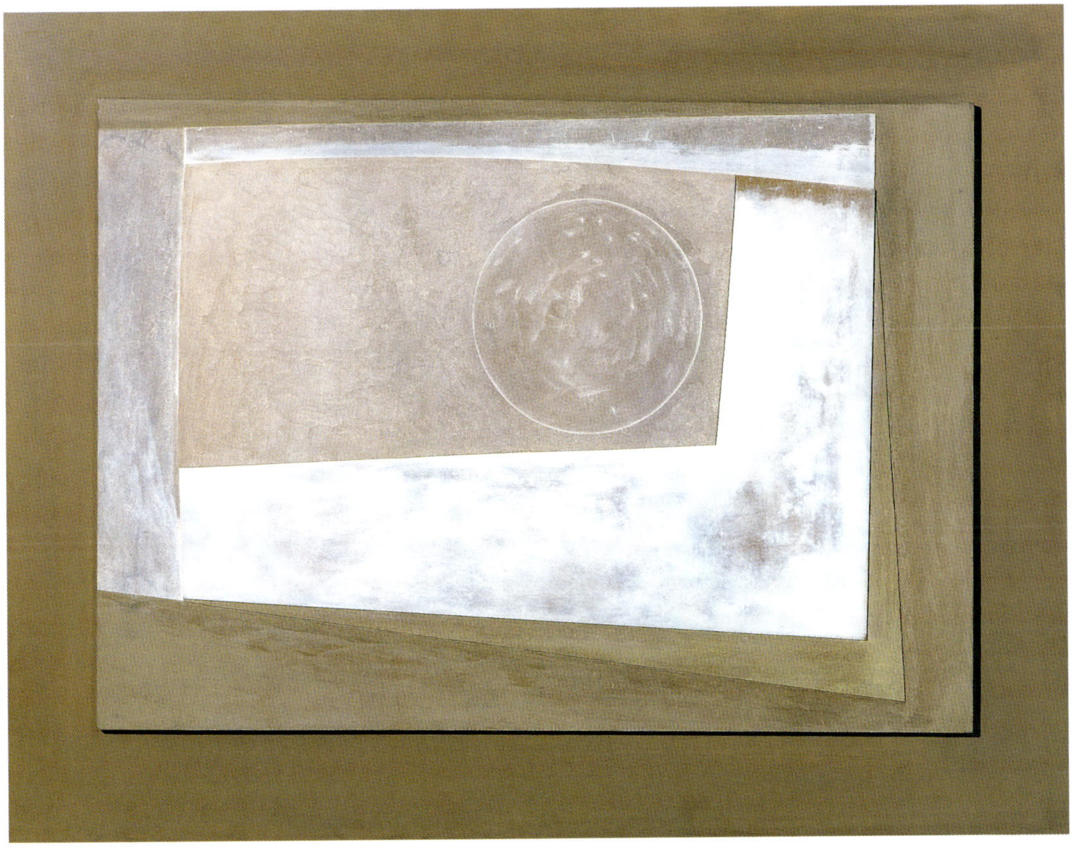

67 *1968 (silver relief)*
oil on carved board
99 × 129.5 cm (39 × 51 in)

the reliefs that bear these titles, and in all of them you will see Nicholson working within the same narrow repertory of square, oblong and L-shaped forms, sometimes tapered or trapezoid so as to create tension, confronting each other, interlocking or ambiguously overlapping in shallow space (a persisting inheritance from Cubism). Textures and colours evoke the natural world but not specific locations, except in a few cases (such as *1969 (monolith – Carnac 5)*, whose form actually suggests a standing stone). To the innocent eye there are no clues that would differentiate the topography of *1964 (valley between Rimini and Urbino)* from that of *1964 (Patmos)*, or *1959 (Lindos)* from *1965 (Amboise)*. Obviously these reliefs are less depictions of place than analogues or memory-traces of landscape, and the name-tags are metaphors for the feelings or associations aroused by each completed work in Nicholson himself. The viewer's experience is essentially an aesthetic one – an appreciation of the forms, colours and textures of the object in front of him. If he contemplates it long enough, doubtless it will give rise to feelings and associations connected with his own experience, perhaps only subliminally of landscape.

Early in 1967 the Marlborough Gallery invited Geoffrey Grigson, who had first written on Nicholson's work in 1933, to write for the catalogue of an exhibition of recent reliefs. Grigson visited Nicholson at Brissago to look at the reliefs, and in his essay ponders on their relationship to landscape.

I saw, in various circumstances of light, these newest Ben Nicholsons in the studio in which they were carved and painted, rather more than a thousand feet above Lago Maggiore. There was one time during which a squarish window in the end wall of the studio became a rectangle of unaccountable blue; there were times outside when the curved mountains across the lake, and rising from the lake, became superimpositions of a matt blue almost drained of blue, to somewhere between blue and grey. These could be trimmed by the razorblade of imagination into straight-sided forms, or more or less regular forms slightly curved instead of straight along their boundaries ... I would not allege that these new reliefs-in-colour are specifically a form of those circumstances and phenomena (despite the blue 'window' which occurs in two of them). What impressed me was rather the way in which the vertical surfaces (and the lake surface) of Nicholson's Swiss-Italian landscape would forego the pretensions of colour, when the sky clouded over, and would acquire a special gravity of tone, and a special absence of clatter, without becoming imprecise or dreamy.

68 Of *1966 (Zennor Quoit 2)* in particular he wrote:

The contemplator, with that tag to alert him, can think of the blue more or less in its middle as a patch of the Atlantic, beyond the edge of Zennor, he can think of the shapes tensely holding it as the stones of a dolmen – if he must ... But for Nicholson, name-label or no, the relief is a relief – 'very horizontal', to quote Nicholson, 'and all browns, and a mysterious blue in the centre ...'. For Nicholson it is a problem solved, in his language of abstraction – 'It's abnormally long and narrow and for that reason exciting to try and solve it'.[95]

After reading Grigson's essay, Nicholson wrote him a letter which, since it expresses his own view of the relationship between his reliefs and landscape, I quote *in extenso*.

The general relationship with the landscapes you mention is certainly true. I think the blue rectangle comes from something much more distant – more from one's imagination than the blue window rectangle. I see it as something connected with the sea on the Zennor side of W. Penwith but even that is too direct a statement. It must be *mental* & must not be *directly* sky or sea & that is why it's a difficult colour to grapple with – it is always trying to become sea or sky? In fact *where do one's ideas come from?* One can only work until the situation is a happy one for oneself – & if it is that then assume there are a few people (very few) for whom it is also a happy & far-reaching solution. And of course it must be actual (a piece of reality). I also think my ignorance & lack of normal education means that I have to discover for myself certain v. simple things & things too which look as though they could be developed in ½ an hour but in fact probably take nearer 20 years – I like to learn & discover but hate being taught – it's as if one's freedom is being interfered with – One *senses* that something is there but it takes years to discover what it is. And a few painters & sculptors & poets help one to discover it?

I think *quietness* is a miraculous & creative spirit & probably the Chinese knew as much or more <as> anyone about this? Again I am ignorant but it looks like that from their ptgs.

You are quite right: colour comes inkstinktively to me, & form I've had to learn about & shall always be learning about. It's a lovely thing to learn about. If you're ever at the Tate, there's a single-line jug dwg I gave them – this has a *form*. The discovery of a carved ptg was merely the same discovery for me as a Lascaux or Altamira were for the chaps who incised the walls there – something *natural*? (Away from picture galleries & museums.) ...

Apart from landscape, what else goes into one's ptg? The long brown relief [= *1966 (Zennor Quoit 2)*] reminded me of a small bird (not a sparrow & not a robin) which I found on the ground early one morning near our big sitting-room window. I thought it was dead or stunned after flying into the window. Then I saw one leg had been torn out. I touched it gently & it opened a most beautiful brown eye – really exquisite – & looked at me quite without fear. I picked it up & put it into the bushes (because I never can revive birds that are stunned or hurt – they seem to prefer to leave this world). When I looked again it had clung to a branch with its one leg – & next time I looked it had flown away. At the same time I had recently met a girl for whom I have a deep affection with lovely brown eyes – & then there were my Mother's brown eyes. Well alright, the relief is a landscape, but it is also these other things . . .

Zennor Quoit of course is wonderful. I believe it is a closed-in tomb-like affair, but I see it open at both ends & a view of the Atlantic at one end & mountain fells at the other. (We once came across a fell fire above Zennor. It had crossed the road & there was an eagle flying above us – a long, smooth, lazy flight & its mate sitting on the road – & a burning fire & the Atlantic beyond.)

That look in the small bird's brown eye – so clear & alive. I think now it must have been attacked by another & larger bird – only a hole where the leg had been, & it lay there shocked & depressed, eyes closed, & then when it found I was friendly it came back to life & I expect all its friends felt a bit overdressed with 2 legs. But it is all simple *& no intellectual confusion?*[96]

Nicholson's works need quiet contemplation. The greater the sympathetic insight brought to this contemplation, the more fully will they disclose themselves. But the viewer's appreciation of a late relief does not depend on his recognizing whatever connotations Nicholson himself may have attached to it. As Helen Sutherland had been the first to understand, it was always with the universal, with the inner reality behind the outer appearance, that Nicholson was concerned, and even after knowing his work for over thirty years this could still strike her with the force of a sudden realization. As she recorded in her diary on 18 November 1957:

We've had grim grey *sunless* days for a week but driving to Grasmere, tho no sunlight appeared, suddenly there was colour: on Saddleback & his neighbours – most moving dark rich sombre yet glowing winter colour while the trees & fields of the valley landscape held their leafyness & lightness still – a looking back towards Summer – & still a sort of Summerlike dancing prevailed.

I suddenly realized that had Ben seen this moving grandeur & solemn rich beauty he cd not have reproduced it by drawing the landscape but would have had to translate it into one of his great deep dark yet radiant *Abstracts* – I suddenly understood this: saw & felt it –[97]

Drawing the landscape was, in fact, something Nicholson did do. In 1961 he reported to Herbert Read: 'We have been in Ticino now 3 years —— and judging by photos, I have done just over 300 works (a large part of this of course oil wash line dwgs). These are probably the ideal foil to the reliefs.'[98] The relation between Nicholson's drawings and his reliefs needs to be made clear. It has in the past been misunderstood as a result of a false dichotomy between the abstract and the representational, which precludes a proper appreciation of his work as a whole – as the consistent expression of one sensibility. Pure abstraction, without reference or

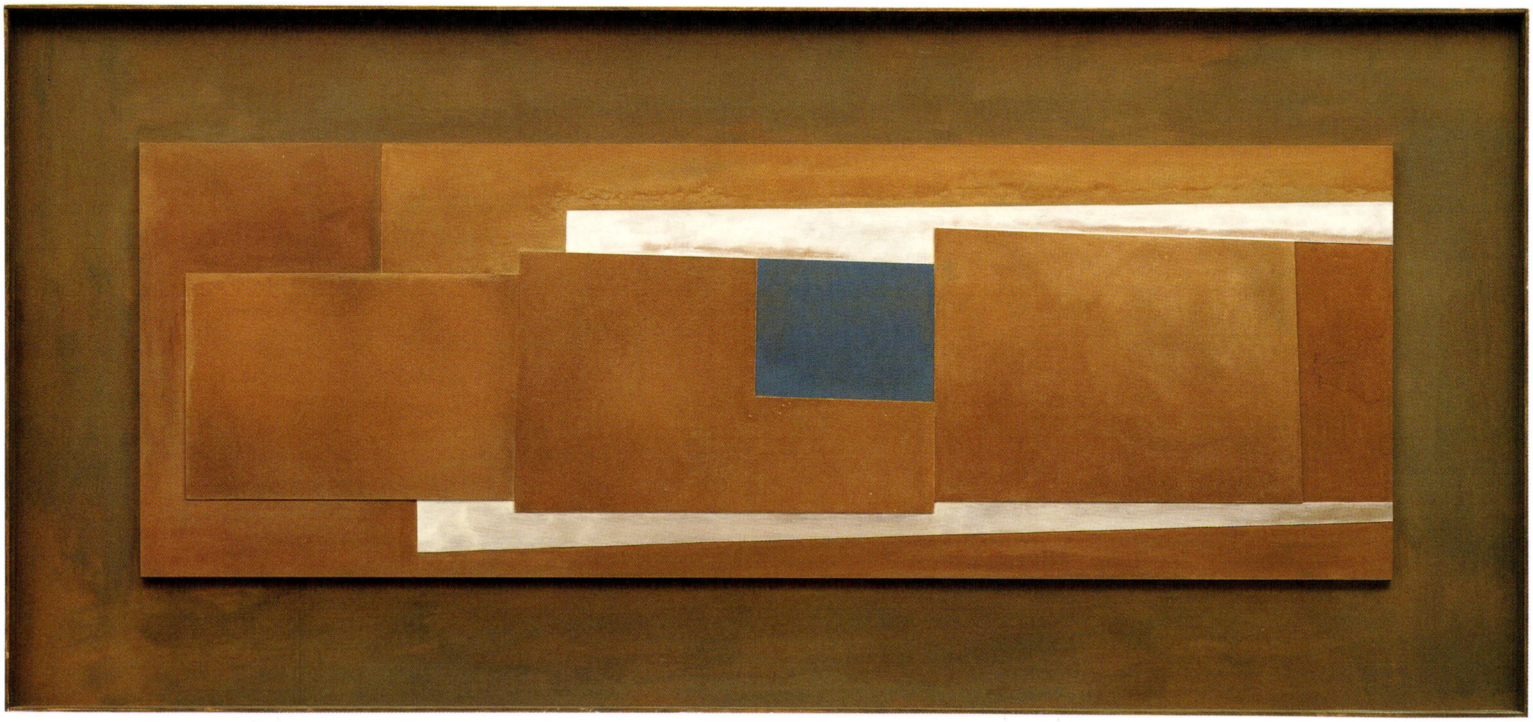

68 *1966 (Zennor Quoit 2)*
oil on carved board
117 × 261 cm (46 × 102¾ in)

→ 69 *July 1959 (Paros with blue)*
oil and pencil on carved board
46 × 86 cm (18 × 34 in)

equivalence to anything outside itself, was for Nicholson just one end of the spectrum of modalities through which he ranged freely, back and forth, not asking himself 'Is this figurative or is it non-figurative?' but following his instinct to 'chase out something *alive*'. In fact the distinction seemed to him irrelevant: 'The kind of painting which I find exciting is not necessarily representational or non-representational, but it is both musical and architectural, where the architectural construction is used to express a "musical" relationship between form, tone and colour and whether this visual, "musical", relationship is slightly more or slightly less abstract is for me beside the point.'[99] The power of interiorization, of going beyond the concrete, does not of necessity entail a lessening of resemblance to outer reality so much as a transfiguration of that outer reality by an inner reality. The poetic 'idea' and the search for the real are paramount for Nicholson, and he adopts whatever medium is most appropriate to the expression of that idea and reality, be it a selectively naturalistic drawing or a non-figurative carving. However much theorists might insist on the essential difference between abstract figuration and non-figuration, for Nicholson there was no divorce between the two.

The drawings, then, are not aids or studies preparatory to the reliefs which are the finished works. They are themselves finished works, independent, and with expressive qualities of their own. Yet the reliefs do owe something to the drawings. Making a drawing focused Nicholson's feeling about a particular place, so that when he came to carve a relief, that feeling was powerful enough to permeate the abstract work and evoke the spirit of that place in general terms, while the link with the particular became correspondingly tenuous.

So far, Nicholson's landscape drawings had been largely of Cornwall, Yorkshire and Italy. Now that he no longer lived on a remote peninsula facing out to the Atlantic, he took full advantage of the opportunities to travel offered by his position in the centre of Europe. His first excursion was to Greece and the Aegean in April–May 1959. Greece had long occupied a place in his imagination: one may recall *1931–6 (still life – Greek landscape)* and the large-scale still-life fantasias of the 1950s – *Delos*, *Cyclades*, *Aegean*, *Crete* – names which he attached to his paintings, just as Hepworth did to her sculptures, to suggest affinities with the light of the Aegean or the massive remains of Greek temples. The Swan Hellenic tour was no more than a preliminary reconnaissance: it was all too hurried, and his fellow-travellers too distracting, for Nicholson to be able to take much in, but certain things were a revelation – the Cycladic figurines (many of which he missed due to his dislike of museums), the landscape of Mycenae and Epidauros, and the island of Paros.

The experience of Paros he recreated in a relief which he made on his return
69 home. To describe *Paros with blue* in terms of squares, rectangles and two circles –

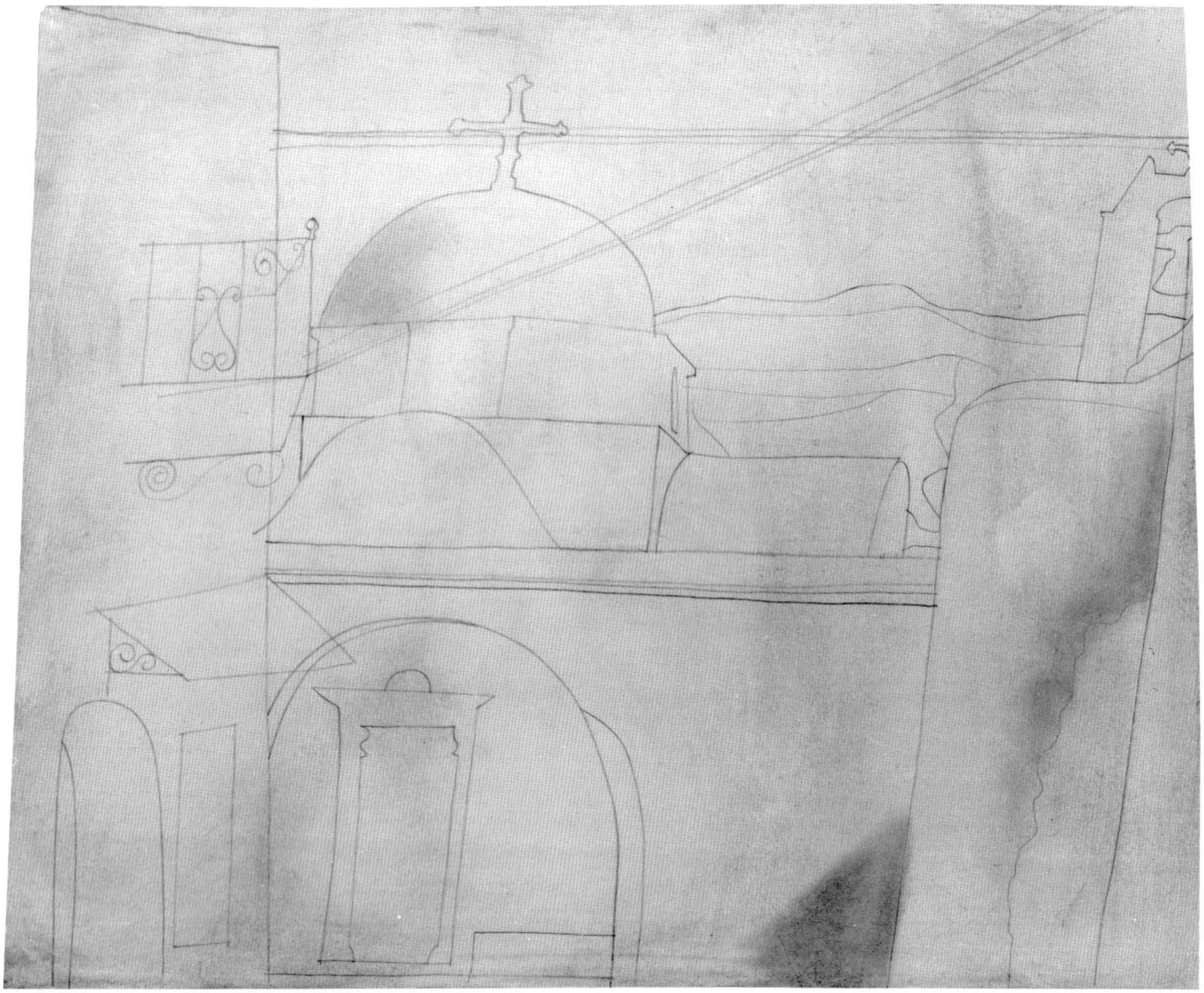

70 *September 1961 (Paros chapel)*
oil wash and pencil on paper
40 × 49.5 cm (15¾ × 19½ in)

one drawn in pencil, the other excavated – does not differentiate it from a hundred other reliefs. Everything depends on the proportion and relationship of its forms, on the subtle deviations from the strictly rectangular, and on the finely graded depths of carving. The whole lightly balanced structure is imbued with the memory of glaring sunlight on whitewashed walls, so that while admiring the beautifully made object we also experience some of the disorientation of being dazed by bright light.

In 1941 Nicholson had written:

> One of the main differences between a representational and an abstract painting is that the former can transport you to Greece by a representation of blue skies and seas, olive trees and marble columns, but in order that you may take part in this you will have to concentrate on the painting, whereas the abstract version by its free use of form and colour will be able to give you the actual quality of Greece itself, and this will become part of the light and space and life in the room – there is no need to concentrate, *it becomes a part of living.*[100]

In *July 1959 (Paros with blue)* Nicholson does indeed convey the sensation of dazzling Aegean light, and in *November 1959 (Mycenae 3, brown and blue)* it would not be difficult to recognize bare brown mountains or cyclopean walls, punctuated by bands of deep-blue sky. But in the majority of his late reliefs such correspondences are far from apparent, even with the clues provided by the titles. This is not to criticize the works but to question the claim Nicholson makes for them. They are such personal, and such generalized equivalents for his experience of place that they cannot communicate to us in such a specific way.

72

Nicholson made three further trips to Greece and the Aegean during the 1960s. In the autumn of 1961 he returned to some of the places that had made the strongest impression on his first visit two years earlier: Mycenae, Olympia and Paros.

> I enjoyed best of all an afternoon dwg in Paros – the light, the architecture white & almost sculpture & whiteness everywhere even underfoot & a cat or two & one or two beautiful children & goats & donkeys & white chapels each with a lovely interior and a kind of Punch & Judy set up with fine Byzantine ptgs & candelabra. The whiteness of course seemed v. close home to my first white reliefs.[101]

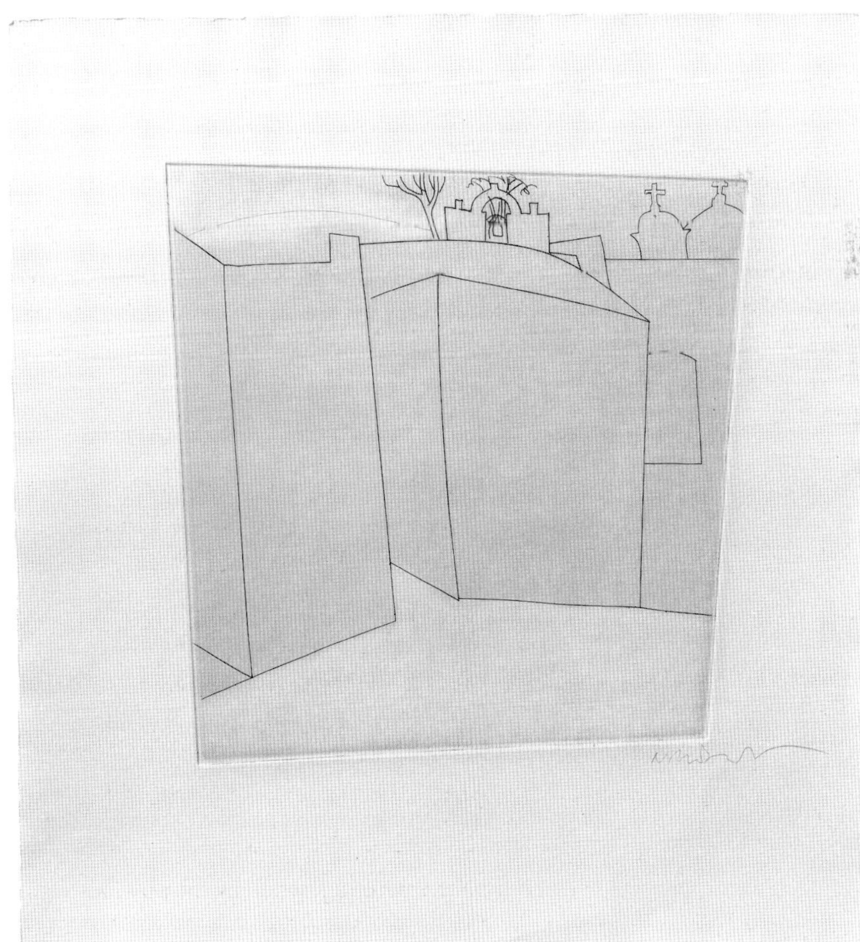

71 *1967 (Paros 2)*
etching with pencil
26 × 26 cm (10¼ × 10¼ in)
paper 41 × 38 cm (16¼ × 15 in)

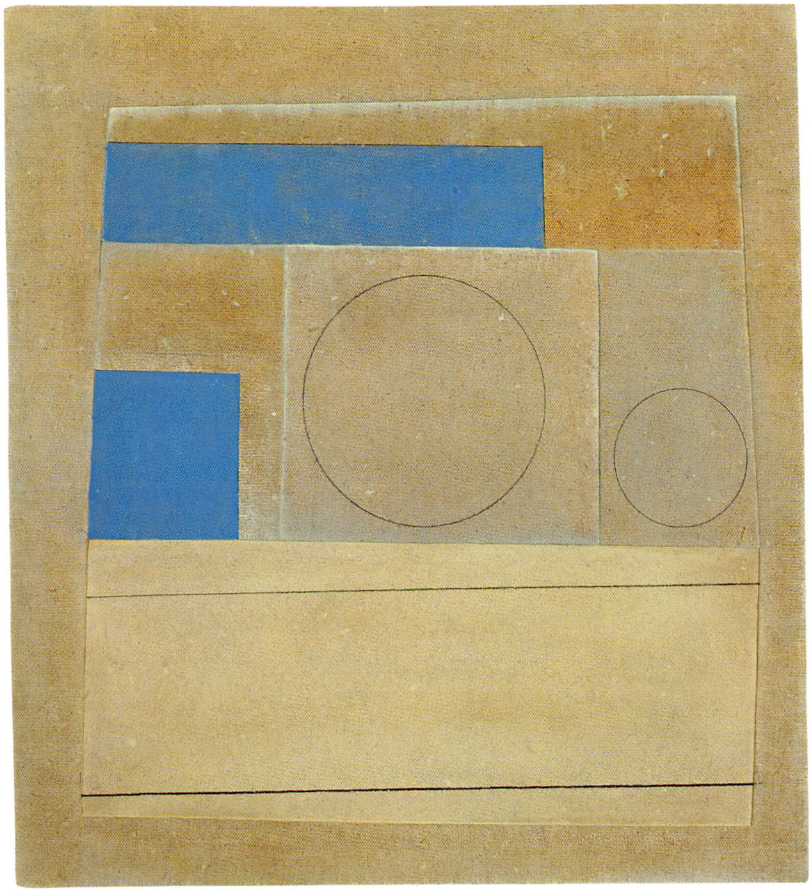

The memory of that whiteness was duly translated into a relief which contrasts
73 with the earlier *Paros with blue* and most of the other reliefs of this period in that variety of texture, tone and colour are entirely absent. As in a relief of the 1930s, the smooth surface is saturated with a uniform white. The tilting planes, however, produce an effect quite different from the ordered serenity of those early reliefs. Closely interlocking forms combine with unrelieved whiteness to baffle and dizzy the
71 viewer's gaze, just as *Paros 2*, an etching made five years later, evokes high walls, narrow alleys and a glaring sun.

74 In his drawing of the *Road near Olympia* Nicholson uses the dash-board, steering-wheel and mirror inside the car as a foil to the landscape seen through the windscreen in the same way as he had earlier contrasted still-life objects on a window-sill foreground with a landscape background. The subject, already treated in several previous drawings,[102] was most probably suggested by Matisse's painting *The Windshield* (1917), a reproduction of which Nicholson had stuck into a scrapbook dated 1922.

Having no antiquarian interest in ancient Greece, what moved him at Olympia was the form and texture of the great drums of the fallen columns – man-made artefacts, contrasting with the landscape but also in harmony with it – these and the atmosphere of the place, which he would gradually absorb until he felt ready to

72 *November 1959 (Mycenae 3, brown and blue)*
oil and pencil on carved board
51.5×48.5 cm ($20\frac{1}{4} \times 19$ in)

→ 73 *January 1962 (white relief, Paros)*
oil on carved board
61×63 cm ($24\frac{1}{4} \times 24\frac{3}{4}$ in)

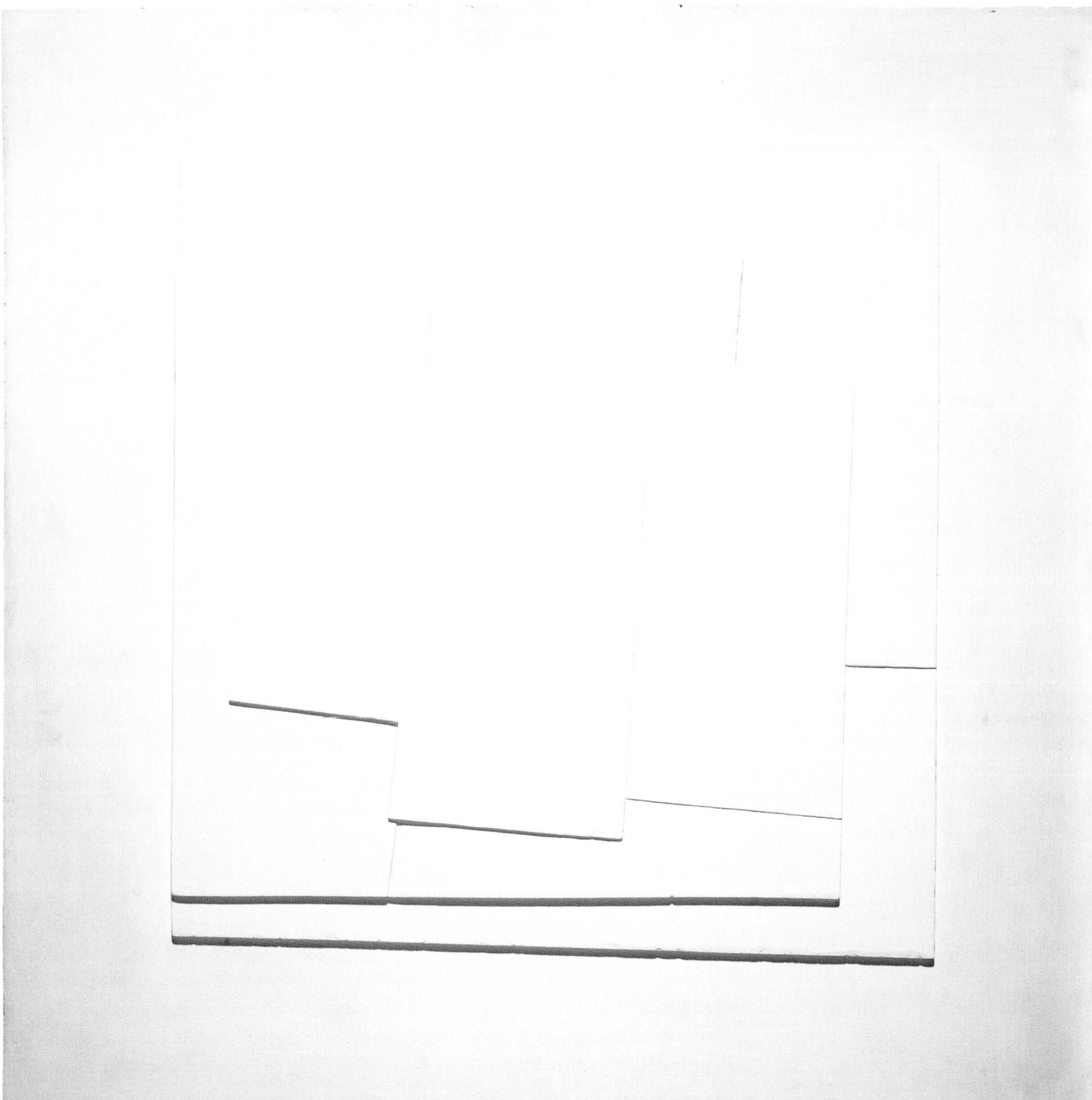

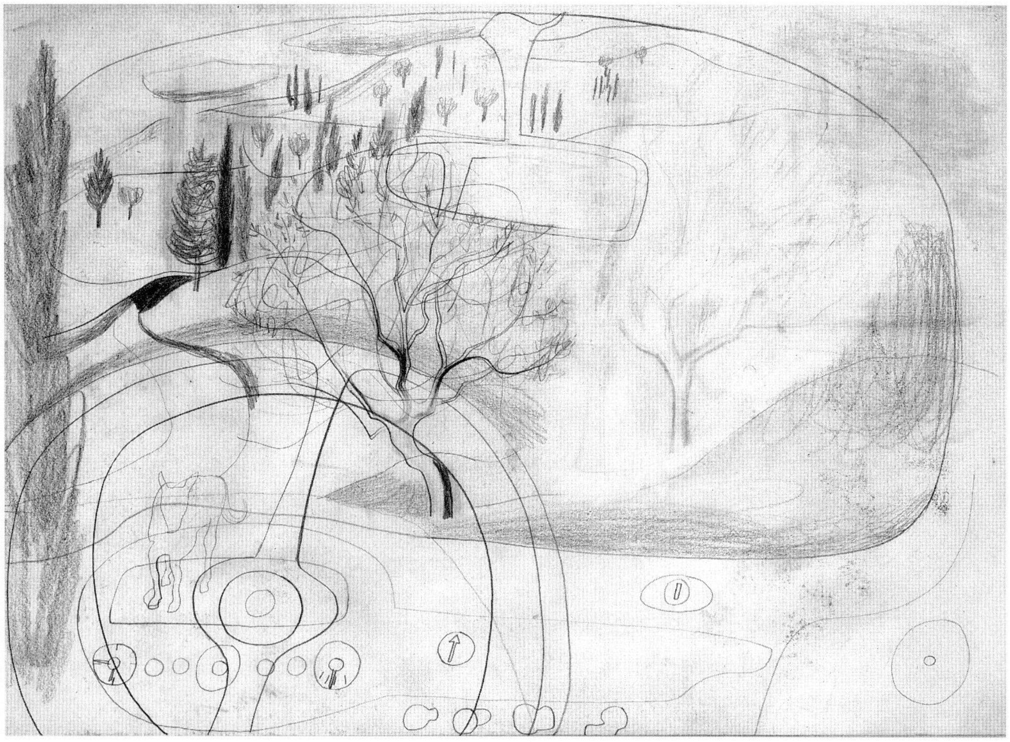

draw, swiftly, decisively and with total concentration. His identification with the subject – his idea – was so intense that it could remain with him for years before being recalled in the making of an abstract relief.[103] The relief was a further distillation of experience, but not consciously planned as such. He cherished the saying of Brancusi – 'Simplicity is not an aim in art: one attains simplicity in spite of oneself by getting nearer to the sense of things'[104] – and he often spoke of his own aim as 'going deeper and deeper into the sense of things'. The long hours spent on the reliefs demanded as much concentration as did the drawings, but now the identification was with the material object in front of him – with colour, texture and space proportion. The movement and angle of line, the depth and sharpness of relief, the relation of forms and planes had all to be reconciled and, ideally, brought into harmony with each other. A hair's-breadth in design divided a vital creation from a tasteful object.

Colour in these late reliefs is more completely integrated with material and form than in any previous work.[105] Many of the paintings based on still life which Nicholson made in the late 1940s and 1950s could be described as coloured drawings. In them colour serves to lend depth to the linear design or guide the eye over it, but often it has hardly more affective power than a harlequin's motley. In the later reliefs, though, colour becomes an altogether subtler, deeper and inseparable element. Nicholson is preeminently a tonal painter. Like his father, he can produce magical effects of space through close intervals of tone, and is at his best when handling a limited range of colours. The key to a work often lies in the expressive qualities he can draw out of just one colour. Paint is brushed onto the carved board,

74 *September 1961 (road near Olympia)*
oil wash and pencil on paper
46 × 60.5 cm (18 × 23¾ in)

scraped off, rubbed in, scoured and smoothed again, so that it becomes one with the support which may then be cut anew. Colour and tone are made to register the finest gradations of light to illuminate a surface and bring it alive.

When Nicholson referred to his later reliefs as 'primitive reliefs', he must have had
75 in mind the monumental and age-worn appearance of such a work as *1966 (Carnac – red and brown)*. In 1965 he revisited Brittany and the prehistoric standing stones at Carnac. No more than at Olympia was he concerned with history or archaeology. What impressed him was the almost living presence of the menhirs, their massive size and their eroded surfaces, blotched with white lichen. These are recalled in the flecked and pocked areas of the relief he made in the following year, but the title alludes only to the atmosphere of Carnac, not to anything specific. As always, the formal composition of the relief is restricted to a few abstract, rectilinear shapes, whose sharply defined edges contrast with the shifting perspectives they enclose. Apart from the near-rectangle of pale terracotta that anchors the work, each of the four main areas suggests a different, and indefinable, space. On the left, the dark stain, like a burn, in the centre of the axe-head shape, can seem to recede far back into its surrounding emptiness. On the right, the vague boulder shape roughly scratched out of the scumbled surface evokes the worn, the weather-stained, the disfiguration of time (a good example of *wabi/sabi*). The fractional tilting of both vertical and horizontal lines brings the component parts together in a more dynamic relation than in the strictly orthogonal grid of the early reliefs. This tight interlock-
76 ing of parts is seen even more clearly in *1967 (Tuscan relief)* whose dynamic power is generated by the large axe-head shape on the right, mirrored by a smaller version on the left, and recapitulated in the overall configuration of the relief held within a rectangle. Beside the square, the rectangle, the trapeziums which are variants of these, and the circle, this axe-head shape in varying proportions, and turning through 360 degrees, is the only other formal element in Nicholson's late reliefs.[106] It is already dominant in *Andrew*, the third abstract painting of 1924 (see p.19). Depending on its proportions, it can have the aggressive power of a hatchet or the angular mobility of a boomerang. Compositionally it acts as a pointer, propelling the eye from one form to another. An added tautness is achieved in *Tuscan relief* by the slight curve of the upper carved edge. Nicholson had previously used the curve to this effect in paintings, such as *1956 (Val d'Orcia)* (see p.73), but only introduced it in his
77 reliefs from the mid-1960s, at first sparingly, as in *1966 (Erymanthos)* whose two answering arcs keep the work in a state of dynamic suspension. But in the reliefs he made in 1970 and 1971, at the end of his time in the Ticino, the curves begin to multiply and strain against one another, creating an effect of restless movement which is
80 further accentuated by the pigment being freely brushed over the surface of the board (the nearest Nicholson ever got, in his mature years, to gestural painting).

No amount of description or analysis, no reproduction, however good, can convey the impact made by the physical presence of these late reliefs. Balance, proportion, controlled energy, texture, colour, reflected light, the sensation of limitless space, precision combined with mystery – all these draw the viewer in to commune

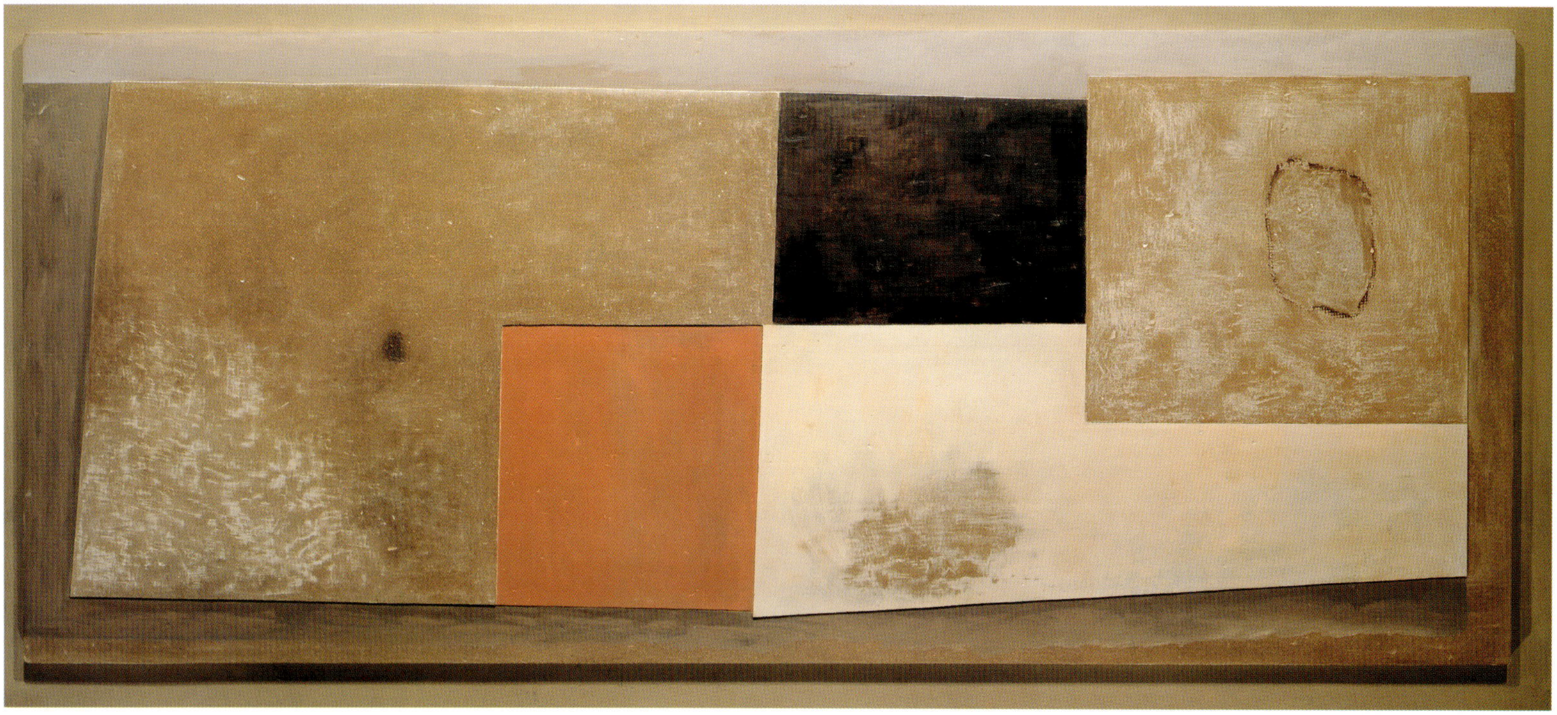

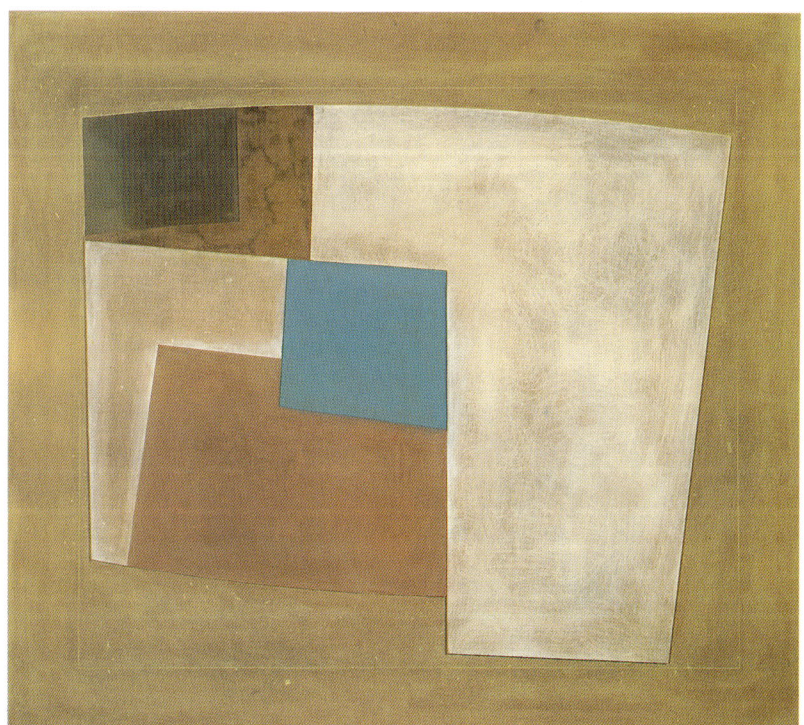

75 *1966 (Carnac – red and brown)*
oil on carved board
101.5 × 206 cm (40 × 81¼ in)

76 *1967 (Tuscan relief)*
oil on carved board
148 × 161 cm (58¼ × 63½ in)

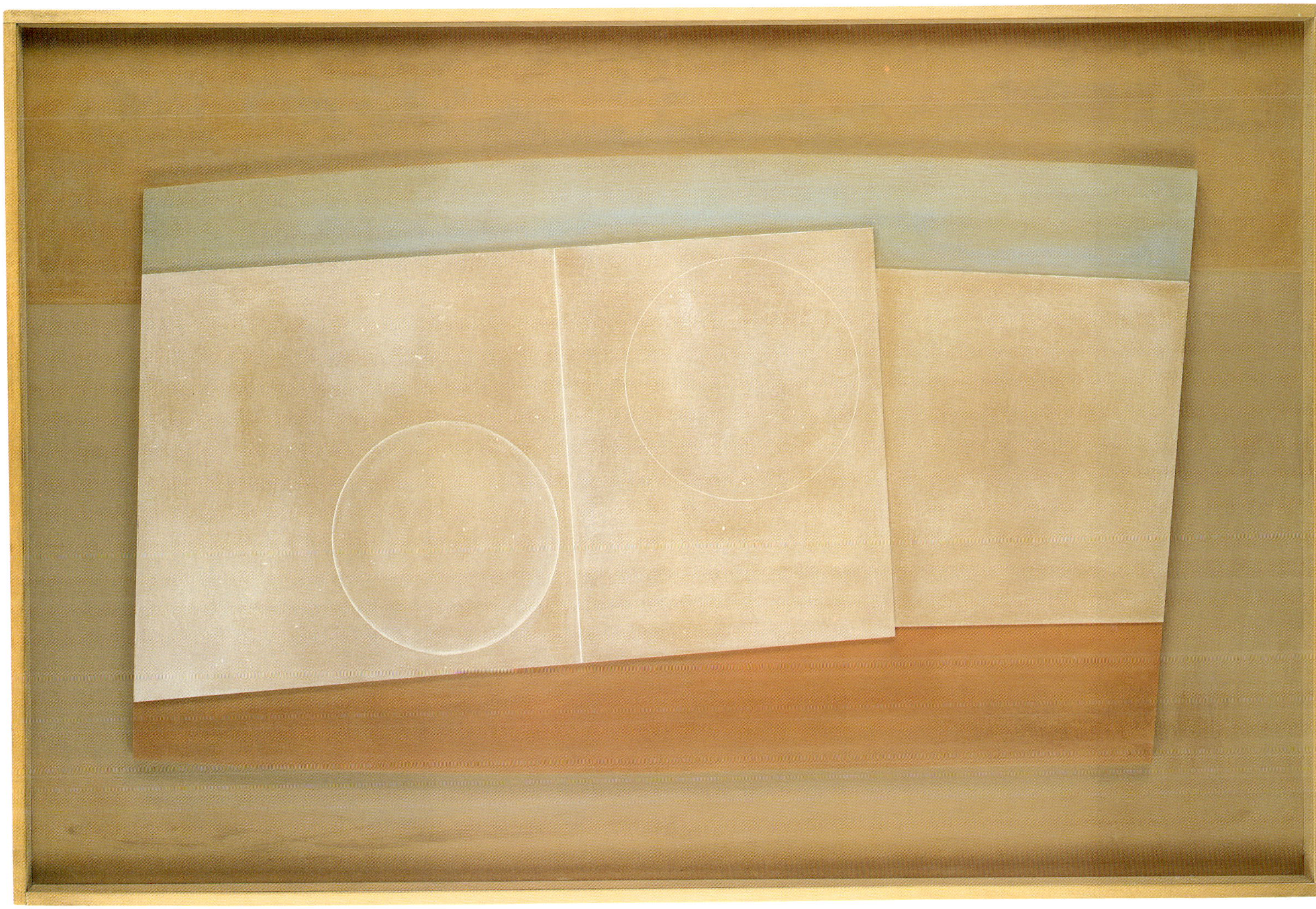

77 *1966 (Erymanthos)*
oil on carved board
121 × 186 cm (47½ × 73¼ in)

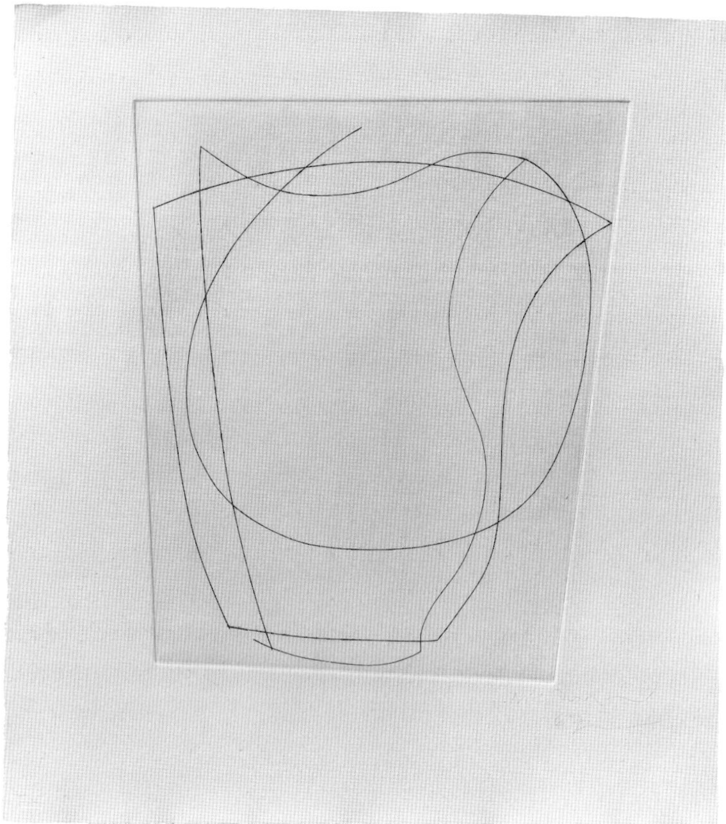

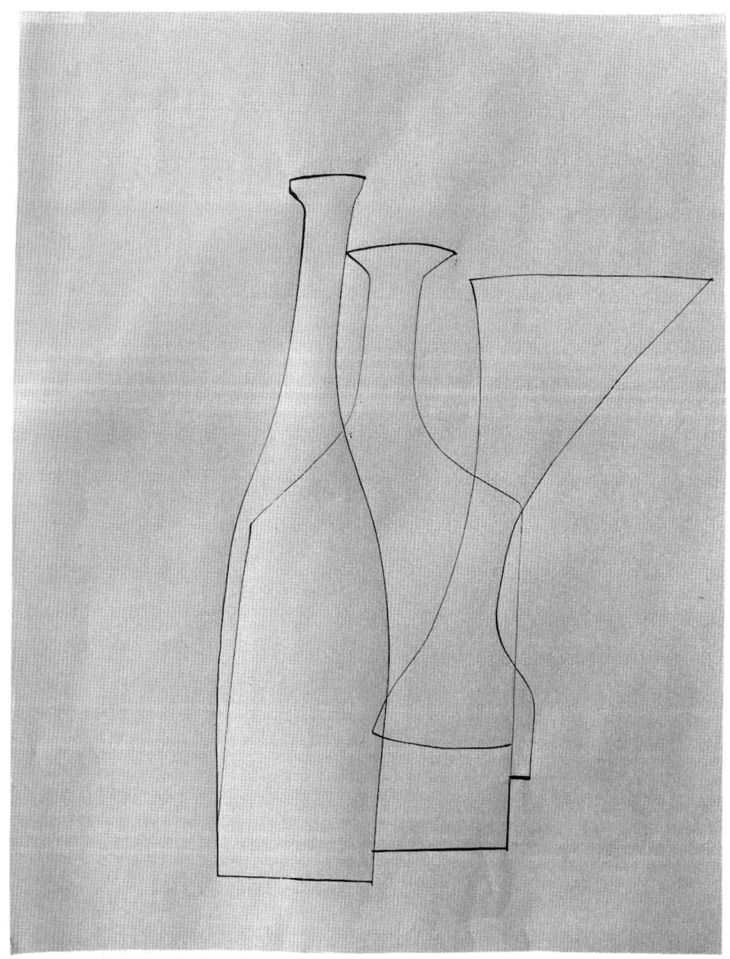

78 *April 1967 (large jug, small mug – Raphael)*
etching
30 × 26 cm (11¾ × 10¼ in)
paper 42 × 38 cm (16½ × 15 in)

79 *February 1964 (three forms)*
ink on paper
44 × 33 cm (17¼ × 13 in)
This photo, showing the drawing in reverse, was used as a basis for the etching *1967 (two bottles and a glass)*.

with the work and submit to its beauty. In these works Nicholson achieved a formal resolution and expressive power greater than ever before, as he himself recognized in a key statement he made in a letter to Herbert Read: 'The reliefs – both the white ones & the later primitive reliefs – are what I'd choose to stand or fall by (— the reliefs, then the dwgs, then the ptgs).'[107] The exhibition of twelve recent works (ten of them reliefs) at the Marlborough Gallery in June 1967 was the last that Read was able to go to before his death a year later. It is fitting that he should have thought it the finest exhibition he had ever seen.[108] The white reliefs remain indisputably a peak in Nicholson's career, but the later reliefs communicate a more ample experience. They sum up, but also surpass, all his previous work.

When ranking his work by genre, in the letter to Read just quoted, Nicholson made no separate mention of his prints. Maybe he subsumed them under his drawings, or, more likely, considered them as peripheral to his main activities. Yet, even though they may be minor works both in size and ambition, they do not deserve to go unheeded. Nicholson made prints at three widely separated periods of his life, each time practising a different technique. Between 1926 and 1938 he made about twenty-five linocuts and one woodcut based on still life, profiles of the human head, or on abstract themes.[109] Four Cornish landscapes and five still-life abstractions are the subjects of drypoints made in 1948, while three further drypoints belong to the 1950s: *Pisa* 1951, *San Gimignano* 1953 (based on an earlier drawing) and *Goblet Forms* 1957. But his fullest commitment to the medium was between 1965 and 1968 when, with the artist-printer François Lafranca, he produced 127 prints, most of them etchings but occasionally drypoint and aquatint as well. Further etchings, dated 1969, complete the corpus and bring its total to over 160 prints.

Nicholson greatly enjoyed the experience of engraving. As he wrote to his friend Geoffrey Jellicoe, the landscape designer: 'Etchings . . . are irresistible to do because of the bite of the hard point & the golden glitter that happens on the dark-as-night plate. It is like cutting, which a pen or pencil is not.'[110] Etching allowed him to combine the spontaneity of drawing with the instinctive desire to carve. But despite his pleasure and skill in the medium, he never considered himself a true engraver.

> I think I am not an 'etcher' as I understand the medium at all – really to be this one should know and have the whole paraphernalia – prepare & print the plates oneself? . . . Off-hand I can only think of a couple of very small Verona & Pisa 'etchings' which seem to me to have the true quality of etching. I suppose mine are really drawings on prepared copper.[111]

This is a modest, but accurate, self-assessment. Just as Nicholson's pencil line can sometimes seem to carve the surface of the paper, so the line engraved by his etching-needle is hardly distinguishable from a freely drawn pencil line. And since many of the etchings are in fact details, variations or copies (slightly simplified so as to accommodate to the smaller scale) of earlier drawings, it is hardly surprising that they are
78, 79 similar in style. In both media Nicholson aims at a rhythmic equivalent of the subject, pared down, reordered, and with a selective minimum of idiosyncratic detail.

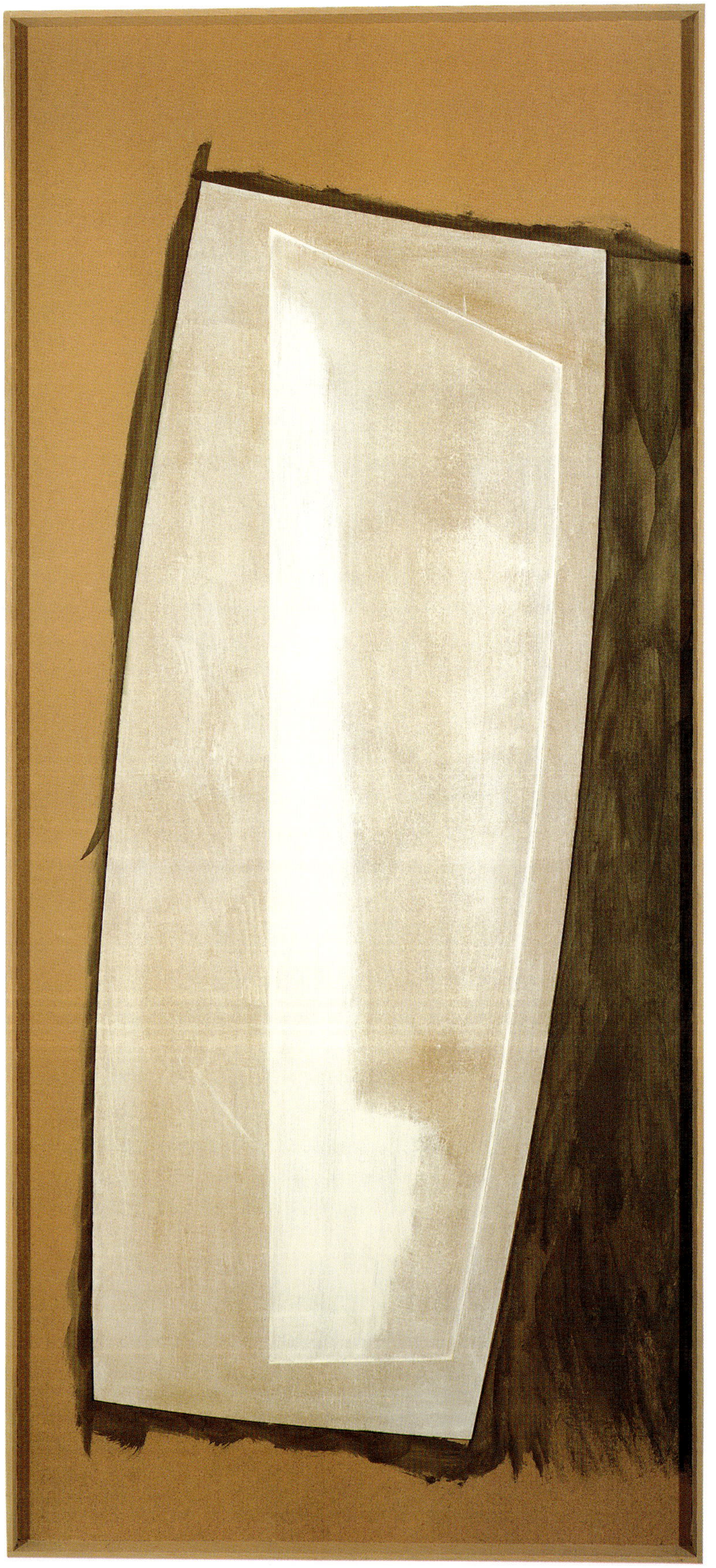

80 *1971 (dolphin)*
oil on carved relief
167 × 68 cm (65¾ × 26¾ in)

→ 81 *October 1958 (moonlight, Lucca)*
oil and pencil on board
17.5 × 23.5 cm (6¾ × 9¼ in) incl. mount

The essence of his drawing lies in the defining outline – William Blake's 'wirey bounding line' – which he would sometimes further enhance by painstakingly varnishing the graphite with a tiny brush. This outline is inflected with such sureness and finesse that it conveys a sense of the volume and the internal modelling of the form it encloses. Naturalistic shading becomes redundant, and the line virtually abolishes itself in the creation of air, space and light. The etchings, even more than the drawings, demonstrate how much can be expressed or suggested by just a few lines.

Nicholson could not resist reworking the proofs of his etchings by cropping them, adding lines in ink or pencil and embellishing them with colour, so that they might just as well not have been etchings in the first place. The result, if unorthodox, is usually an enhancement, even if at times such tinkerings verge on the whimsical to precious. We have already noted the evolution from drawing to painting to etching in the San Gimignano balcony scene (see pp.60–1). Another such group was inspired
81 by Lucca, beginning with *October 1958 (moonlight, Lucca)*, a jewel-like miniature, measuring only 5 × 7 in, in which the architectural pattern of roof, dome and tower is enriched with colour and texture by loosely brushed-in patches of paint and thick scribblings of pencil to conjure up a romantic, moonlit townscape. This is Nicholson

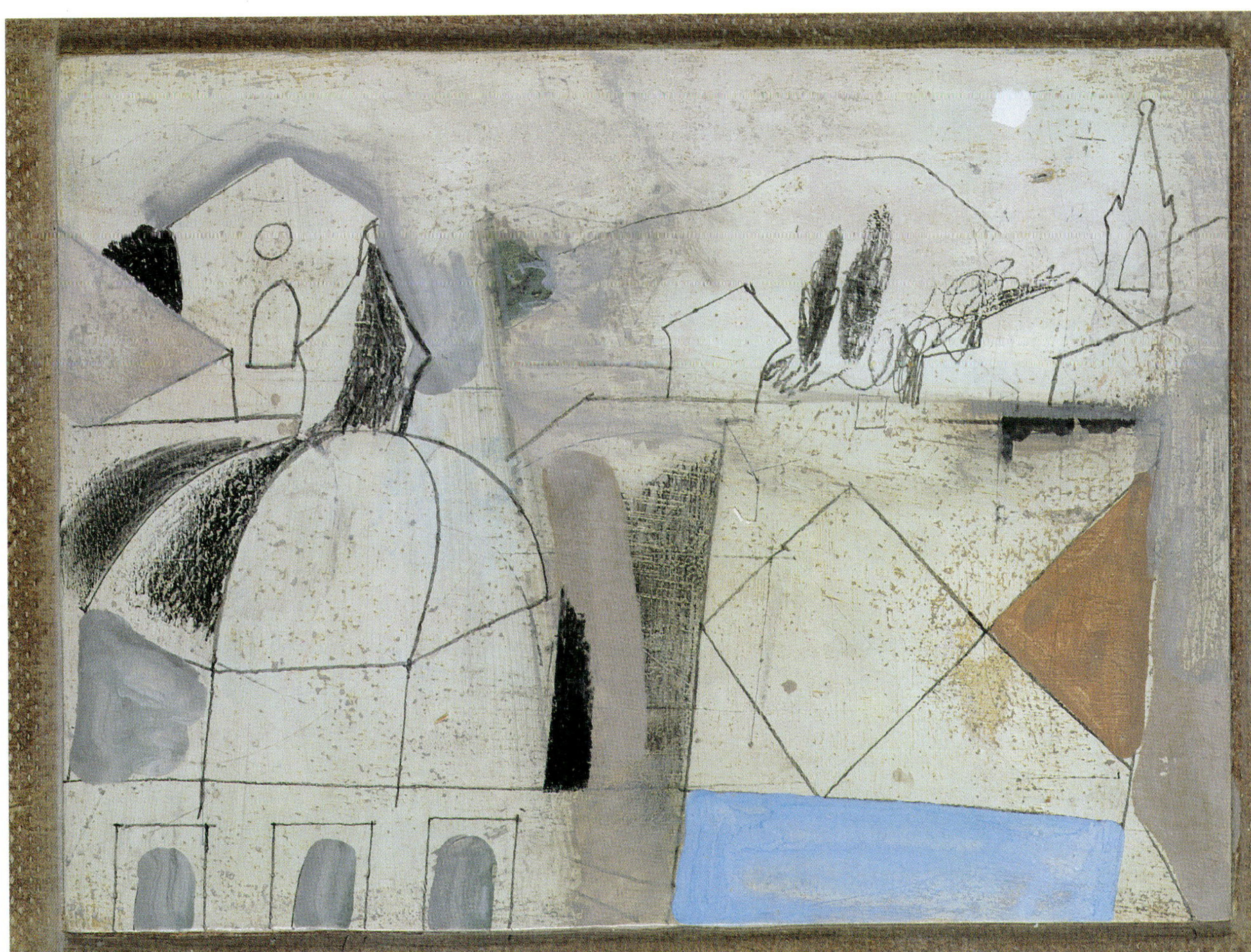

working like a smith on some cloisonné enamel the size of a hand, far removed, one might think, from the austere creator of the white reliefs. Directly based on this is the
82 etching *1967 (Lucca, small version)*, actually a little larger than the painting but, allowing for the reversal in printing, a close copy of it. The same motif inspired two
83 other etchings, *1966 (Lucca)* and *August/September 1967 (Italian mountain village (Lucca))*. Nicholson then worked on proofs of the latter, cropping them more or less severely, and adding lines in ink and patches of gouache colour until they came to
84 resemble in quality the original painting *October 1958 (moonlight, Lucca)*.

The etching process gave rise to another kind of hybrid: the 'relief drawings' made
87 on the back of discarded pulls whose surface had been indented by the copper plate. The irregular shapes of the plate impress add to the individual character and vitality of each drawing in a playfully inventive series inspired by some hand-forged scissors which his daughter Kate brought back from Argos. The early variations are vivid
85 portraits of the scissors in different moods and guises, but then the image is complicated by the gradual infiltration of still life and landscape elements until the scissors themselves are in danger of being overlooked. The drawing's reference expands from the particular to the universal, figurative merges with abstract, and the contempla-
86 tive viewer finds himself experiencing a whole complex of sensations, all mysteriously interacting in a perpetual motion which is also the stillness of infinity.

When not based on still life, Nicholson's drawings and etchings of the 1960s take their inspiration from his travels in France, Portugal, Italy, Greece and the Aegean. His wife often took photographs of the landscape and architecture which he drew, and her finest work shares some of the abstract and poetic qualities of his.[112] In May 1967 they joined some friends on a small yacht for a ten-day cruise in the Aegean. The experience of going ashore in Turkey is reflected in a group of etchings Nicholson made later that year. Like the drawings of minarets he had made earlier
89 at Rhodes and Kos, these 'Turkish forms' are just sufficiently tinged with the East to jolt one into realizing how entirely European the sources of Nicholson's inspiration otherwise are. One may find the occasional reference to China, Tibet or Peru in the subtitles of his works, but these are mere metaphors: Nicholson's allegiance was to Europe. The places that stirred the deepest response in him and fed his imagination – Carnac, Mycenae, Altamira, Olympia, where the works of man have taken on the timelessness of the works of nature; Siena, Urbino, Pisa, Torcello, the spirit of whose buildings he seemed to recognize as something out of his own past – all these memorials to the passing generations of man were an intrinsic part of the landscape of Europe. And so it is fitting that in 1974 Nicholson should have been chosen to receive the Rembrandt Prize, which goes to an artist whose work is deemed to be a significant enhancement of the European cultural heritage. Bestowed by the aptly named Goethe Foundation of Basel, which exists to promote European culture and unity, it was one of the few public honours Nicholson was willing to accept, apart from the Order of Merit which had been conferred on him in 1968. Otherwise, he shunned publicity and was sceptical about prizes for the arts.

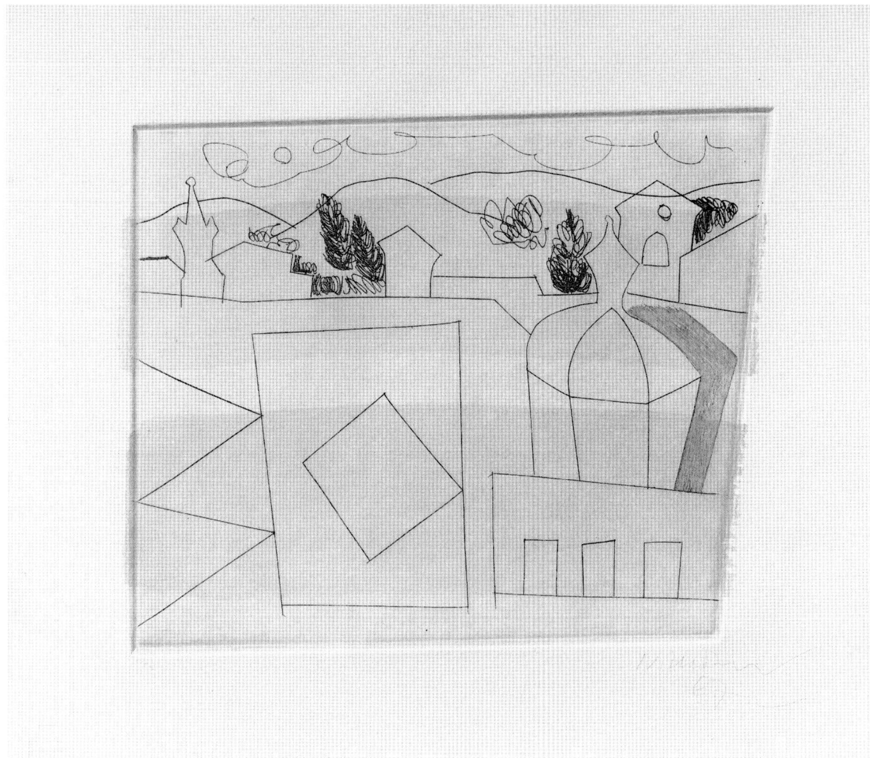

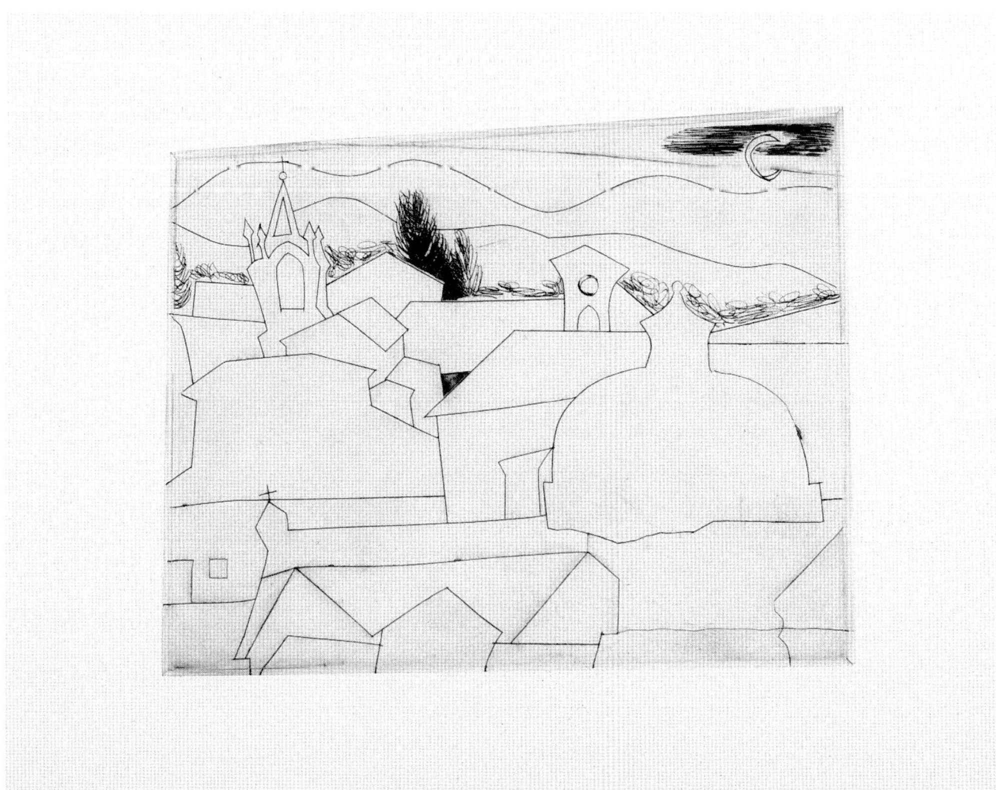

82 *1967 (Lucca, small version)*
etching with wash
18 × 22.5 cm (7 × 9 in)
paper 27 × 31.5 cm (10½ × 12½ in)

83 *August/September 1967 (Italian mountain village (Lucca))*
etching
20.5 × 26 cm (8 × 10¼ in)
paper 32 × 41 cm (12½ × 16 in)

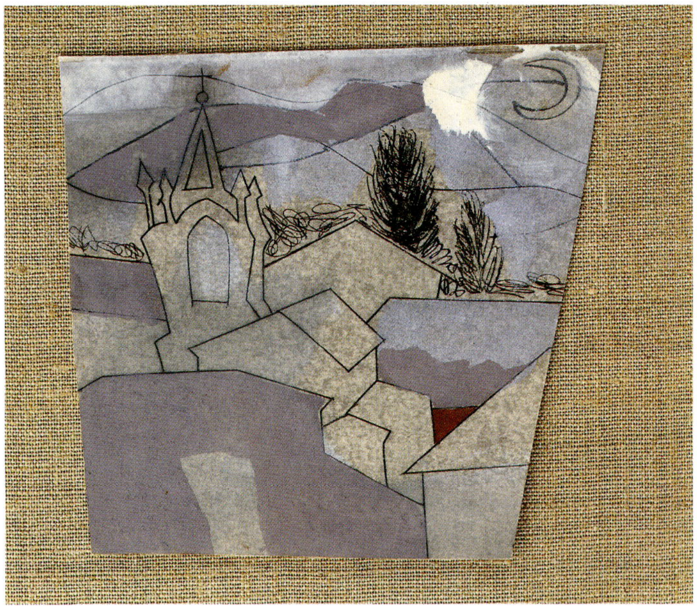

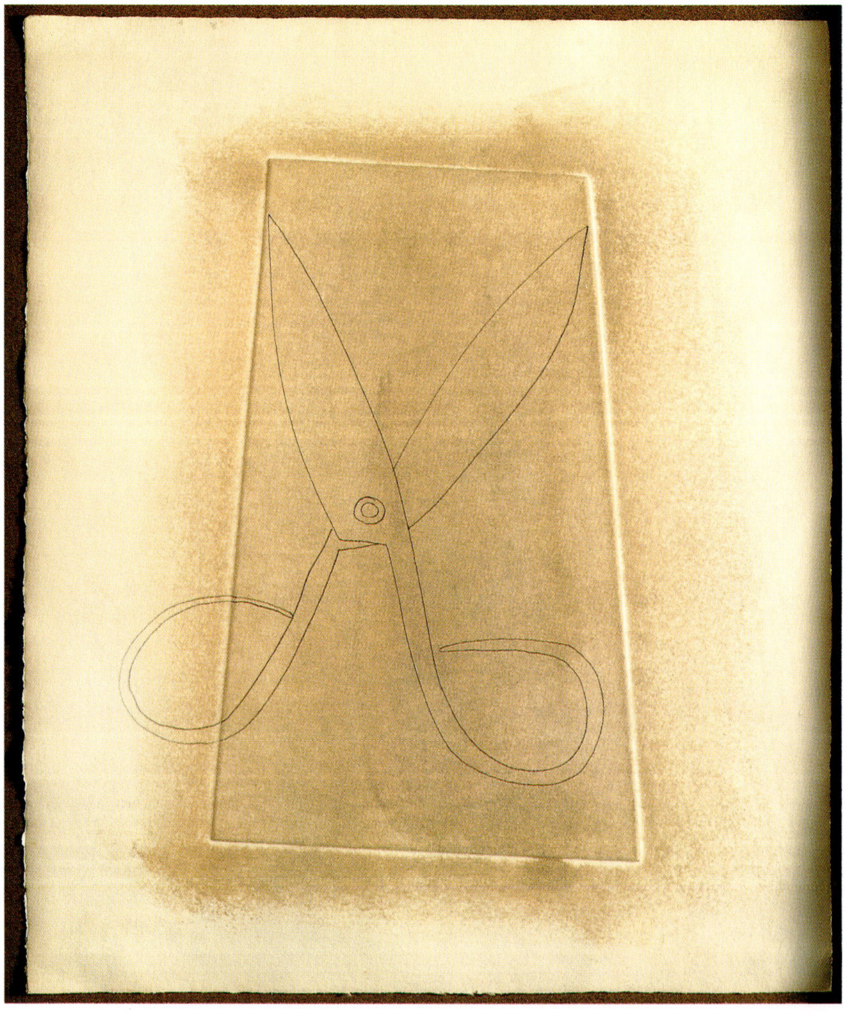

84 *1965 (Italian mountain village, variation on a theme no.3)*
etching with ink and gouache
12.5 × 13.5 cm (5 × 5¼ in)

85 *1968 (scissors, variation on a theme no.2)*
oil wash and pencil on paper with relief
38 × 32 cm (15 × 12½ in)

→ 86 *1966–8 (still life with scissors)*
oil wash and pencil on paper with relief
60 × 45 cm (23½ × 17¾ in)

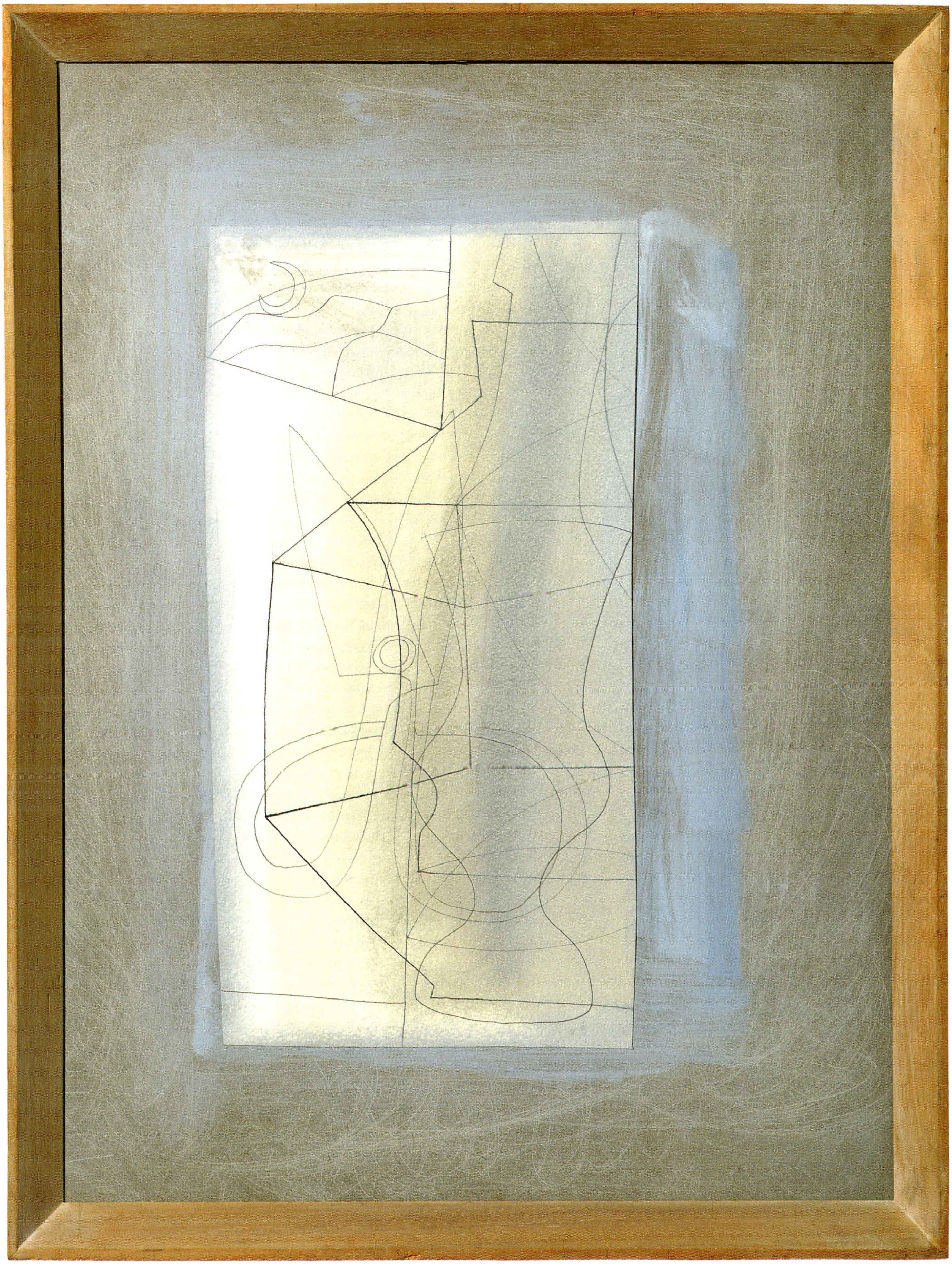

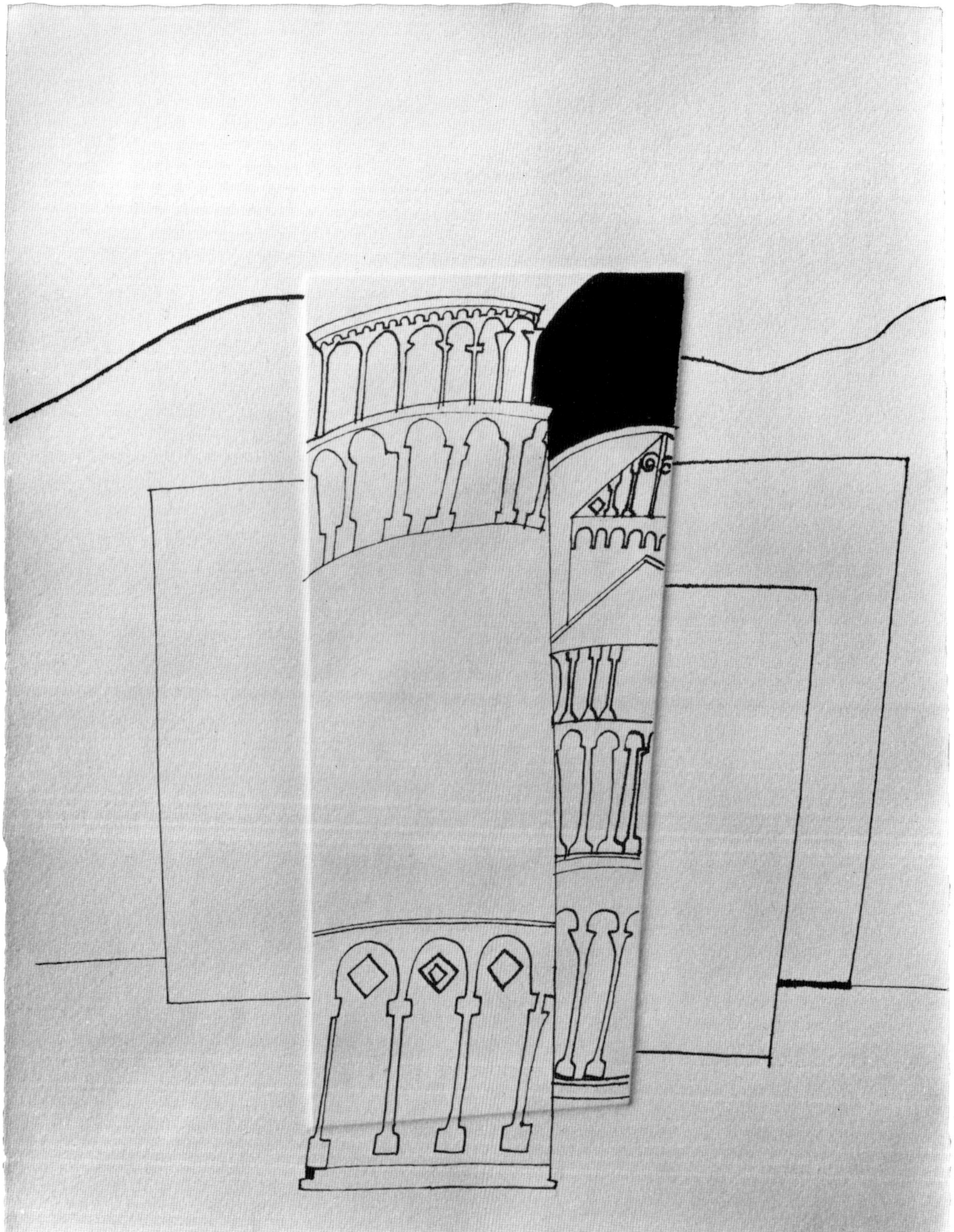

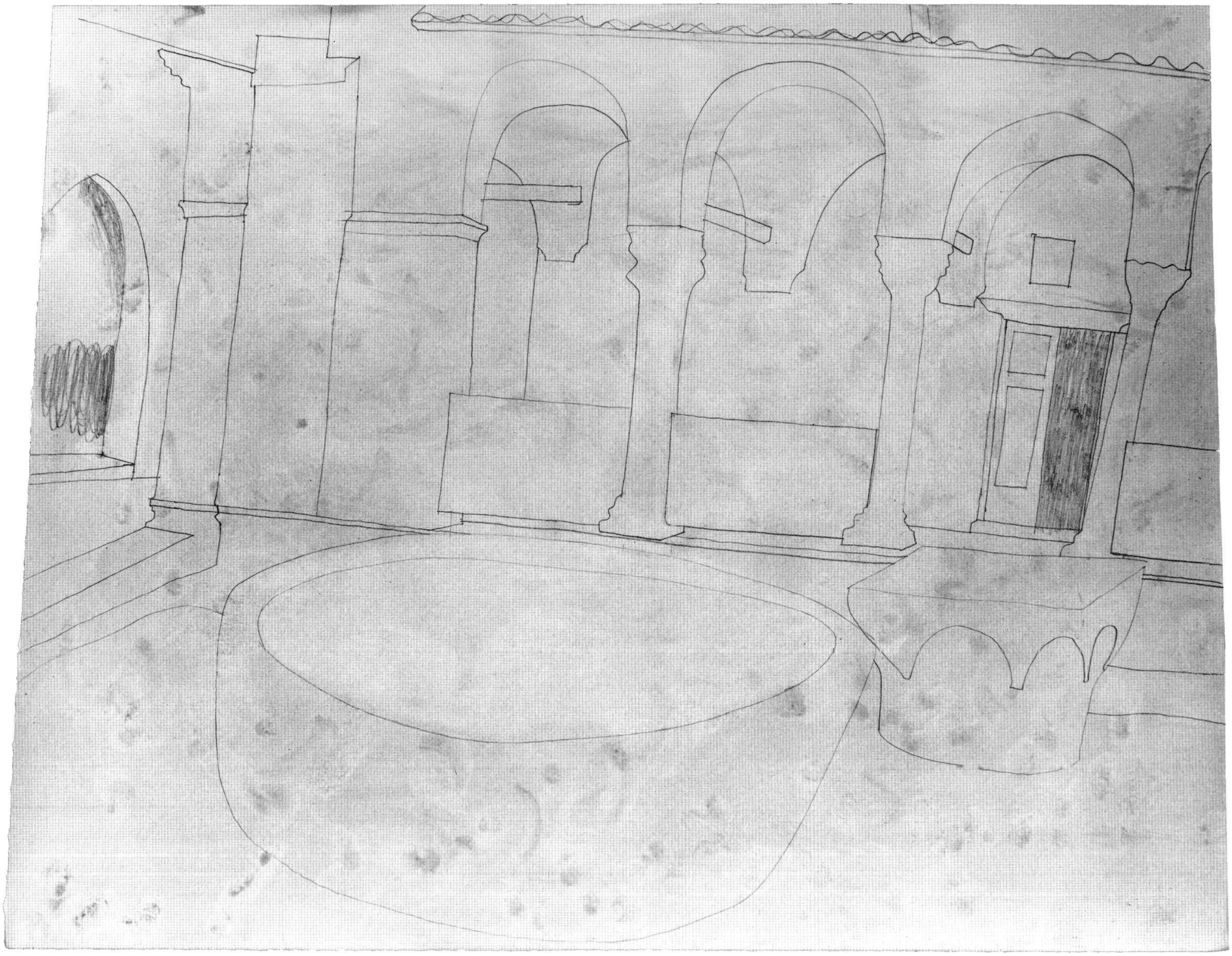

← 87 *1967 (Pisa as intended)*
ink on paper with relief
49 × 42 cm (19¼ × 16½ in)

88 *1962 (Torcello)*
oil wash and pencil on paper
36.5 × 47.5 cm (14½ × 18¾ in)

Nicholson – it hardly needs saying – lived for his work. Not only did it give him acute pleasure and satisfaction to search for and find the living reality in a new work, it was a necessity of his being. His wish to create calm and exact balance in so many of his compositions may, in part, reflect a need to resolve an inner unrest. Certainly he required a peaceful environment and long stretches of virtual solitude for his work, took care to safeguard his privacy, and was wary of the slightest infringement of his freedom. Like many artists, he simply wanted to be left alone. A female presence was always very necessary to him to provide the right kind of sympathetic support, but otherwise he was largely self-sufficient. 'The two essentials to my painting,' he confessed to Geoffrey Jellicoe, 'are a love-affair with a woman (even if it's only a

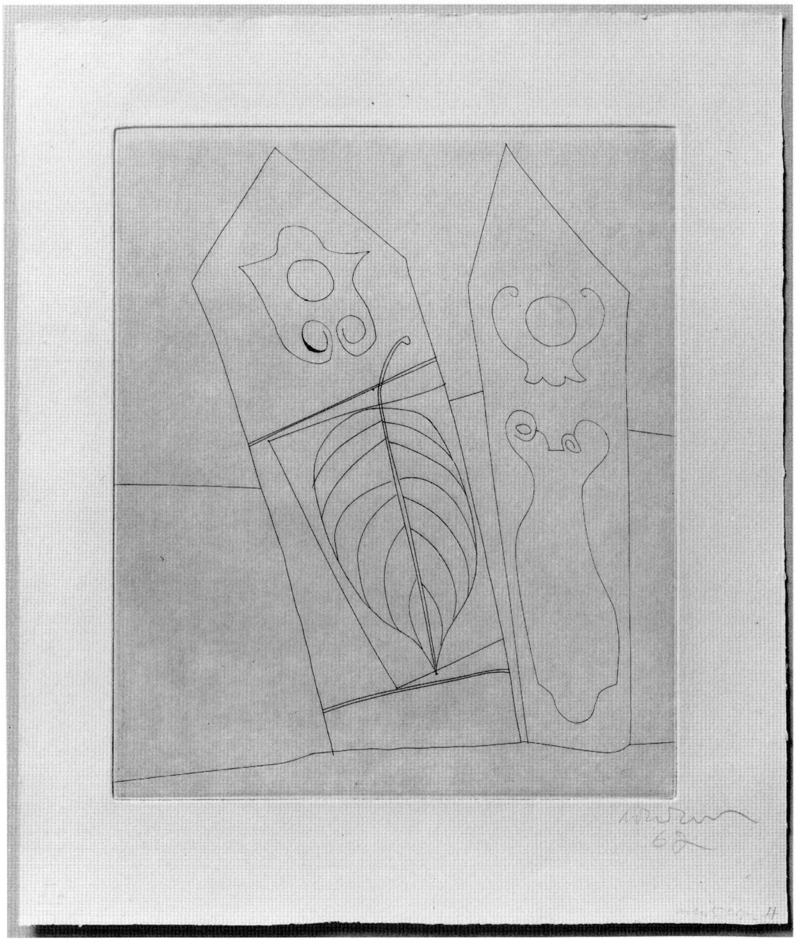

89 *August 1967 (Turkish forms with leaf)*
etching
32.5 × 28.5 cm (12¾ × 11¼ in)
paper 43 × 38 cm
(17 × 15 in)

→ 90 *1965 (Pisa with black)*
oil wash and ink on paper with relief
55.5 × 48 cm (21¾ × 19 in)

look — —) & a ditto with a landscape (from which architecture is certainly not excluded) – in fact ideally all three together! What a life — — — .'[113]

Though he did not seek close intimacy, he enjoyed seeing a wide variety of friends and was himself delightful and stimulating company. It happened that, just at the time he was living in the Ticino, a number of other artists had migrated there. As he wrote to Jim Ede in August 1963:

> There are several amusing artists in the district ... Bissier as a character would amuse you a lot. His forms are not sculptural enough for me (too many socks and frogs?) but the quality, the texture of his ptgs is marvellous and the *depths* behind the forms. Certainly the quality of the fine linen on which he works is quite remarkable and not seen or felt in reproductions.
>
> Arp is also here ½ the year – a singularly nice chap ... Tobey wld be right up your street these days and lives at Basel (expect you knew him at Dartington) – I think among the 2 or 3 best of all ptrs today.[114]

Nicholson had been much taken with Julius Bissier's retrospective exhibition in Hanover in 1958 and had visited him at his home at Hagnau on Lake Constance before they became neighbours in the Ticino. Though he was primarily attracted by the aesthetic refinement of Bissier's paintings in tempera on linen, he may also have

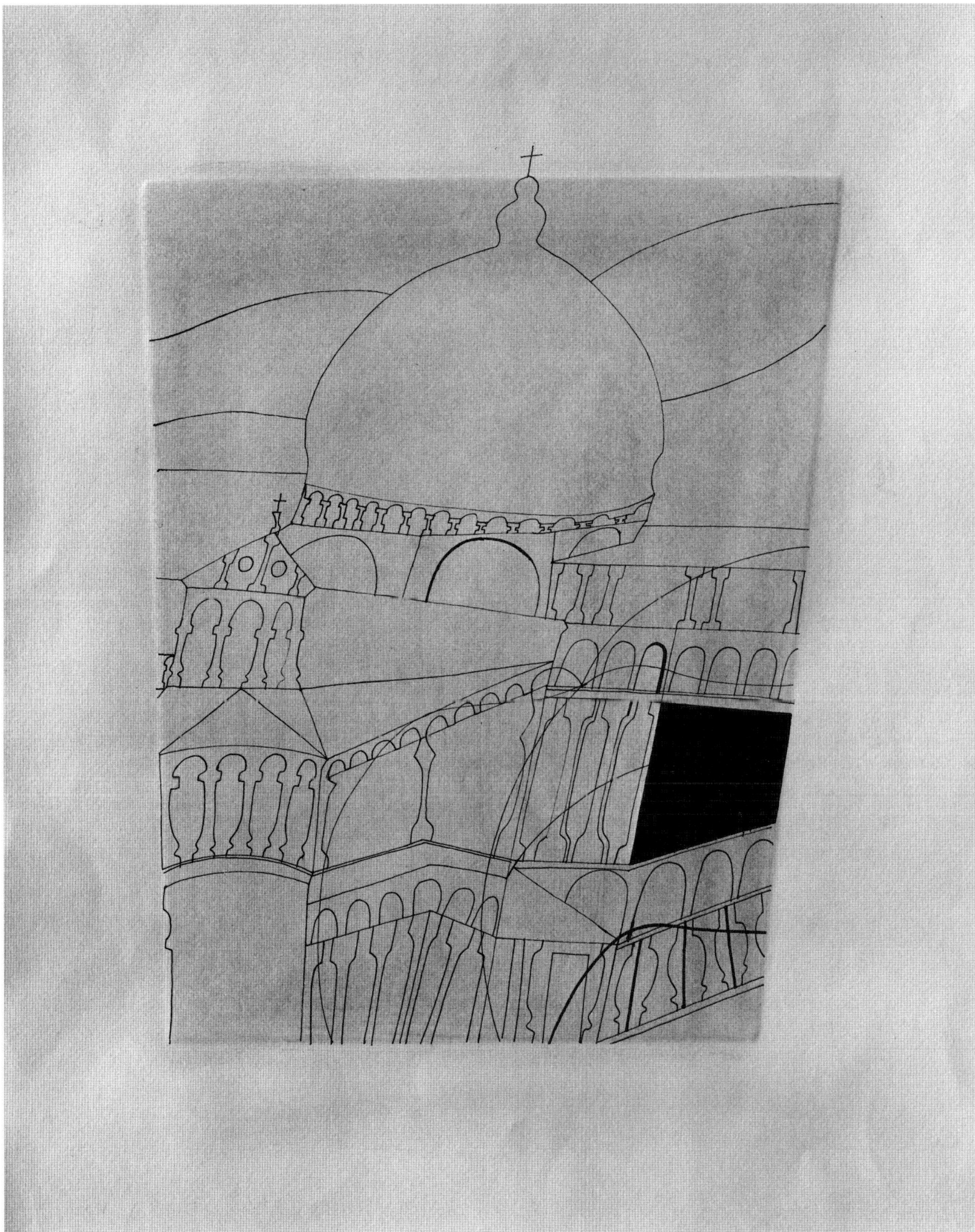

felt in sympathy with its Far-Eastern inspiration which, in turn, was a link with Tobey's work. Arp had influenced Nicholson in the formative early 1930s (see p.35) but since then they had lost touch. Now, just at the time of his letter to Ede, Nicholson was sharing an exhibition at St Gallen with Arp, Tobey, Bissier and another 'local artist' (also a friend of Ede's), Italo Valenti. His relations with these and other artists, some of whom he met on his regular visits to the *Venice Biennale*, were purely social: they did not talk art. With Zoran Music, for instance, he invented a sort of fives, which they played with a golf ball in an empty swimming pool. He admired the work of Tobey, Mark Rothko, Sam Francis, Alberto Burri, Pierre Soulages, Victor Pasmore and others, but at this late stage of his career it is wiser to speak of sympathies or affinities than to claim influences from their work.[115]

Links with England and the past were not severed. Nicholson paid brief visits to London (usually at the time of his exhibitions there) and stayed with friends in the country, while they in turn came to see him in Switzerland. Helen Sutherland, now in her eighties and very lame, travelled out in March 1962 for what was to be their last meeting (she died four years later). Herbert Read participated in some of the Eranos conferences held each August at Ascona and was glad to escape to the shade and tranquillity of Nicholson's terrace-garden. There were visits from Cyril Reddihough, Margaret Gardiner, Geoffrey and Jane Grigson, John and Elizabeth Summerson, Leslie and Sadie Martin – all of whom he had known for over thirty years – and other special friends such as Geoffrey Jellicoe and the Pasmores. But these brief contacts could not banish a growing sense of isolation. Language, in particular, was a cause of frustration: conversations were conducted in French, German, Italian, English or any combination of these, but all too often only one of the parties was speaking his native tongue. The others had to get by with approximations. Nicholson could express himself in French and Italian, but not with ease or nuance, and he longed to be able to speak to someone who would really get the point of what he was saying in English – who would understand his jokes, which were often verbal.

He missed the English landscape and ambience, was conscious of having no roots in the Ticino, and feared a lonely old-age. In short, he wanted to return home. Felicitas, however, wished to remain in Switzerland, on the Continent. For some time they had tended to lead increasingly separate lives, so that parting was accepted on both sides as inevitable.[116] In May 1971 Nicholson left the mountains and the great lake – the slate-grey mountains wreathed in bands of white cloud, the waters of the lake hourly changing from deep blue to green to turquoise to grey – exchanging them for the more placid, but more reassuring countryside of England.

1971–82

'going deeper into the sense of things'

Between the grandeur of the Ticino and the humble ordinariness of Cambridgeshire there could hardly be a greater contrast. But Nicholson, now in a mood to relish everything English, saw it differently: '5 miles from Cambridge & complete ENGLISH countryside – such a quietness & 2 streams & huge chestnut trees & willows & English green orchards & grass'.[117] His old friends Leslie and Sadie Martin, who lived in a converted mill at Great Shelford, near Cambridge, had recently turned the grain store next to the mill into a four-storey 'flat' and invited Nicholson to live there. It was a tall, narrow building, which meant that his studio would be quite small, but he was delighted with it: the position was idyllic, with trees and grass, swans on the mill pool, and only the sound of the weir to disturb the silence. He immediately invested the place with his own poetry, naming his new home 'The Flying Fox' after a weather-vane he could see from his window.

At a party given by the Martins that Christmas of 1971, Nicholson met Angela Taunt, the wife of a mathematician who, like Leslie Martin, was a Fellow of Jesus College. She was interested in painting and already greatly admired his work, while Nicholson found in her the enthusiasm, vivacity and feminine sympathy that he needed so much. The meeting ripened into friendship, with outings by car into the country around Cambridge and to churches in Suffolk, while three times a week Angela had the opportunity to work at her painting in an attic studio of the Flying Fox and benefit from Nicholson's comments.

In May 1972 they went for ten days to Wharfedale, the first of many productive drawing trips they made together over the next six years – to Greece, to Cyprus and to Tuscany, as well as regularly to Yorkshire. The weather was so awful that Nicholson was forced to do much of his drawing inside the car. As he reported to Geoffrey Grigson: 'I have never drawn under such fiendish and delightful conditions – cold winter winds and incessant rain but what a landscape – I think one of the most beautiful in England – that and W. Penwith. . . . I did make 2 rather spiffing dwgs of Burnsall Bridge – and of a small squat church with the sky going by at a tremendous pace – and also one of the whole landscape going by ditto.'[118]

He liked to make these drawings on irregular-shaped sheets of paper whose trapezoid forms and slightly curved edges, like those of the etching plates in the relief drawings, are integral to the character and expressiveness of the work. In *1972*
91 *(Burnsall bridge no.1)* the piers of the bridge are reduced to a series of diminishing rectangles connected by springing arcs. The strength, speed and rhythm of the line is perfectly controlled, while all decorative detail is obliterated in favour of this purely abstract notation of a bridge. Though much is also omitted in his view of the squat
93 church at Hubberholme, the character of the drawing largely depends on the treatment of selected details: the weather-vane, the window in the tower, the transparent gravestones and the typically childlike versions of cows stepping out of the drawing

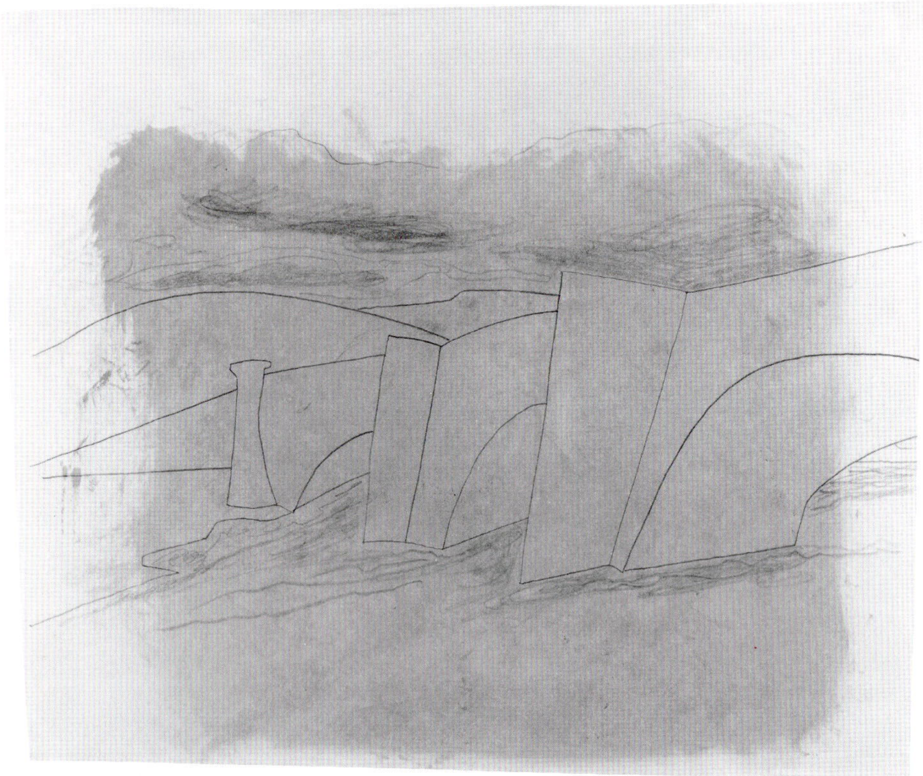

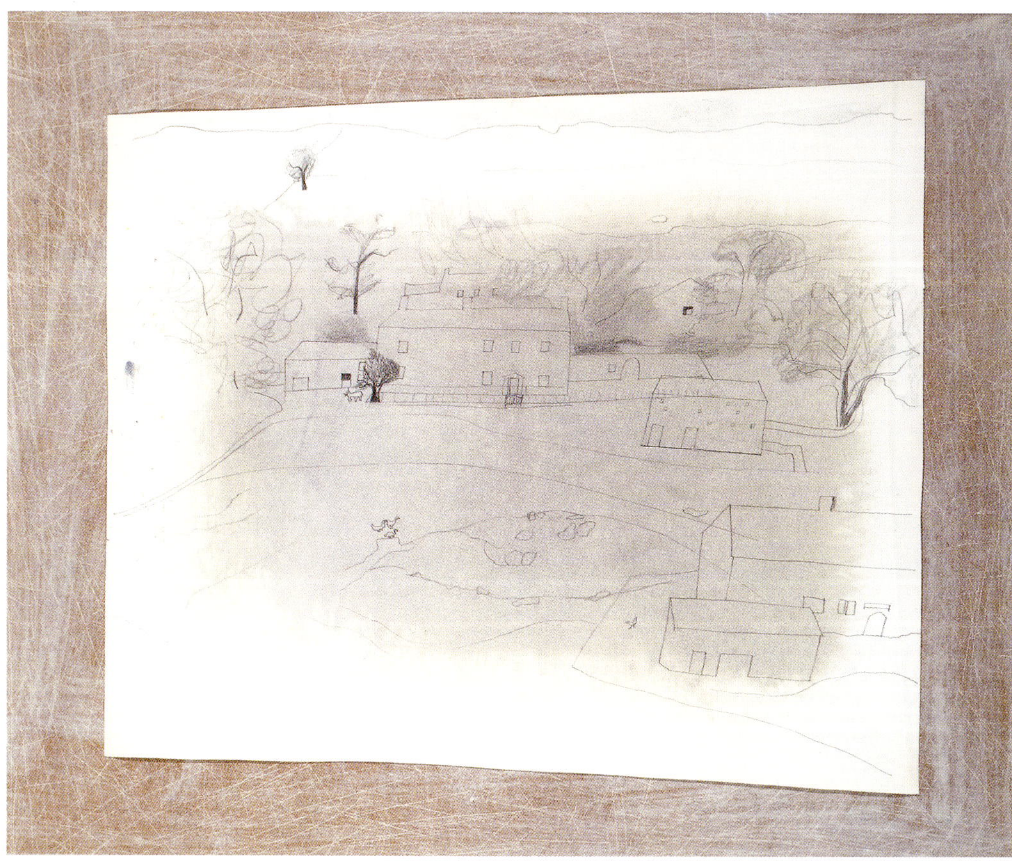

91 *1972 (Burnsall bridge no.1)*
oil wash and pencil on paper
39.5 × 50 cm (15½ × 19¾ in)

92 *1972 (Yockenthwaite in rain)*
oil wash and pencil on paper
40 × 48 cm (15¾ × 18¾ in)

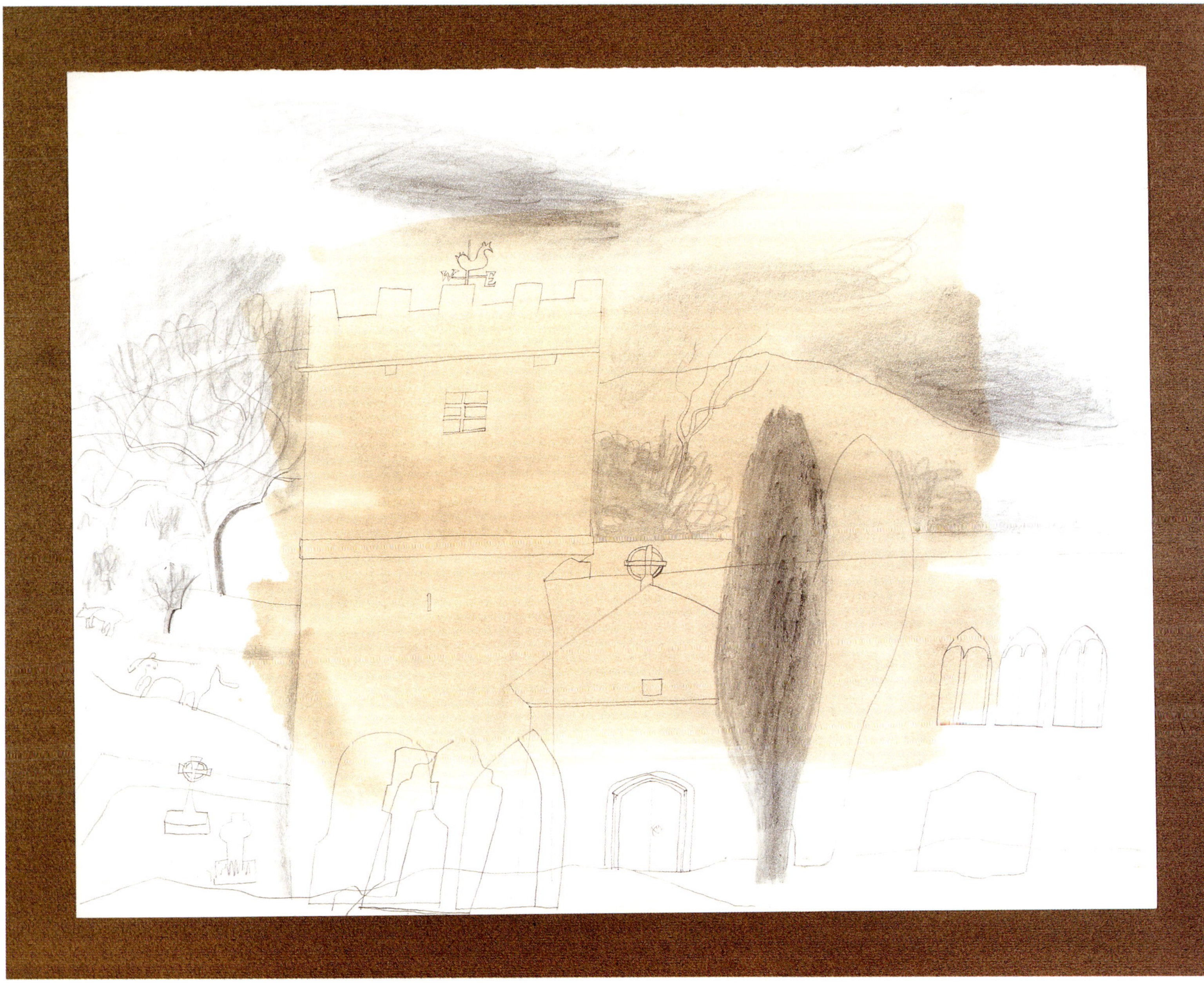

93 *1972 (Hubberholme)*
oil wash and pencil on paper
38 × 51 cm (15 × 20¼ in)

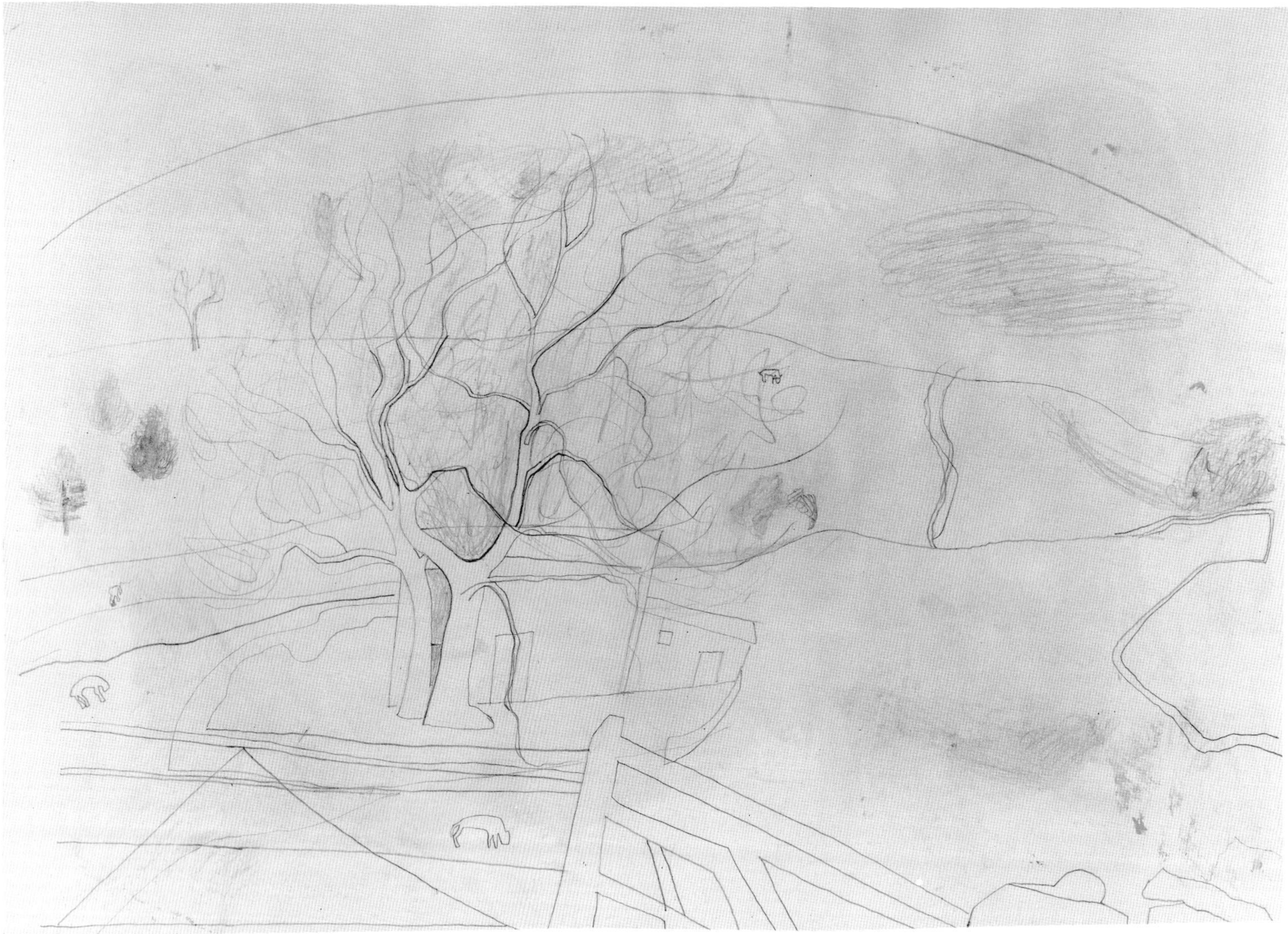

like the truncated horses in the *Peter Pan* poster of 1904 (see p.10). The same 'child's drawing' effect is even more evident in the farm buildings of *1972 (Yockenthwaite in*
92 *rain)*.[119] Rain-softened outlines and delicate, more tentative drawing characterize
94 *1972 (Wharfedale in rain)*. Its rhythm is similar to that of *January 4 1953 (Thorpe, Wharfedale in snow)* (p.68), but the lines are freer, less emphatic, and Nicholson is not afraid to simplify the outline of the hilltop to a shallow arc. His first concern, when drawing a tree, is to show its structure and the springing tracery of its branches. Foliage is either stylized in a violent scribble of black, or, as here, stripped away to reveal an equally stylized tree-anatomy – bare branches whirling out as if to free themselves from the main boughs. It was the bareness of the landscape of the Yorkshire dales that he loved, and the clear lines of stone wall, road and hilltop moving in counter-rhythm.

94 *1972 (Wharfedale in rain)*
oil wash and pencil on paper
36 × 51 cm (14¼ × 20 in)

→ **95** *1972 (Gythian theatre)*
oil wash and pencil on paper
37 × 52 cm (14½ × 20½ in)

95 A drawing of the ancient theatre at 'Gythian' (*ie* Yithion, on the Laconic Gulf), shows the same riotous abandon in the branches of two trees, contrasted with the tense horseshoe curve of its tiered seats. The lines, particularly of the criss-cross of twigs and branches in the centre, look as though they had been etched, not drawn, on the paper. Another drawing, made on the same visit to Greece with Angela Taunt in October 1972, is unusual for showing a landscape without buildings – the mountainous landscape at Ligourion, on the road between Nauplion and Epidauros. Here
96 the lean of the tree to the left is reinforced by cutting the paper's edge at an angle to create a real tension before releasing a branch (and the viewer's gaze) to the right, over the wavy outline of the mountain ridge and the calmer undulation of the hills below. This, one may think, is a different Nicholson from the Nicholson of the white reliefs, but it is the same poetic idea which he is expressing, with greater freedom and a looser, gentler line, the same reduction to a few essentials and suggestion of the infinite.

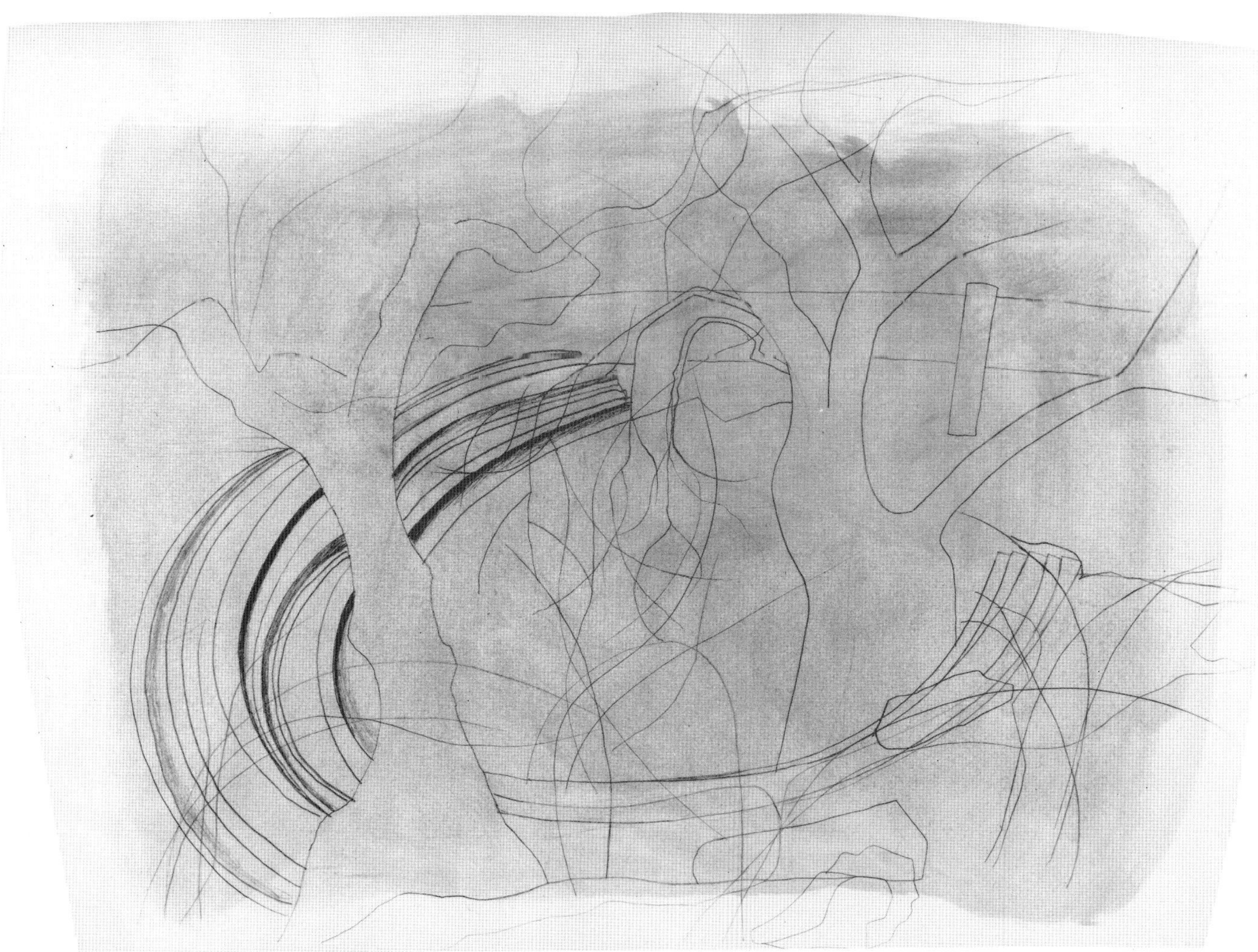

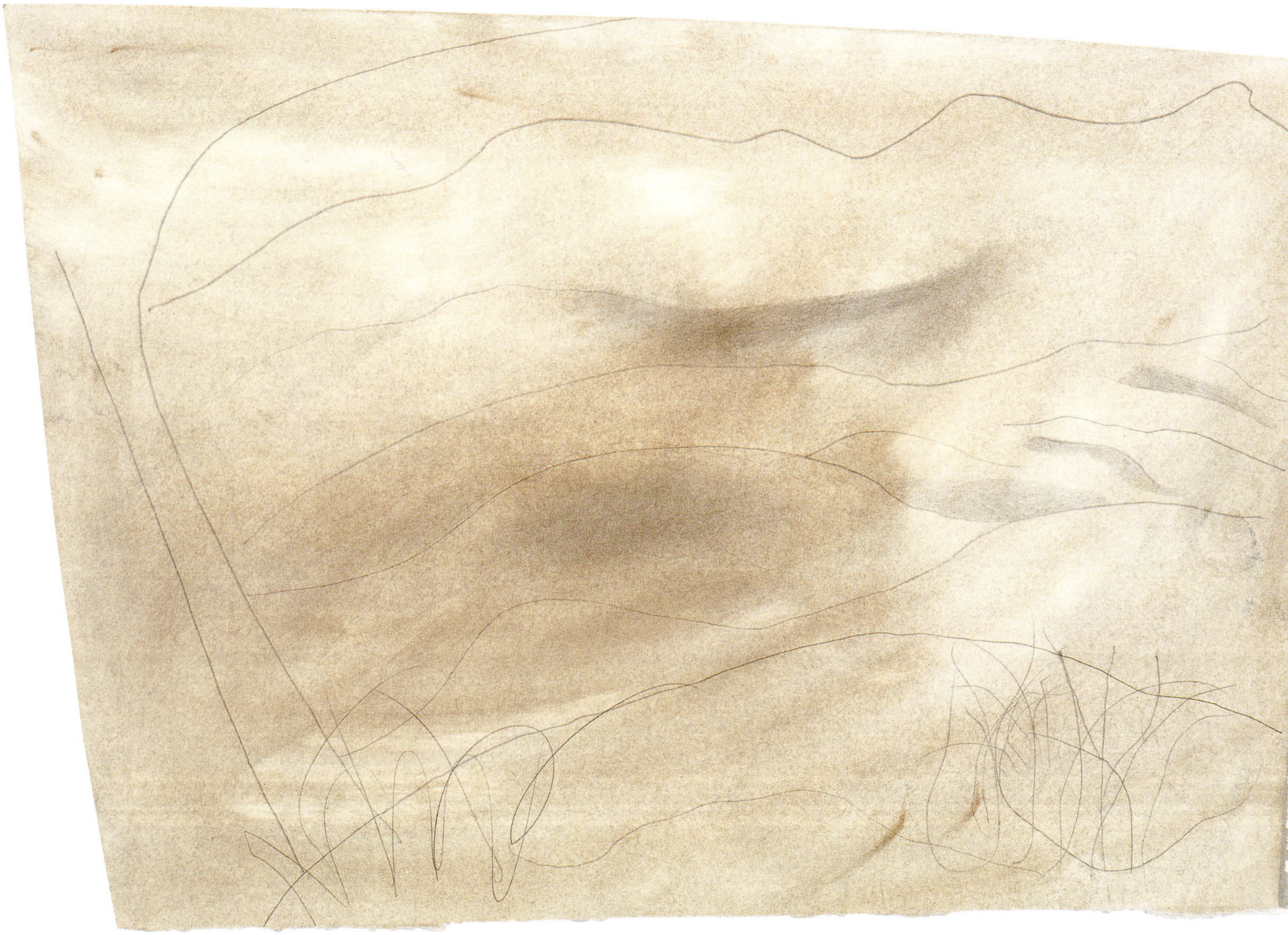

96 *1972 (Ligourion)*
oil wash and pencil on paper
43 × 55 cm (17 × 21¾ in)

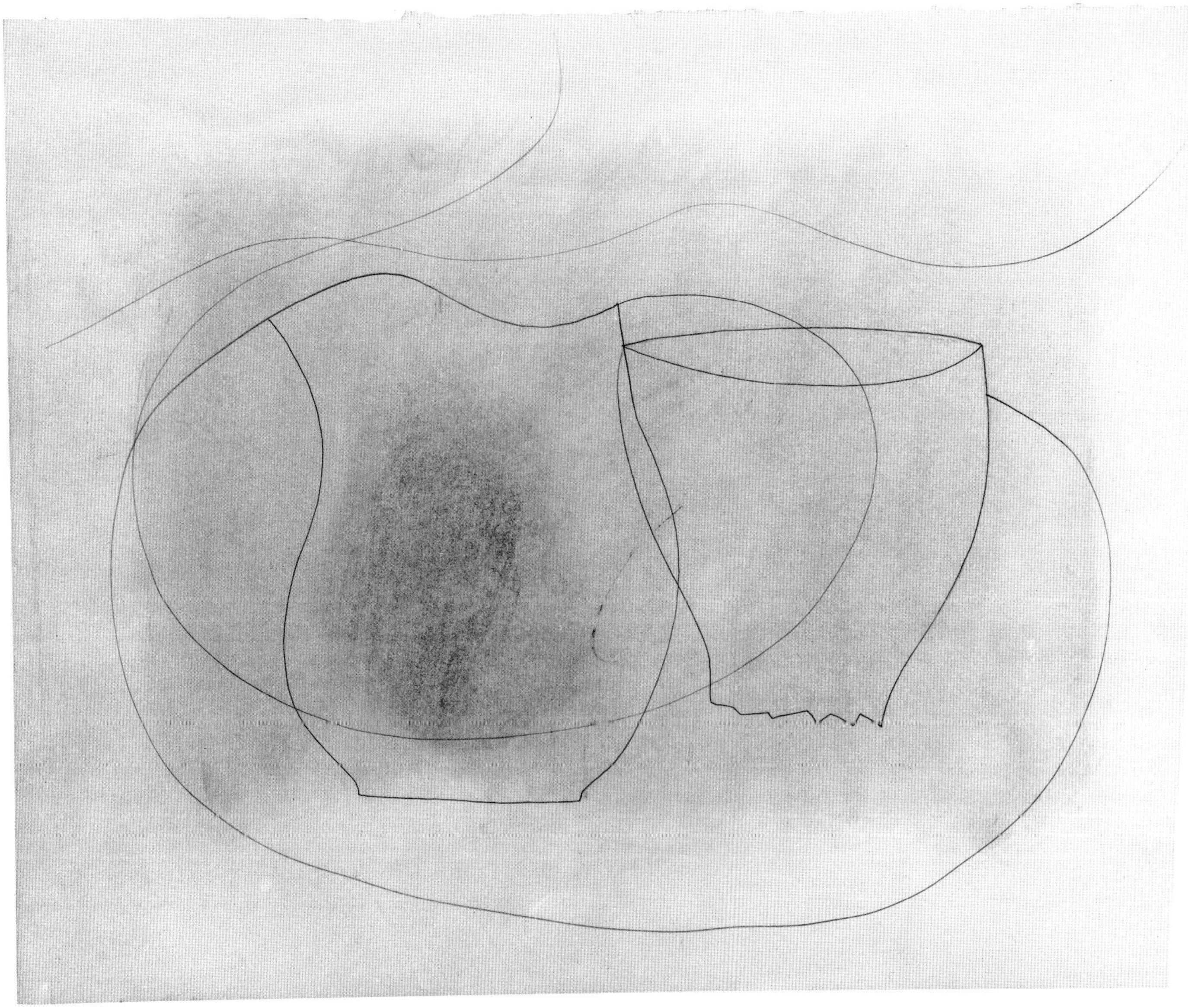

97 *1970 (Greek forms)*
oil wash and pencil on paper
38 × 47 cm (15 × 18½ in)

Many of the drawings Nicholson made in the 1970s are of architecture. Though they vary in character, most often one element in them is played off another to create
99 movement, tension, life. In *1974 (Siena)* the empty foreground and high walls funnel one's curiosity towards the detail of the teasingly obscured, rakishly leaning tower. Compared with *May 1957 (Siena campanile)* (see p.77), the touch is gentler, the line less virtuosic (Nicholson was eighty when he made this); he allows himself greater licence in the interpretation of his subject, often with an element of surprise or of caricature; he is happy to leave large areas blank; and there is a relaxed, devil-may-care
100 assurance in his handling which comes from long practice. In *1974 (Certaldo)* he places the same quirky detail against a marvellous springing counterpoint of archway, staircase and window embrasure (with a tiny landscape visible through it of cypresses on a hilltop). Humour and fantasy take over in his re-creation of the
98 Gothick gateway at Madingley Hall, a Tudor house outside Cambridge. Without any illusionism the character of the place is captured by means of selection, caricature and an overall reshaping dictated by imaginative empathy. As he realized, 'the problem in dwg things which are already a work of art is to be able to take the necessary physical liberties with them & at the same time take no liberties at all with the spirit, in a kind of re-creation'. [120]

A survey of Nicholson's drawings, over a period of fifty years, would reveal a remarkable constancy of style. Having once arrived at a personal, essentially linear, method of notation in the late 1920s, he developed this with increasing verve and assurance until it reached full maturity in the Italian drawings of the early 1950s. From then on he had at his disposal a technique perfectly suited to express whatever he wished. Some of the drawings he made in the 1970s are strikingly sparse, others abound in detail. In some the line may be softer, looser, less insistent, the atmosphere gentler and more relaxed than in earlier drawings, but others exist to confute any attempt at generalization. One may say only that the drawings of Nicholson's lively old-age bear very few traces of after-thoughts or erasures, and give the impression of having been made, more than ever before, for the pleasure of the making.

Returning to England – to where he felt he belonged – renewing old friendships and finding a new companion in Angela Taunt, all gave Nicholson a fresh optimism and zest for life. He continued to delight in his surroundings at the Flying Fox but, predictably, found the provincial, academic atmosphere of Cambridge uncongenial. He had always considered himself a Londoner, and as he felt more and more isolated and out of his element in Cambridge, his thoughts turned in particular to Hampstead where he had lived in the heroic years of the 1930s. In July 1974 he found a 'studio house' at 2B Pilgrim's Lane, off Rosslyn Hill, and finally moved there in September. There was double reason to regard this as a homecoming since he was now living practically opposite the site of one of his childhood homes.

As a result of the move he could return to making reliefs: the lack of space at the Flying Fox had meant a three-year interruption. However, he was not sure whether he still had the stamina to take up carving again. Already in 1967 he had bewailed

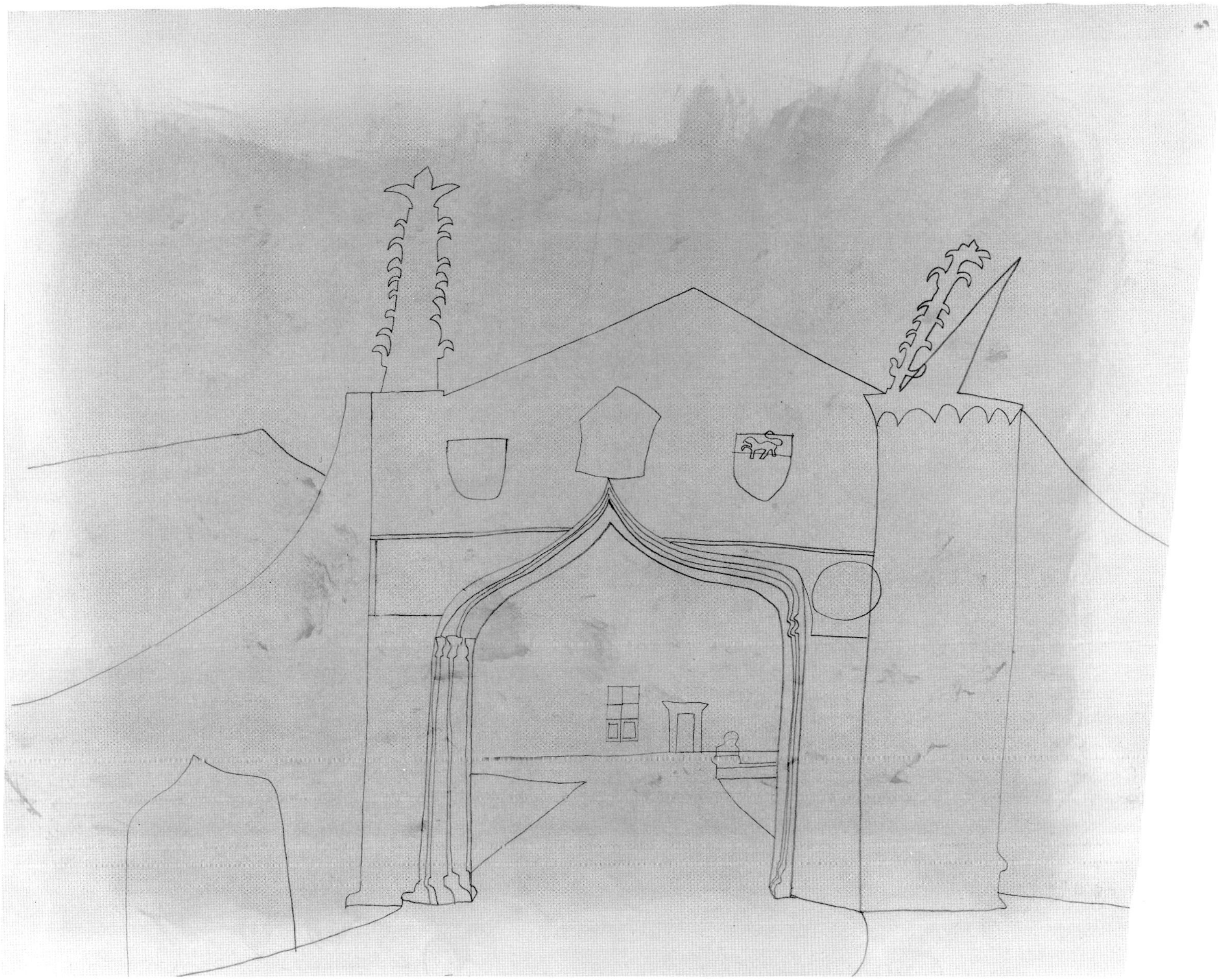

98 *1972 (Madingly no.1)*
oil wash and pencil on paper
38 × 49.5 cm (15 × 19½ in)

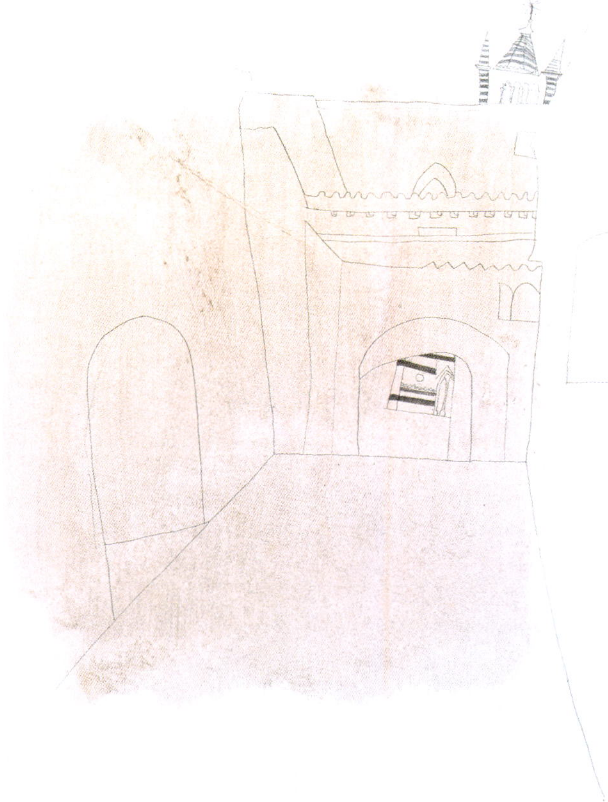

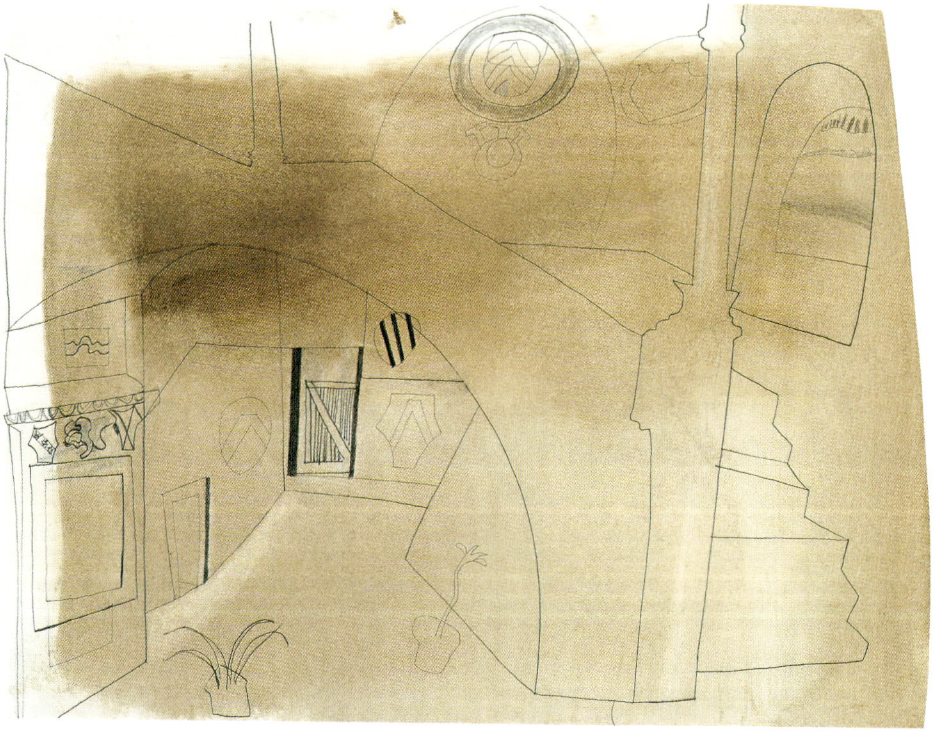

99 *1974 (Siena)*
oil wash and pencil on paper
59 × 49 cm (23¼ × 19¼ in)

100 *1974 (Certaldo)*
oil wash, pencil and ink on paper
54 × 68.5 cm (21¼ × 27 in)

→ **101** *1972 (three red stripes on blue)*
oil wash and pencil on cardboard
40.5 × 30.5 cm (16 × 12 in)

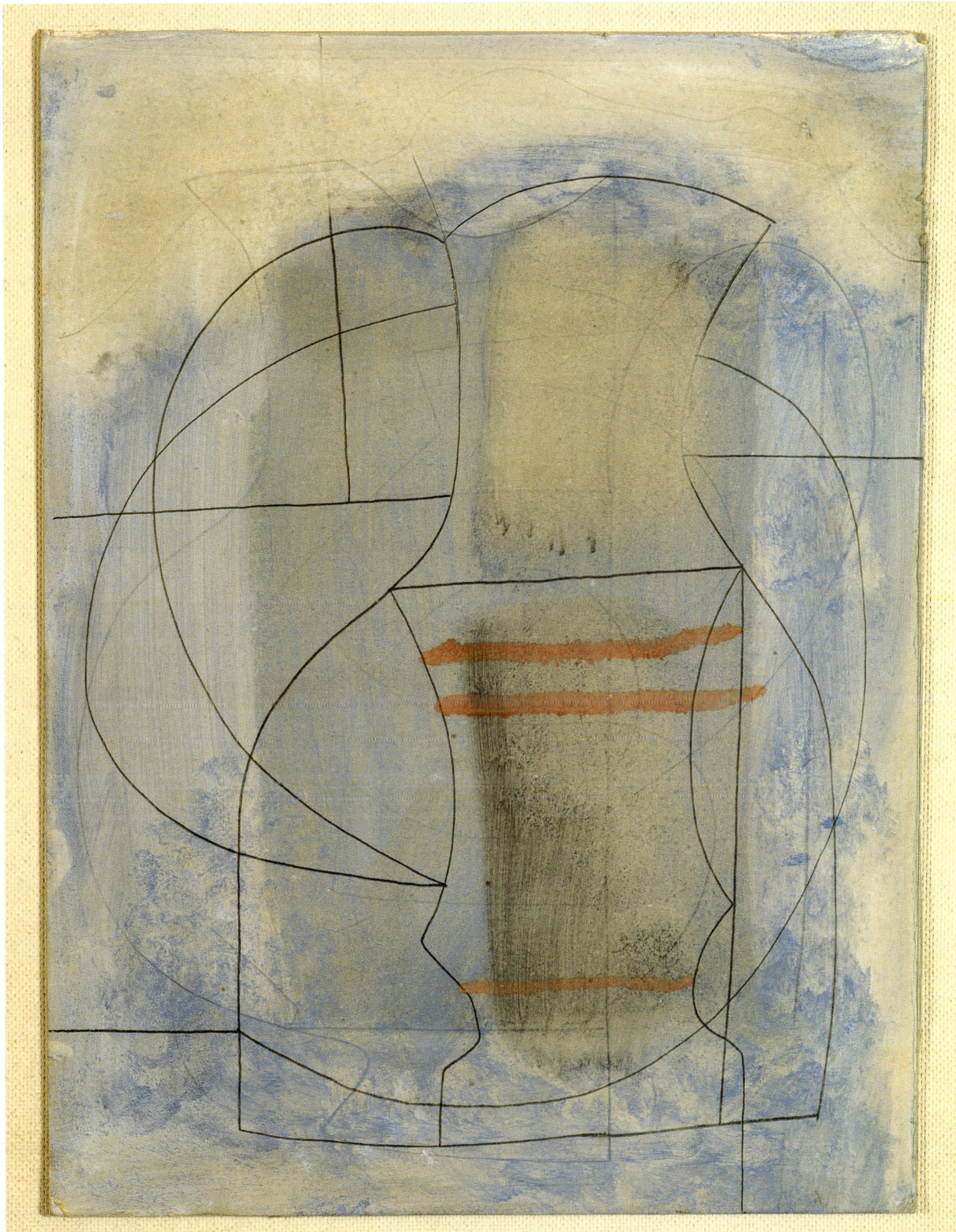

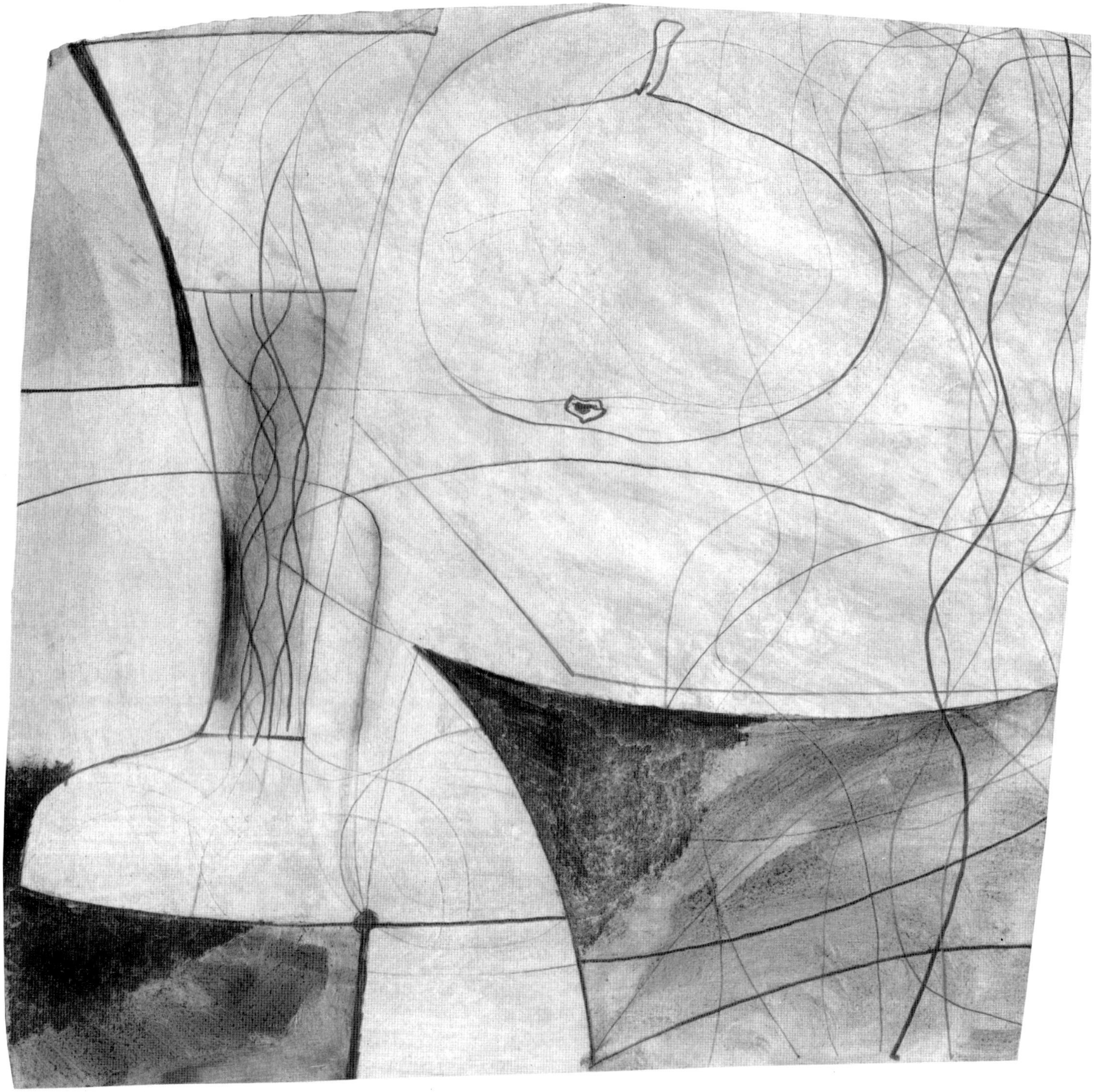

102 *1972 (apple and glass)*
oil wash and pencil on paper
21 × 21 cm (8¼ × 8¼ in)

the fact that he no longer had the necessary energy. 'My major problem,' he then wrote, 'is that I like to work 10 hours non-stop and the last 2 hours are those which count – when the relief takes control itself – and with increasing years this is increasingly difficult & to find a new working rhythm after so long is a problem.'[121] Foreseeing this difficulty, Nicholson, before leaving Switzerland, had drawn designs for new reliefs and asked a carpenter friend to cut out these basic shapes for him. He now had the prepared boards as a starting-point and could therefore concentrate all his energies on bringing them alive by scraping them with razor blades, by scrubbing, scratching and cutting them, and by rubbing paint on and off so as finally to create those luminous, infinitely subtle surfaces that seem the result of centuries of time and weather. Soon he was jubilantly reporting to Jim Ede: 'At last I have a studio again large enough to make *reliefs* & have 2 or 3 corkers – better than anything you've seen – by this I mean that they go deeper into the matter.'[122] Failing energy could even be turned to advantage since he found 'the tireder one gets the more subconscious one
103 goes & the deeper into one's idea'.[123] Some of these reliefs, *eg Celestial, Moonrise* and *Night blue – brown circle*, by their luminosity and evocation of vast distances, and as their titles suggest, lead us beyond landscape to contemplate the infinity of outer space. The void or cosmos as the subject of a picture that is to be contemplated recalls Chinese landscape painting and the numinous impression it creates by empty distance. And though there is no reference to landscape, either terrestrial or extra-terrestrial, in Rothko's late works, their enveloping spaciousness, inviting a contemplative engagement, is akin to these latest of Nicholson's reliefs. Nicholson especially admired the depth of colour and sense of huge scale in Rothko's work and on a visit to New York in 1965, at the time of an exhibition of his own, visited Rothko in his studio and, significantly, exchanged works with him.

Nicholson firmly believed in an after-life, in the power of thought and in the immaterial nature of ultimate reality. It is surely not fanciful to sense in the reliefs which he made in his eighties, and indeed in some of the drawings made at this time
105 which are equally imbued with ethereal mystery, a subconscious reaching out to the world beyond. In this context it is telling that at the Turner bicentenary exhibition held at the Royal Academy in 1975, he should have particularly admired the magnificent vision, 'both deep and subtle', of the late works and 'only think of Cezanne in our own times who more consistently pierced deeper'.[124]

As remarked earlier, many of Nicholson's reliefs, whose actual dimensions may be quite small, nonetheless give the impression of monumentality and would seem to lend themselves naturally to being magnified. The idea of creating a large-scale relief to function as a free-standing wall, in either an architectural or a natural setting, began to grip Nicholson seriously in the early 1960s, and he made a number of quite small reliefs either specifically subtitled 'project for free-standing relief wall' or else,
108 like *1968 (ramparts)*, obviously suited to such a purpose. In 1959 six works of his had been shown at the second of the *Documenta* exhibitions at Kassel initiated by Arnold Bode, and it was through Bode's vision and enthusiasm that he was able to

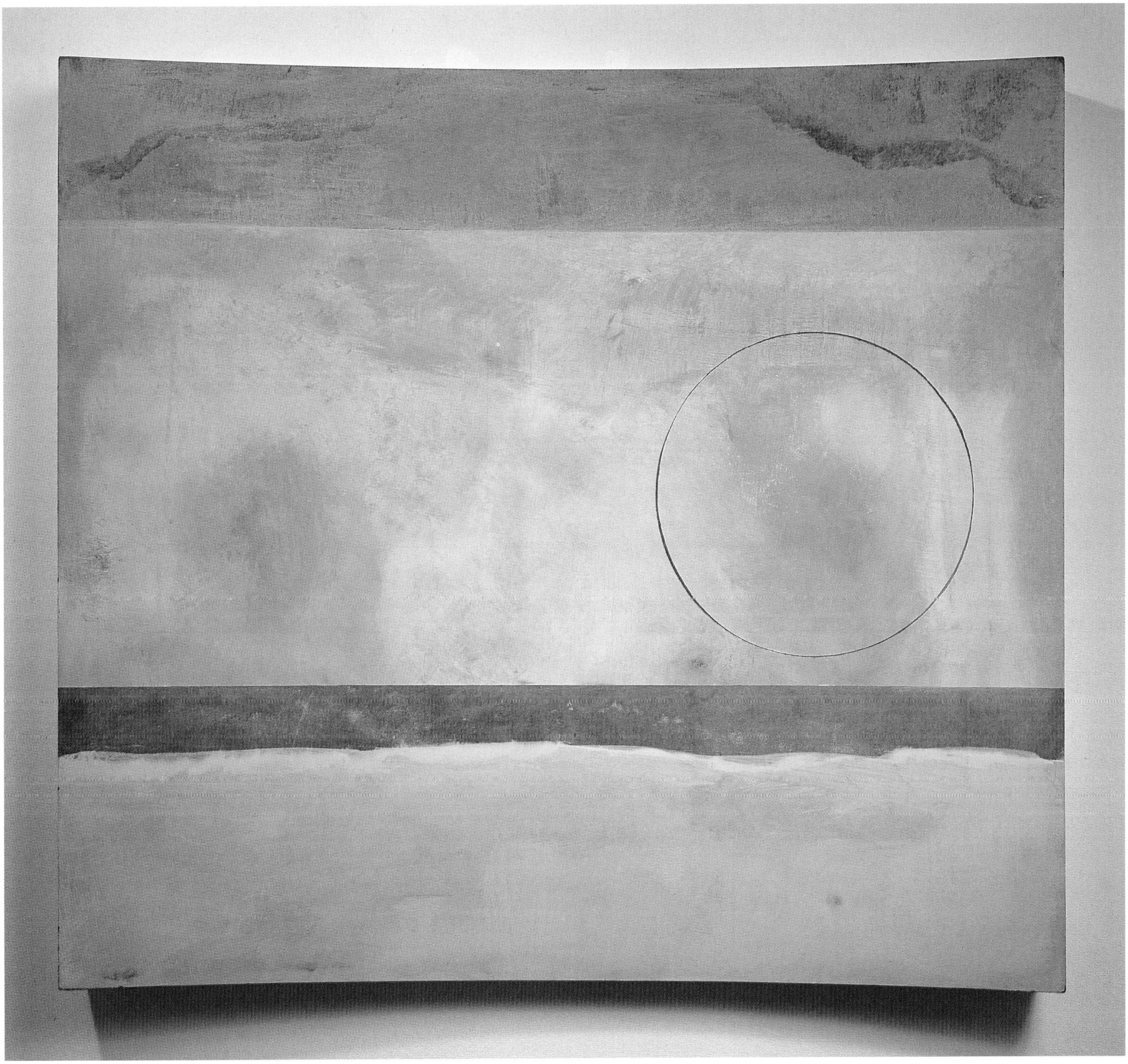

← 103 *1974 (moonrise)*
oil on carved board
72 × 62 cm (28¼ × 24½ in)

104 *1975 (one curve – one circle)*
oil and pencil on board mounted on curved panel
110 × 121 cm (43¼ × 47½ in)

109 see his idea of a monumental wall realized at *Documenta III* in 1964. Nicholson reported his satisfaction to Jim Ede:

> We've at last been able to realize this *free standing wall* idea & there it is as large & in fact a good deal larger than life and very well translated – water in front of it & sky beyond – and looks (to me) like a large chunk of Greece. It's 4m × 15m but what fascinates me is that it looks at least twice that size. . . . It is I suppose a kind of fulfilment of all one has been working for & it does set up I believe a new poetic kind of architecture which has been lacking since religion ceased to produce this, & I think too it could shake up the present day lifeless architecture into some kind of *life* —— & where a functional bldg is of necessity a bit 'dry', if it were related (but not joined onto) to this kind of poetic affair it could (without knowing that it was doing so?) begin to live.

In a further letter he explained his conception of what a relief wall should be: 'How they should function is to relate to landscape (trees, birds, water, fishes, sky) & when possible to some good contemp. piece of architecture, but standing *free* from this.'[125] After going out to Kassel, at Nicholson's expense, to see the wall for himself, Ede fully shared his enthusiasm: 'Your wall is so modest, so right, & so beautiful that I could not find it! I walked past enjoying the feeling of space! It enchants me. I did not feel it large or small – for like right things they have [*ie* it has] no special size – I could take it home in my suitcase (!) or make it hide a whole city. What lovely tone & colour – I wonder how this will last & how vulnerable it is.'[126]

The problem of durability and vulnerability was indeed to prove the main obstacle to realizing Nicholson's relief-walls. At Kassel the wall, which had been built in non-durable foamed concrete, was pulled down at the end of the exhibition, never to be re-created elsewhere in a more permanent material. In the late 1960s Nicholson collaborated with Geoffrey Jellicoe on a relief-wall for Pitville Park in Cheltenham, but though their plans reached an advanced stage, the wall never materialized due to Nicholson's fear that it would weather badly or else be vandalized. Unfortunately such fears were not unfounded: his large (7 × 16 ft), curved panel, commissioned for the Festival of Britain in 1951 and placed outside the Riverside Restaurant on the South Bank, had been damaged by rain and further spoilt when it was later set up in a vulnerable position at London Airport.[127] Nevertheless one suspects that Nicholson's perfectionism and unwillingness to compromise were at least partly the reason for the failure to realize any permanent wall project until the very end of his life.[128] And the successful completion of this one work was largely due to his friend Geoffrey Jellicoe.

In 1980 Jellicoe was asked to redesign and extend the gardens of Sutton Place, one of the finest surviving Tudor mansions, built in the 1520s near Guildford, Surrey. At the beginning of the last century Gertrude Jekyll had created an enclosed garden at some distance from the house, with a sunken pond in the form of a stepped cross, surrounded by grass and hedged in with clipped yew. Jellicoe now proposed to set up a Nicholson relief-wall on a raised bank at the far end of this rectangular enclosure. None of Nicholson's actual projects for relief-walls was chosen for this site. It was decided instead to enlarge, by more than seven times (15 × 30 ft), one of

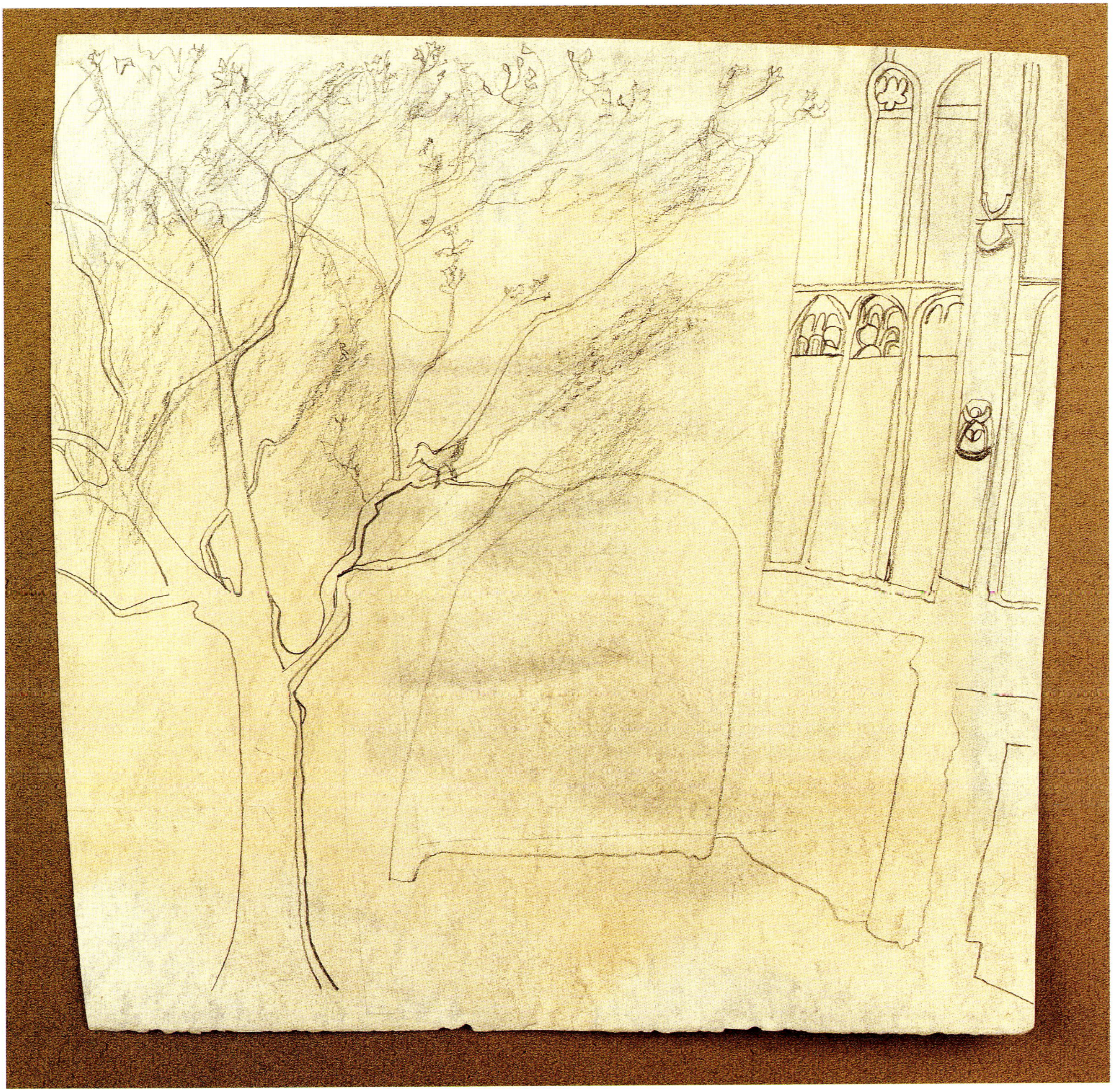

105 *1976 (Muchelney Abbey with bird)*
oil wash and pencil on paper
55 × 55 cm (21¾ × 21¾ in)

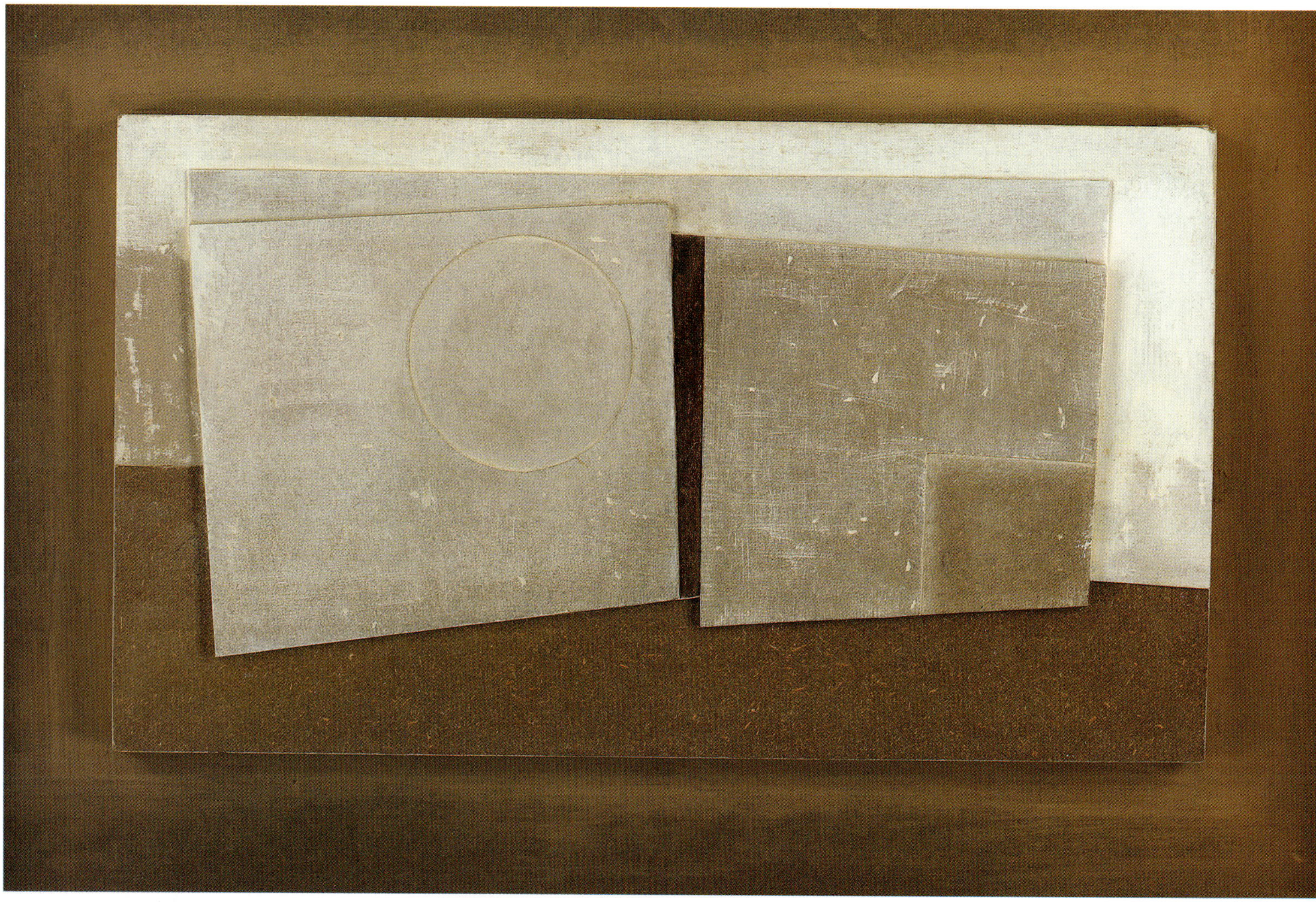

106 *April 1964 (Patmos – project for free-standing relief wall)*
oil on carved board
41 × 62.5 cm (16 × 24½ in)

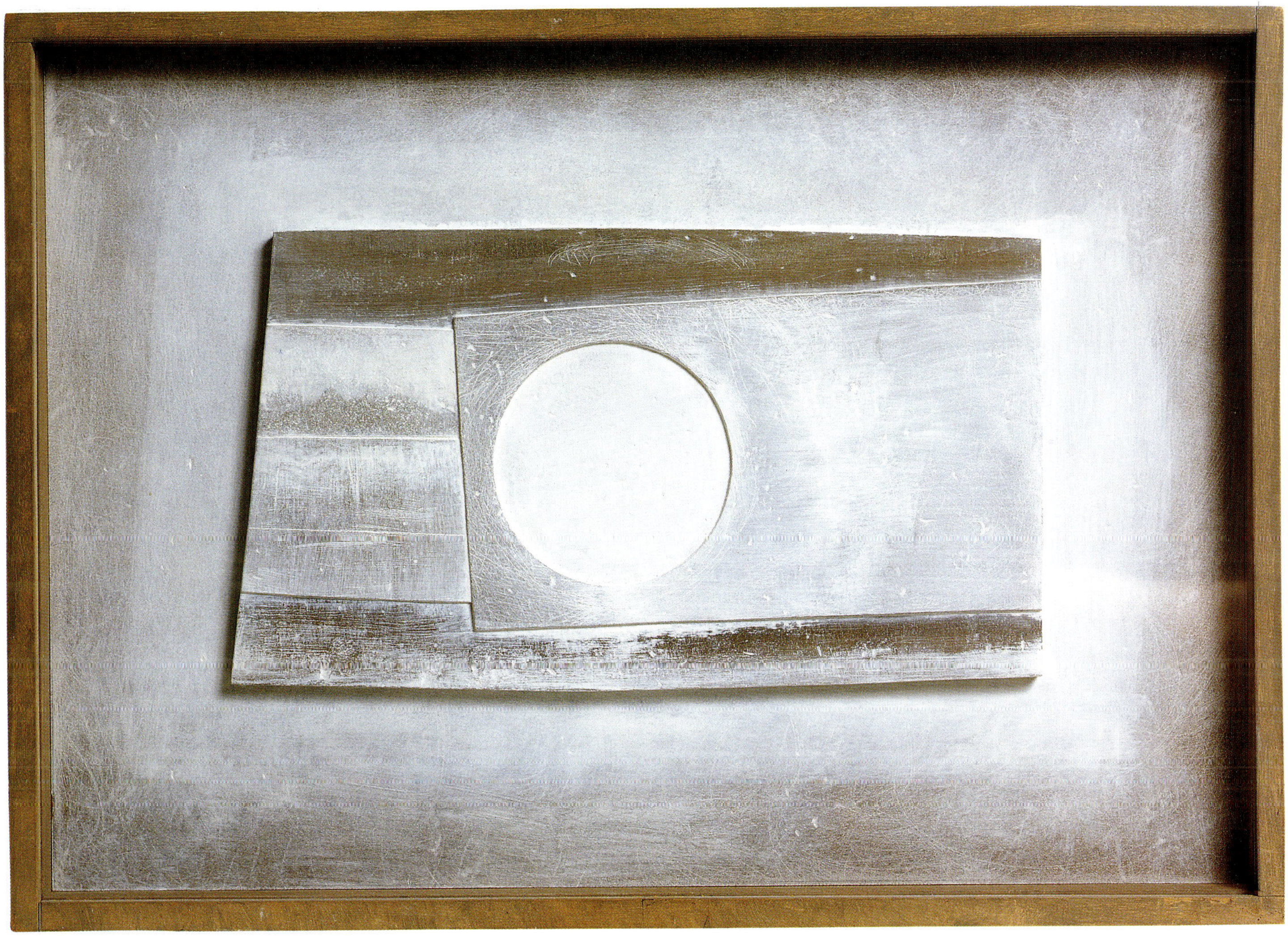

107 *1965 (Kos – project for free-standing relief wall)*
oil on carved board
32 × 47 cm (12½ × 18½ in)

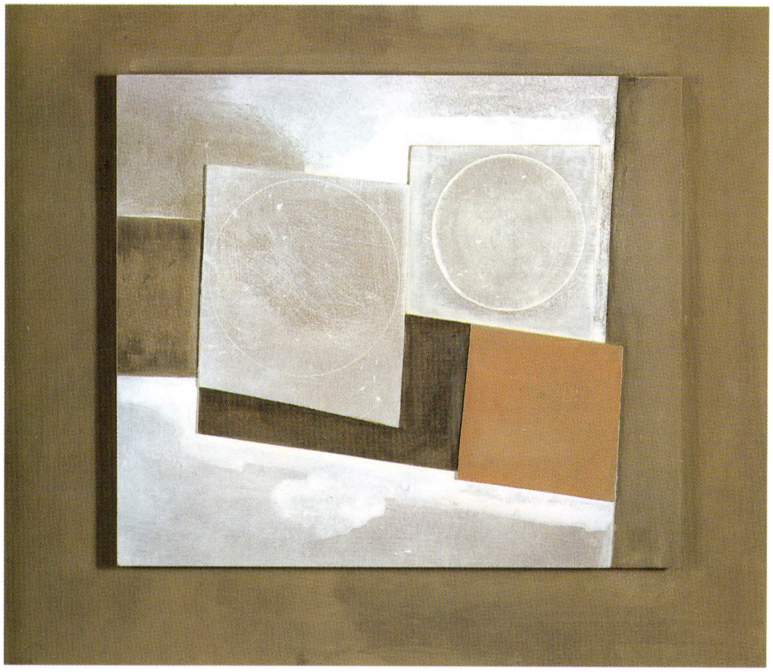

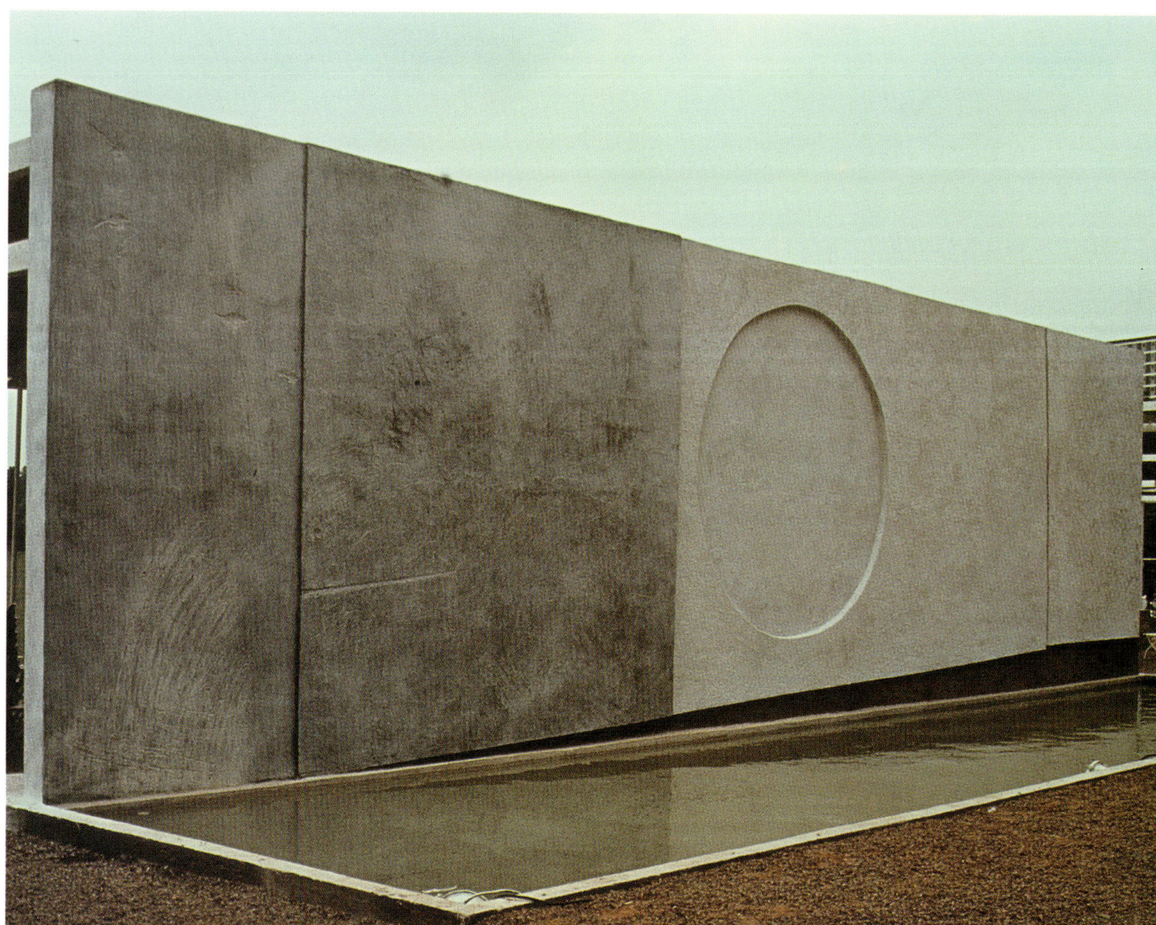

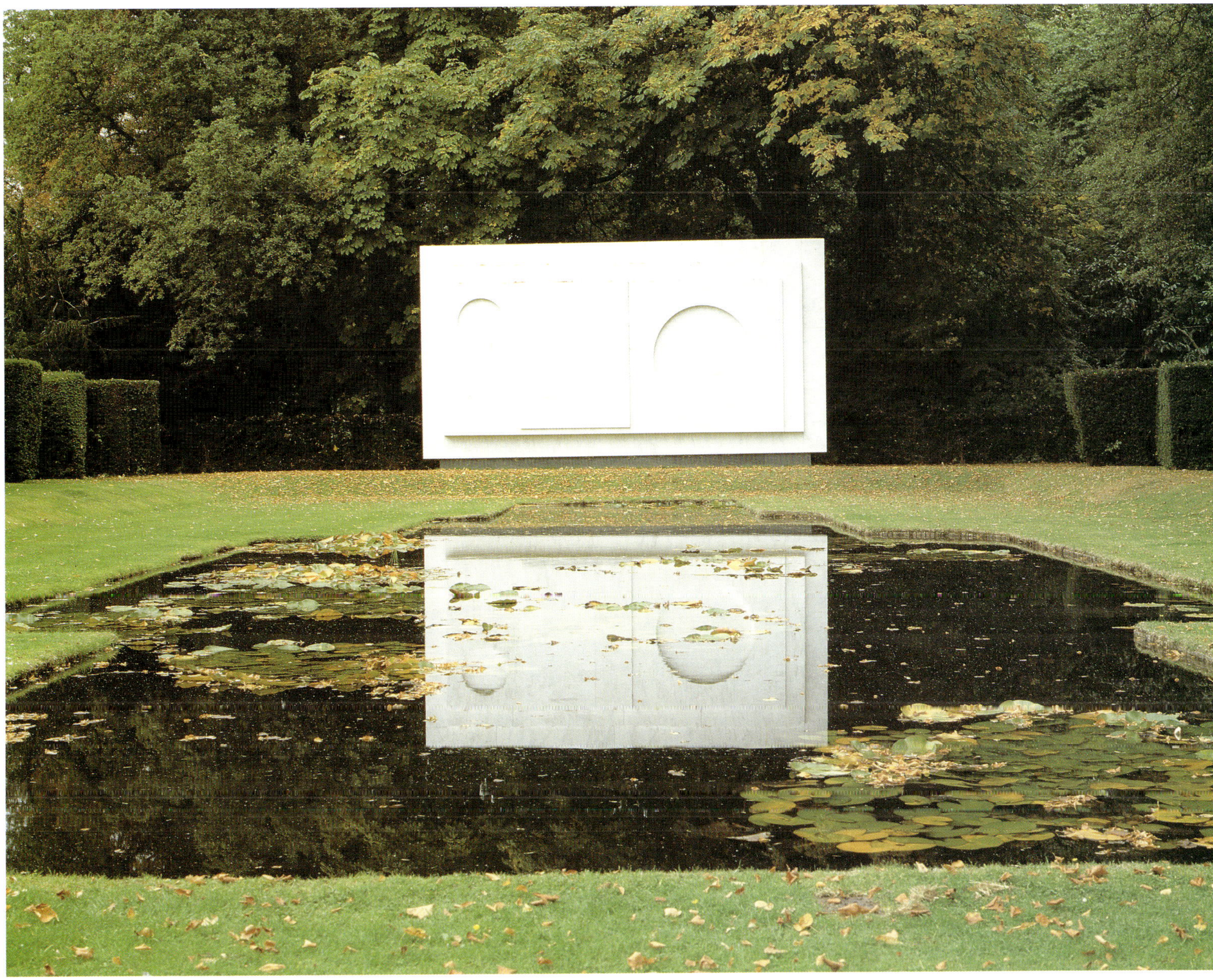

← 108 *1968 (ramparts)*
oil on carved board
47.5 × 53.5 cm (18¾ × 21 in)

← 109 *1964 (relief wall at* Documenta III, *Kassel)*
concrete
4 × 15 m (13ft 1½ in × 49 ft 2½ in)

110 *1982 (relief wall at Sutton Place, Guildford)*
marble
4.67 × 9.14 m (15ft 4 in × 30 ft)

his white reliefs dating from 1937/8 (now at the Albright-Knox Art Gallery, Buffalo, New York), and to make it out of white Carrara marble with a core of concrete.

110 The result is imposing but some may feel that the white marble is in too stark contrast with the greens of the grass, the yew hedge and the backdrop of chestnut trees – that it dominates, rather than harmonizes with, its surroundings. The relief is reflected in the lily-pond but does not itself register the constant changes of light with much subtlety. Considering the *Documenta* wall and the relief-projects Nicholson made in the 1960s, all of which are notable for colour, tone, texture and a strong vertical or horizontal axis suggestive of movement, one may question whether a relief in white Carrara marble and double-square format, for all its monumental presence, truly corresponds to Nicholson's intentions. Though consulted about the relief and its positioning, the initiative had not been his. At eighty-six, his powers were failing, and he did not live to see the wall in its finished state.

The idea behind the relief-wall was essentially no different from that in Nicholson's paintings and drawings where landscape is articulated by buildings (as, for instance, in *1930 (Birch Craig, winter)*, see p.30), abstract rectilinear shapes played off against natural forms – a practice learnt from Cézanne. Throughout Nicholson's work landscape and architecture are intrinsic to one another, and the relief-wall physically present in a landscape – reflecting light and relating to trees, water, sky – was a logical extension of this. In a letter to Geoffrey Jellicoe he recalled:

> I once walked with Robt. Graves from Boar's Hill down into Oxford across the fields & asked him what kind of a poem he'd best like to be able to write & he said one that could be buried & dug up in 2000 years' time & rewritten – & then buried again, & again dug up at suitable intervals. I like this idea, & feel that a re-interpretation of my <wall> project onto a much bigger scale by someone 'sensitive' to the original idea could be v. successful.[129]

Given Nicholson's interest in architecture, his personal friendship with a number of distinguished architects, and conversely the appeal of his work to architects, it is surprising that he was never invited to collaborate in a building scheme in which a relief-wall would feature as an integral part. It is the might-have-been in his career that one most regrets.

Although there are carved reliefs dated as late as 1979, the fourteen works exhibited at the Waddington Galleries in May 1976 – most of them completed in the previous two years – were, in effect, Nicholson's farewell to the medium which he had made his own. In them he gave form to a total experience – of the macrocosm outside himself and the microcosm within – at the furthest remove from the illusionistic view-through-a-window of the conventional painting on canvas in its rectangular frame. The sophisticated *gaucherie* of his early Cumberland paintings is similarly transmuted, in these so-called primitive reliefs, into a completely integrated art form which, by the extreme of refinement, rejoins the natural world.

By 1978 he no longer had the requisite energy for long hours of concentrated

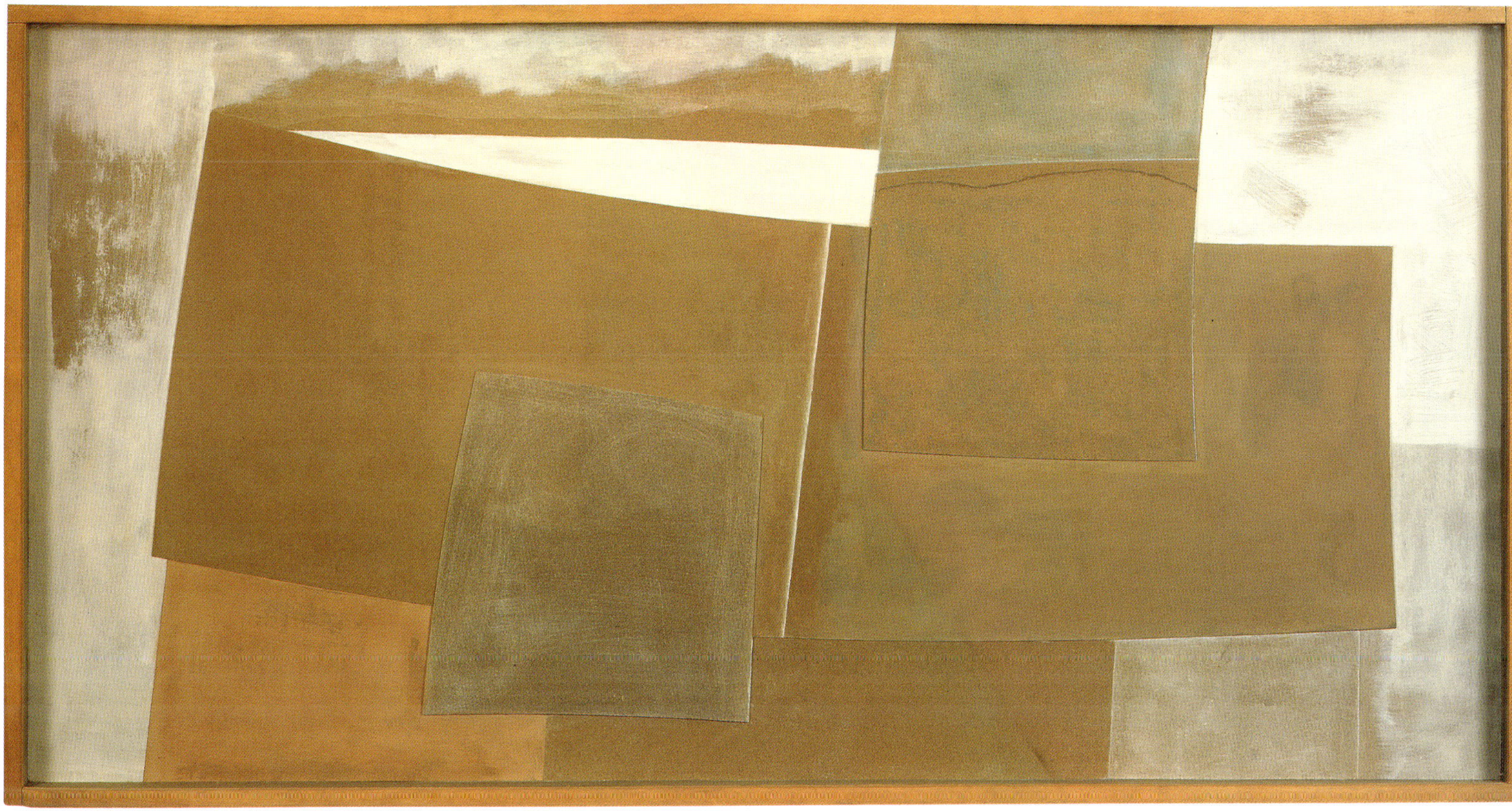

111 *1971–5 (rock landscape)*
oil on carved board
81 × 163 cm (32 × 64¼ in)

work on reliefs. He also began to have trouble with the muscles in his lower eyelids, which meant that he could not lean over his work without dripping tears onto it. Successful surgery eventually solved this problem, but meanwhile there were periods when he was unable to work at all, which, for someone whose creative imagination was still fecund, was hard to endure. But the last four years of his life, far from showing a gradual decline, proved to be a period of distinctively new invention – a coda to his life's work.

Forced to keep to a relatively small scale, Nicholson, by the spring of 1978, had begun to make paintings on paper. They were called such when exhibited later that autumn, but they are at least as much drawings as they are paintings – a direct development out of still-life drawings made in the 1960s. In character and execution, though, they are a new departure. Jug, mug and goblet, familiar since the linocuts of

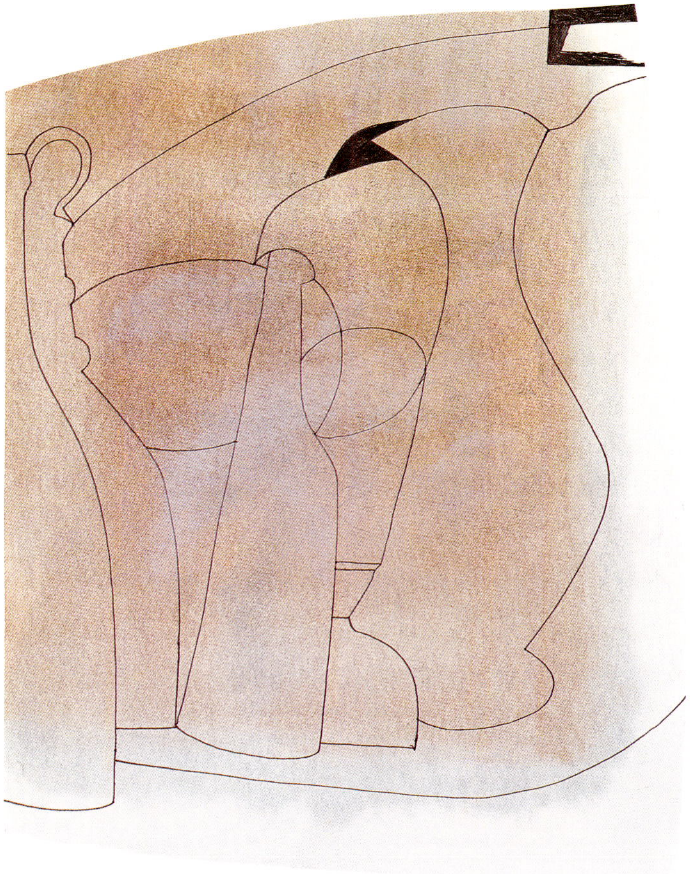

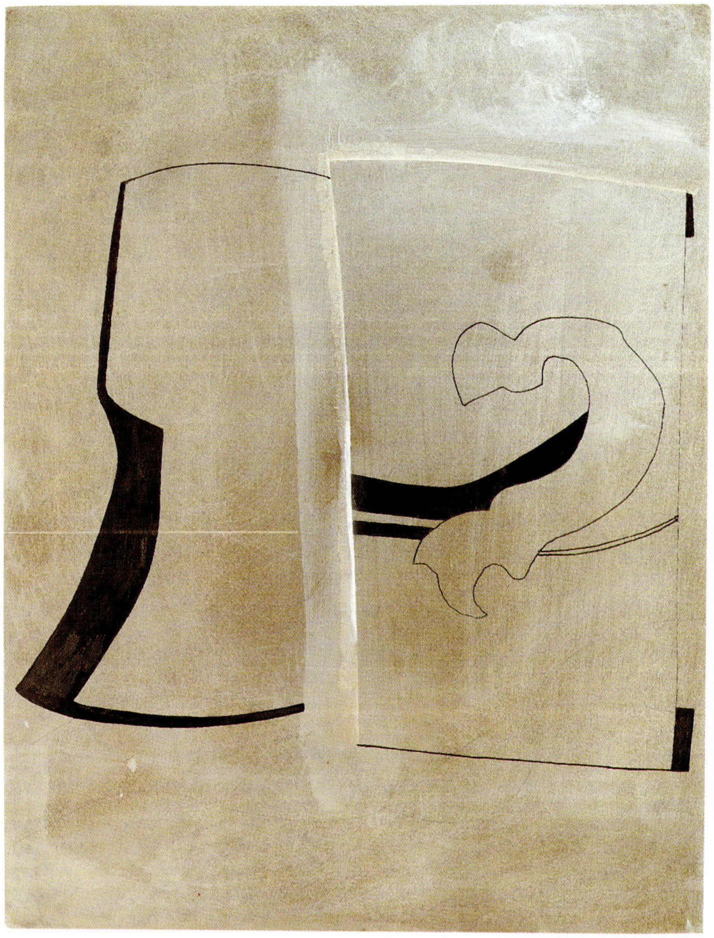

112 *March 1978 (still life, half a dozen objects)*
oil wash and ink on paper
57 × 49.5 cm (22½ × 19½ in)

113 *1979 (goblet, jug and landscape)*
ink and oil on board
64 × 51 cm (25¼ × 20 in)

→ 114 *March 1979 (with blue)*
ink, oil and wash on paper
89 × 76 cm (35 × 30 in)

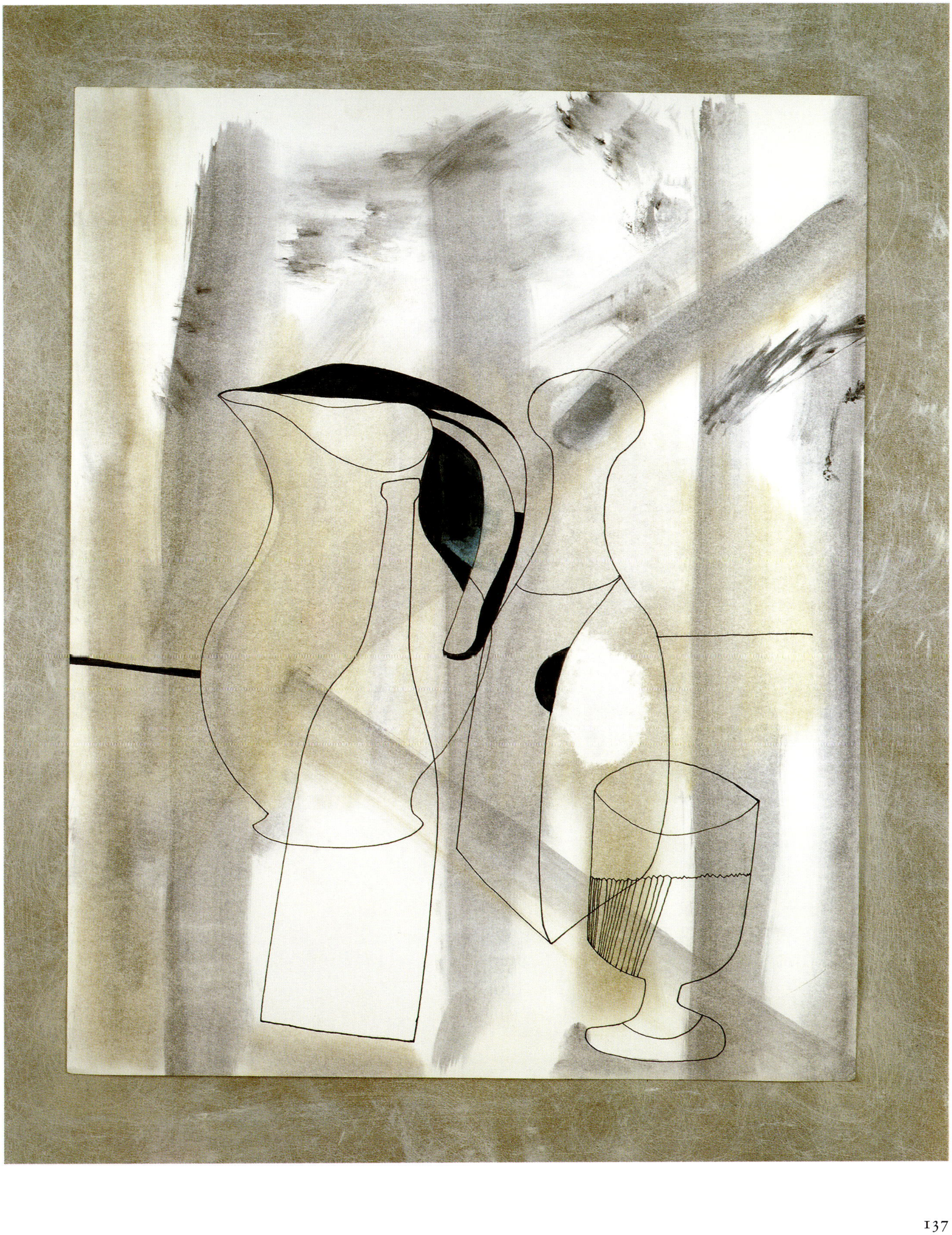

1928 (see p.24), reappear, each seemingly with a life of its own. Their forms may still interlock or grow out of one another, but they are as likely to loom large in the foreground like actors on a stage, each displaying its vivid personality, or to stand poised as if about to fly away, or else to coalesce in a pattern of freely reassembled fragments that refuse any prosaic explanation. The colours too are new: terracotta powerfully confronting black; pale blue against mauve and magenta, and a disturbing blue-green. Large blocks of black are more than shadows. They have a separate existence, invading the still-life object, breaking it apart, at times even threatening to engulf it. In these it would be easy to read a psychological significance were it not for other works, with muted colour, closer to oil-wash drawings, where all is poised and serene and the sharp accents of black animate rather than dominate the composition. As in *1933 (still life, Mediterranean)* (see p.36), a single wavy line, suggesting a background of hill or mountain, provides a foil to the still life or architectural segment
115 and gives to these small-scale works a larger dimension. In *1981 (Ticino Maggiore)* the outlines of landscape, still life and architecture – all three treated on an equal scale – follow a mysterious logic of their own, yet combine in a monumental whole. Such seemingly effortless reconciliations within a small compass are a visual sleight-of-hand.

Nicholson sustained the first outflow of spring and summer 1978 into the following year. Then, after an enforced interruption due to eye-trouble, he rallied for a final spell of activity in 1981.[130] Increasingly a quaver in the line betrays the faltering hand of old-age (a touching weakness, when one recalls the taut, unerring line of former times) but the line is also heavier, less supple, due to his using a fibre-tip pen instead of a pencil. Any qualms about the long-term durability of these lines, and of the areas of densely scribbled black ink, are forgotten under the immediate impact of shape and colour. Just as the still-life forms are often fragmented, so the deftly trimmed scraps of paper on which they are painted can look like potsherds, mounted with fastidious elegance on scoured grey-brown board. Like the cropped and painted etchings, like Alfred Wallis's scraps of painted cardboard, these are talismans – small pieces of living reality to be held in the hand, then propped on the mantelpiece. The
117 springing lines of *June 1981* in which mug and goblet, enclosed by carafe and bottle, are about to soar into the bright air of the Ticino – in which the taut area of black, with its triangular window of white, is neither threatening nor inert but rather a compact mass of energy – show Nicholson still capable of summoning up images full of radiance and exhilaration, of swift-flowing movement and high spirits. But when the exhibition *Ben Nicholson – new work* opened at the Waddington Galleries on 3 March 1982, it was valedictory: Nicholson had died a month before, on February 6, after suffering a stroke.

In giving paramount importance to an inner reality, Nicholson was only one among many artists, from the late nineteenth century onwards, whose pictorial styles differed widely. Had he ever bothered to read his friend Mondrian's *Dialogue on the New Plastic* (1919), he would have found much in it which articulated the ideas and

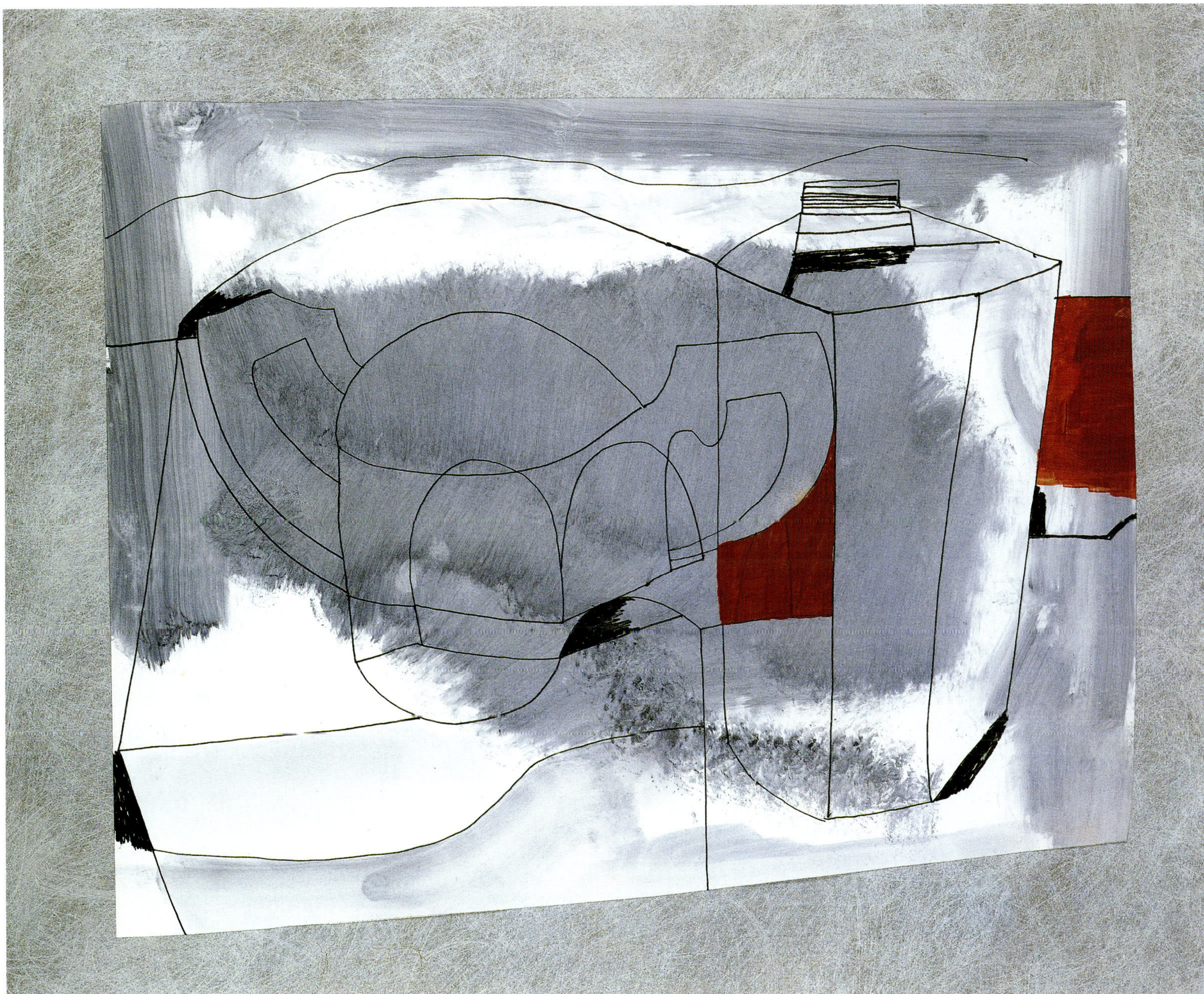

115 *1981 (Ticino Maggiore)*
ink, oil and wash on paper
55.5 × 65.5 cm (21¾ × 25¾ in)

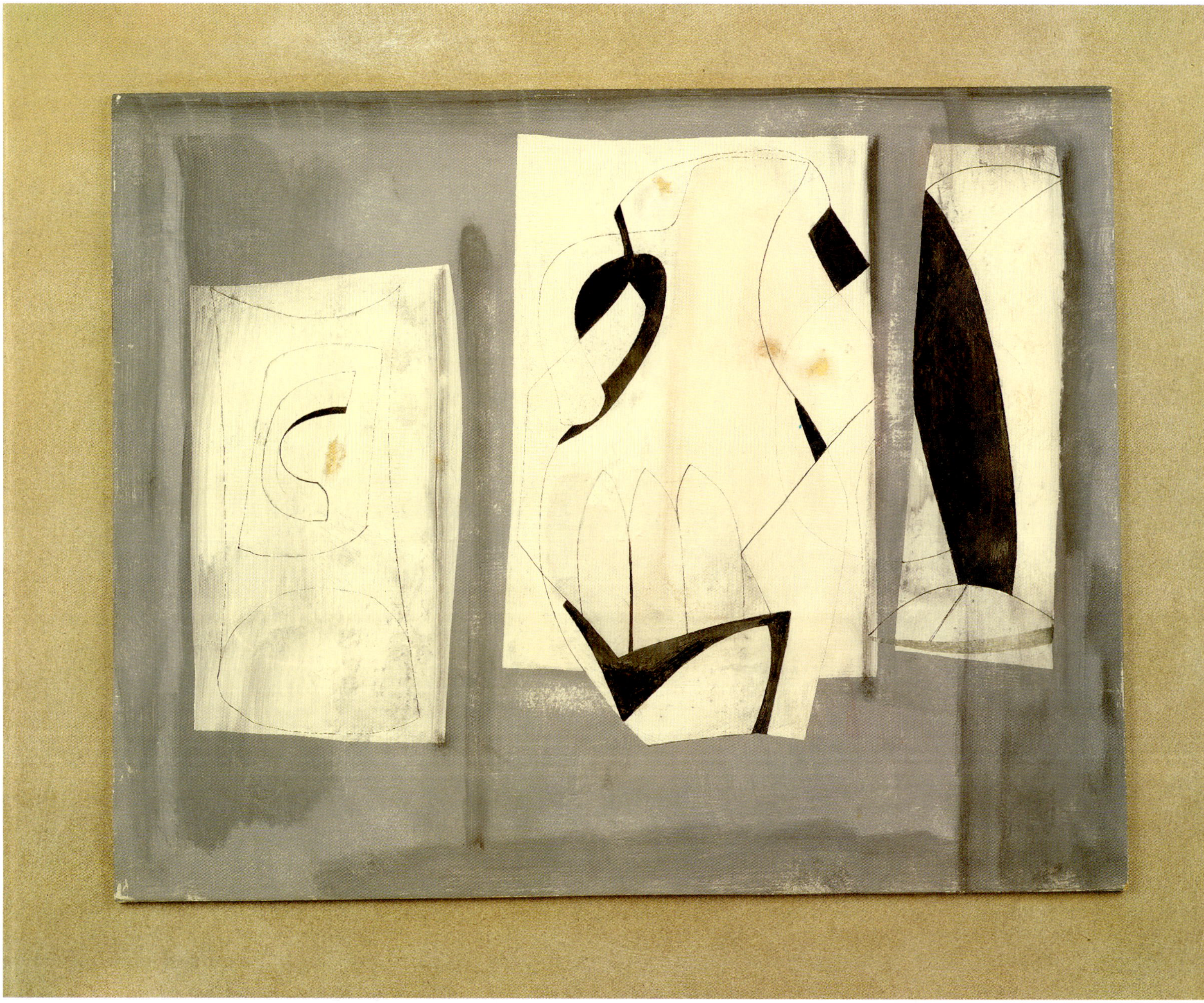

116 *1979 (three forms with blue, ivory and black)*
ink and oil on board
77 × 92 cm (30¼ × 36¼ in)

→ **117** *June 1981*
ink, oil and wash on paper
57.5 × 49.5 (22¾ × 19½ in)

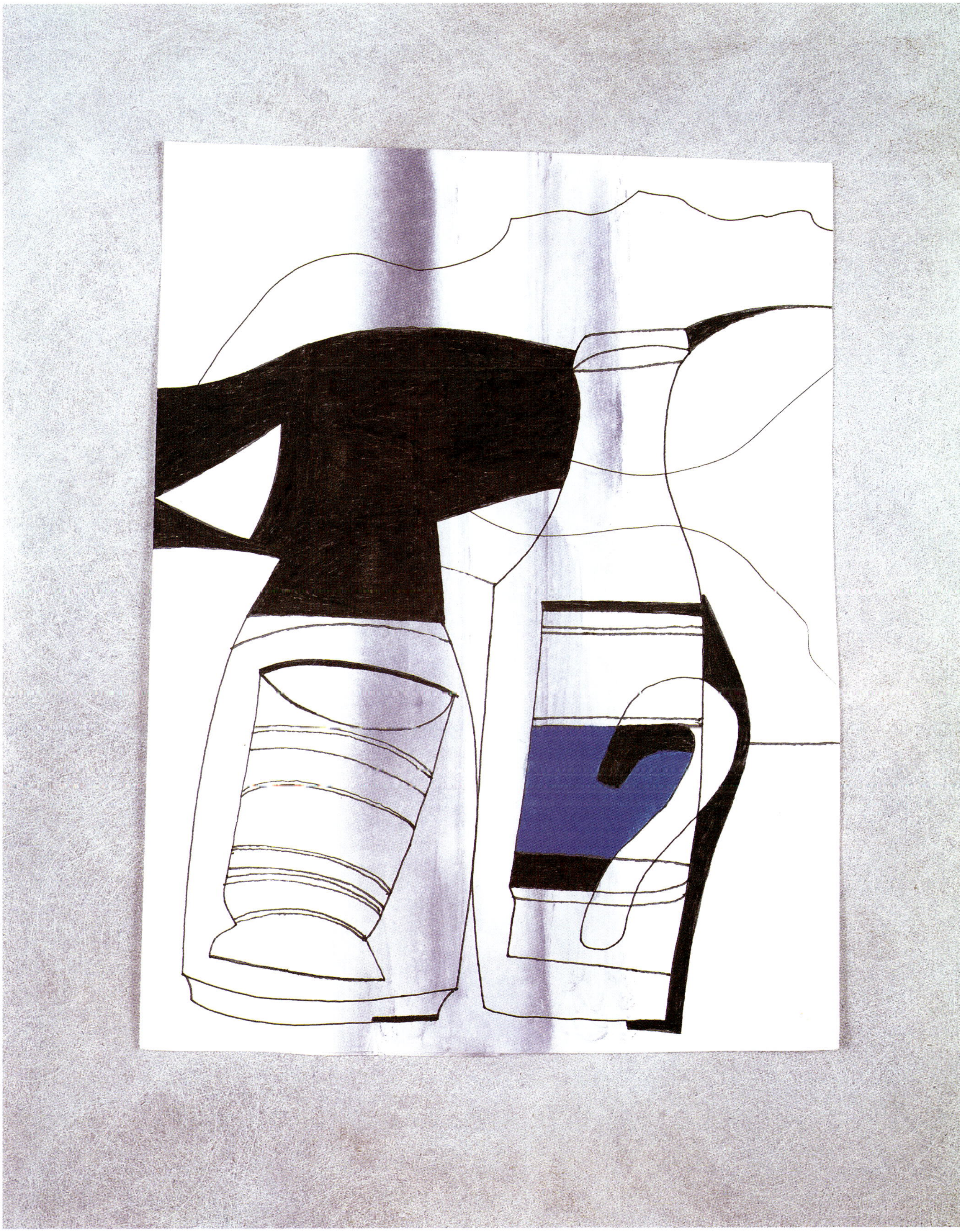

ideals which he gradually, and perhaps not wholly consciously, arrived at by his own experience. He would have agreed with Mondrian's basic proposition that 'art is a duality of *nature-and-man* and not nature *alone*', that 'man transforms nature according to his own image', and that 'when man expresses his deepest being, thus manifesting his *inwardness*, he must necessarily *interiorize* natural appearance'. He would also have endorsed Mondrian's belief that art is 'pure expression of the incomprehensible force that is universally active and that we can therefore call *the universal*'. Mondrian saw it as a limitation that 'with our *unconscious* we always *subjectivize* the universal',[131] and so he sought a conscious, and therefore supposedly objective, expression of the universal. But here Nicholson differs. He is less narrowly concerned to banish all trace of the particular and the naturalistic from his art. Memory of outward appearances is not as completely transformed by him as it is by Mondrian: he still makes powerful allusion to the colours, textures and even forms of the natural world. In other words he does not invent a purely symbolic language with which to express his apprehension of the universal reality free from all accidentals. In this, perhaps, he shows a typically English distaste for the absolute. But, by taking account of the radical changes in outlook and practice among European artists in the early years of the twentieth century, and by adapting these to his own expressive needs, he was able to extend the range of English art.

One purpose of this book has been to show Nicholson not as an inhabitant of some no-man's-land called Modernism or Abstraction, but as someone with a deep attachment to particular places and a highly developed sense of the poetry of the everyday. Following his intuition, he moved from the particular to the universal, from illusion to allusion, until in his late reliefs he created objects whose beauty and vitality provide the viewer with an aesthetic experience independent of any direct reference to place yet which contain a whole complex response to it. It is hard to conceive of a more severe screening of experience or of a more tightly stretched link between material reality and the art it inspires. Yet Nicholson's work derives its charge of energy precisely from such self-imposed restrictions – restriction of forms, restriction of expressive means, and, in his still life, restriction of subject-matter. These are all tokens of a pent-up passion which finds release in a ceaseless flow of poetic invention – precise yet mysterious, contemplative yet vital, cool yet passionate, austere yet richly suggestive, asymmetrical yet in dynamic equilibrium. An art that forgoes so much in the desire to achieve a deeper, more enduring experience makes corresponding demands on the viewer. Nicholson realized that his work would be appreciated only by those willing to give it the sensitive contemplation it demands.[132] Those who do make contact with his 'idea' will feel a growing elation.

→ 118 *1967 (untitled circle)*
oil wash and pencil on paper with relief
45.5 × 38 cm (18 × 15 in)

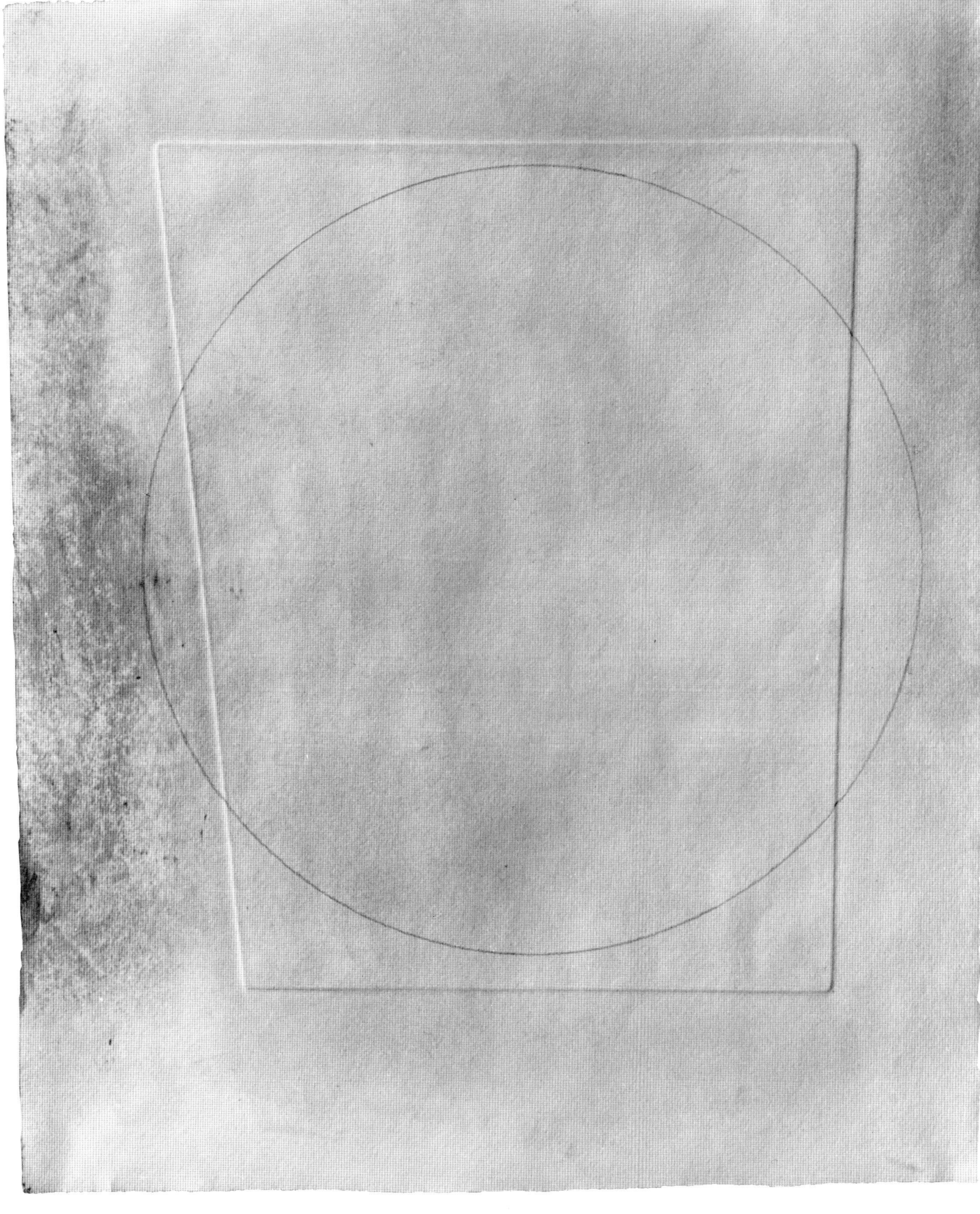

NOTES

1 See p.101.
2 See n.56.
3 Conveniently, though not comprehensively, collected in Maurice de Sausmarez (ed.), *Ben Nicholson*, Studio International Special, London, 1969 (henceforth *SIS* 1969), they take up no more than twenty generously spaced pages.
4 G. Braque, *Cahiers 1917–1952*, Paris, 1952, p.12; BN, *SIS* 1969, pp.52, 59.
5 *eg* John Summerson in *The Architects' Journal*, vol.175, no.7, 17 February 1982, p.29.
6 Paul Nash, 'Ben Nicholson's Carved Reliefs', *Architectural Review*, vol.LXXVIII, no.467, October 1935, pp.142–3.
7 The letter (private collection) is headed simply, but evocatively, 'Café Royal, Thursday'. Its contents suggest a date in late 1912. Between 1909 and 1914 the Nicholsons spent weekends and summers at The Grange, Rottingdean, on the Sussex coast.
8 NN to her nephew Tim Nicholson, pers.com., 30 May 1990.
9 WN to Oliver Brown, a director of the Leicester Galleries: 'Oliver, I believe Ben's going to get away with it!' Quoted in Oliver Brown, *Exhibition*, Evelyn, Adams & MacKay, 1968, p.147.
10 For a mock-solemn appraisal see 'Mr Barrie's Boy Artist. *Peter Pan* Poster for the New Play', *Daily Mail*, 19 December 1904, p.3. In adapting his water-colour, Ben could call upon the expertise of his father, and of his uncle, James Pryde, who, as J & W Beggarstaff, had made a name as poster designers.
11 See BN, 'Memoirs: William Nicholson', *London Magazine*, vol.VII, no.3, June 1967, p.71 (reprinted in *SIS* 1969, pp.53–4).
12 See BN in SIS 1969, pp.50–1.
13 BN reminiscence to Angela Taunt, pers.com., 5 September 1992.
14 BN letter to John Summerson, 6 May 1944 (Tate Gallery Archive, henceforth *TGA*).
15 Among these, Robert Scott Lauder (1803–69) and his brother James Eckford Lauder (1811–69) were Mabel Pryde's great-uncles. Both were members of the Royal Scottish Academy and RSL was also an influential teacher. Before he changed his name by deed-poll in June 1932, Ben Nicholson was Benjamin Lauder Nicholson.
16 BN letter to Herbert Read, 25 September 1944 (McPherson Library, University of Victoria, Victoria BC, Canada, henceforth *Read Archive*).
17 See n.11.
18 T. S. Eliot, *On Poetry and Poets*, Faber, 1957, p.252.
19 BN to John Summerson, 3 January 1944 (*TGA*). BN only met Lewis twice. Though he felt that Lewis's painting lacked a generous sense of scale, he was attracted by the acidity and pungency of his colour (see BN letter to Jane Grigson, (?)5 January 1969, by courtesy of Dr Caroline Grigson). It is curious that he should have singled out Lewis's use of colour, as he did Picasso's soon after (see p.15).
20 Review by 'Z' in the Art Notes of *The Woman's Leader*, 3 December 1920. With BN's portrait of Graves compare Lewis's *Portrait of Ezra Pound* (1919) and his self-portrait, *Portrait of the Artist* (1920/1), reproduced in Walter Michel, *Wyndham Lewis, Paintings and Drawings*, Thames & Hudson, 1971, plate 45/cat. P 26, plate 66/cat. P 28.

21 BN letter to John Summerson, 5 September 1944 (*TGA*). In a letter to Ronald Alley, 27 July 1962, BN wrote: 'Wyndham Lewis & "X" Group acted for me as an emetic'.

22 For an evocation of their time at Castagnola, see *Unknown Colour, Paintings, Letters, Writings by Winifred Nicholson*, compiled by Andrew Nicholson, Faber, 1987, pp.33ff., 171 (henceforth *Unknown Colour*).

23 BN letter to John Summerson, 3 January 1944 (*TGA*) (reprinted in *SIS* 1969, p.57). The same startling green seems to have struck Winifred Nicholson, though she later remembered it as 'bright emerald . . . swift as a viper' (*Unknown Colour*, p.35). In a letter to her brother Wilfrid, 2 December 1921, she records having seen 'a gem' of a Picasso with 'green of young dog Mercury black and pure white. Vital as quicksilver.' Whatever the shade of green, the reference here is to the plant Dog's Mercury, so that Jeremy Lewison, in his puzzled note (*Ben Nicholson*, Tate Gallery, 1993, p.95 n.4) about Picasso's depiction of dogs, is barking up the wrong tree. The dominant green points to one of the still lifes painted by Picasso at Avignon in the summer of 1914.

24 BN letters to John Summerson, 3 and 4 January 1944 (*TGA*).

25 H. H. Asquith to Mrs Hilda Harrisson, 29 May 1923, in Desmond MacCarthy (ed.), *H.H.A. – Letters of the Earl of Oxford and Asquith to a Friend*, Second Series 1922–7, Geoffrey Bles, 1934, p.62.

26 Paul Nash letter to John Drinkwater, May 1923, in Andrew Causey, *Paul Nash*, Oxford, 1980, p.128, n.j.

27 Frank Rutter, *The Sunday Times*, 24 June 1923.

28 Between 1919 and 1925 Nash made the shore at Dymchurch the theme of twenty or more works – drawings, lithographs, water-colours and oils – which together constitute a distinctive phase in his output. See Causey, *op.cit.* in n.26, p.112.

29 BN letters to Lady Cecilia Roberts, 1 January <1923> and Edith Jenkinson, 3 April <1923> (*TGA*).

30 Though only three 'abstractions' are known to survive, evidence exists of at least three others. See Jeremy Lewison, *Ben Nicholson*, Tate Gallery, 1993, p.24.

31 Helen Sutherland, Notebook 1 (copied from diaries 1920–7), January 1926, pp.63v, 66, 67v, 68v, 80v, 81v, 82r (by permission of the Executors of the Estate of Nicolete Gray).

32 These are some of the influences BN lists in a letter to Wilfrid Roberts, 7 April 1923 (*TGA*).

33 'Mr Ben Nicholson continues his wayward ways, giving evidence now and then of real ability . . . indulging at other times in childish pranks which, in fairness to him, should not be taken *au sérieux*.' P. G. Konody reviewing the seventh exhibition of the *Seven and Five Society* in *The Observer*, 23 January 1927, p.5.

34 Robert Graves, *The Less Familiar Nursery Rhymes*, Augustan Books of Poetry, Ernest Benn, <1927>.

35 Winifred Nicholson, *Unknown Colour*, p.91.

36 BN letters to Andras Kalman, 24 December 1966 and 13 January 1968 (by courtesy of Mr Andras Kalman), and BN, 'Alfred Wallis', *Horizon*, vol.VII, no.37, 1943, pp.50–4 (reprinted in *SIS* 1969, pp.37–8).

37 *Art.cit.* in n.36.

38 BN letter to WN, 11 March <1967> (*TGA*), in *Unknown Colour*, p.183, together with her reply (p.185).

39 *Ibid*, p.173.

40 See Alan Wilkinson, *Barbara Hepworth*, Tate Gallery Liverpool, 1994, p.35, and BH in *Barbara Hepworth, Carvings and Drawings*, Lund Humphries, 1952, n.p.

41 BN letter to Helen Sutherland, 13 June 1932 (*TGA*).

42 Paul Nash, 'A Painter and a Sculptor', *Weekend Review*, 19 November 1932, p.613.

43 BN letter to Herbert Read, 16 August 1965 (*Read Archive*).

44 BN letter to John Summerson, 13 May 1944 (*TGA*).

45 BN letter to Herbert Read, 11 February 1962 (*Read Archive*).

46 BN letter to Charles Harrison, November 1966 (*TGA*).

47 Adrian Stokes, reviewing the joint exhibition of BN and BH at the Lefevre Gallery in Oct.–Nov. 1933 (*The Spectator*, 27 October 1933, p.575), remarked how 'Mr Nicholson's canvases and panels ... serve him more in the role of the carver's block. Just as the carver consults the stone for the reinforcement of his idea, so Mr Nicholson has started to paint when he prepares his canvases.'

48 See BN, 'More or Less about Abstract Art', *London Magazine*, vol.1, no.4, July 1961, pp.64–6 (reprinted in *SIS* 1969, pp.48–9), in reply to Victor Pasmore, 'What is Abstract Art?', *The Sunday Times*, 5 February 1961, p.21. Pasmore, influenced by Charles Biederman's *Art as the Evolution of Visual Knowledge*, claimed that painting, being two-dimensional, is inevitably illusionistic and therefore can never be entirely non-referential, hence the necessity for a fully autonomous abstract work to be three-dimensional.

Early in 1936 Nicholson did make some small free-standing objects intended to be seen in the round. He chose to call them sculptures, but the name hardly suits either of the two surviving examples. The first, cut out of mahogany and painted white, measures 23 × 30.5 × 24 cm (9 × 12 × 9½ in) and looks like a simplified version of one of Vantongerloo's architectural models, which prefigure the De Stijl-type house. Nicholson himself likened it to the white farmhouse near Cannes where he had just been staying with friends (BN letter to H. S. Ede, 17 March 1936, *Kettle's Yard Archive, University of Cambridge*). The other so-called sculpture, also made in March 1936, is carved out of plaster and measures 19 × 17 × 11.5 cm (7½ × 6¾ × 4½ in). In conception it is closer to a white relief with its interlocking planes and shallow, scooped-out circle (to be appreciated only from a frontal view). It too suggests a model, for a free-standing monument perhaps, or for an architectural feature. Though excited by their novelty at the time of making them, Nicholson was never again tempted to make any sculpture.

49 BN letter to John Summerson, 13 May 1944 (*TGA*).

50 BN letters to WN, 30 December 1933 and 12 April 1934, in *Unknown Colour*, pp.143, 146.

51 Judith Collins, *Winifred Nicholson*, Tate Gallery, 1987, p.22, points out that a painting by WN of white dahlias on a white background was shown at the same *7 & 5* exhibition as BN's *Two Circles* in March 1934.

52 Herbert Read (ed.), *Unit One*, Cassell, 1934, p.89 (reprinted in *SIS* 1969, p.31).

53 A. S. Eddington, *Science and the Unseen World*, Allen & Unwin, 1929, pp.22–3, 31.

54 BN again equated painting and religious experience in one of four brief statements he made in Ben Nicholson, Naum Gabo and J. L. Martin (eds), *Circle: International Survey of Constructive Art*, Faber, 1937, p.75 (reprinted in *SIS* 1969, p.32), and yet

again in *Ben Nicholson: Works on Paper*, André Emmerich Gallery, New York, 1974, with the modification 'Painting and so-called religious experience'.

55 BN in *Circle* (see previous note): '"Realism" has been abandoned in the search for reality: the "principal objective" of abstract art is precisely this reality.'

56 Herbert Read, 'Ben Nicholson and the Future of Painting', *The Listener*, vol.XIV, no.352, 9 October 1935, p.605 – a riposte to Kenneth Clark, 'The Future of Painting', *The Listener*, vol.XIV, no.351, 2 October 1935, p.544, complaining of the spiritual exhaustion and poverty of invention in abstract art. Read later adapted his *Listener* article for an essay on BN in his book *A Coat of Many Colours*, Routledge, 1945, pp.79–87. BN's reaction, on reading the proofs, shows his unconcern with metaphysics: 'When you write about my believing that there's a reality underlying appearances this is true now since you & others pointed it out to me but it didn't consciously enter my head – one just goes on chasing out something *alive*.' BN letter to Herbert Read, 21 August 1944 (*Read Archive*).

57 Geoffrey Grigson, 'Comment on England', *Axis*, no.1, 1935, p.10.

58 BN letter to Charles Harrison, 11 February 1967 (*TGA*). Typical in regarding *Two Circles* as no more than a leg-pull were Douglas Goldring in *The Studio*, vol.107, May 1934, p.269 and H[erbert] F[urst] in *Apollo*, vol.XIX, no.112, April 1934, p.226. Paul Nash, though, recognized in the white reliefs 'the discovery of a new world' (*art.cit.* in n.6).

59 BN letter to John Summerson, 3 January 1944 (*TGA*), retouched by BN for publication in John Summerson, *Ben Nicholson*, Penguin, 1948, pp.12–13. Nancy Joslin Troy, 'Piet Mondrian's Atelier', *Arts Magazine*, December 1978, pp.82–7, discusses the studio as a work of art in its own right.

60 BN letter to Herbert Read, 25 September 1944 (*Read Archive*), and see *SIS* 1969, pp.14, 50.

61 See Leslie Martin letter to BN, 21 January 1946 (*TGA*).

62 It is misleading to describe BN's work as 'Euclidean' or 'Pythagorean' as does, *eg*, J. P. Hodin, *The Dilemma of Being Modern*, Routledge, 1956, p.111 and *Ben Nicholson – the Meaning of his Art*, Alec Tiranti, 1957, pp.11, 16, 18. Harmony arrived at by intuition may nonetheless coincide with mathematical proportion.

63 Reminiscences, in conversation with the author, by Rachel Nicholson, 10 March 1993, Cyril Reddihough, 26 June 1990, Lady Read, 27 June 1990 and Sir John Summerson, 17 May 1991. One is reminded also of William Nicholson's exquisite arrangement of his studio at Apple Tree Yard.

64 BN letter to Geoffrey Jellicoe, 24 May 1964 (*TGA*).

65 BN in *Statements: A Review of Abstract Art* in 1956, ICA, London, 1957 (reprinted in *SIS* 1969, p.40).

66 At the time BN was making his first white reliefs, in 1934, Mark Tobey was staying in a Zen temple in Kyoto. Hanging in his room was a large, freely-brushed *ensō* on which he meditated day after day, wondering 'Was it selflessness? Was it the Universe – where I could lose my identity?' See MT in *Mark Tobey – Retrospective Exhibition of Paintings and Drawings 1925–1961*, Whitechapel Gallery, 1962, p.18.

67 BN letter to John Summerson, 28 September 1939 (*TGA*). For a description of Little Park Owles and the surrounding country, as well as an evocation of the war years in St Ives, see Adrian Stokes, *Smooth and Rough*, Faber, 1951, ch.1. Also Margaret

Mellis in *St. Ives 1939–64*, Tate Gallery, 1985, p.100. (Stokes and Mellis left L.P.O. in 1946 and in 1955 it became the home of Peter Lanyon and his family.)

68 BN letter to H. S. Ede, 29 August <1942> (*Kettle's Yard Archive, University of Cambridge*).

69 BN letter to Margaret Gardiner, (?)13 April 1949 (*TGA*).

70 BN letter to Helen Sutherland, 13 June 1949 (*TGA*).

71 Quoted by Nash, *art.cit.* in n.6.

72 For information on BN's working methods I am grateful to Cyril Reddihough (in conversation, 18 September 1991).

73 BN letter to F. L. S. Murray, 1 May 1951 (*TGA*).

74 It is in the 'abstract' lines that flow out from, and back into, the lines of the still-life objects that one sees the 'eternal movement' that BN so much admired in such works of Raphael as the *Sposalizio*. 'Rafael's continuous movement – something "eternal" – has been & is a big influence with me.' BN letter to Jane Grigson, 24 January 1967 (by courtesy of Dr Caroline Grigson).

75 BN letter to John Summerson, 10 December 1949 (*TGA*).

76 BN letter to Helen Sutherland, 12 August 1956 (*TGA*).

77 BN in *Statements: A Review of British Abstract Art in 1956*, ICA, London, January 1957 (reprinted in *SIS* 1969, p.40).

78 When Herbert Read speaks of tachism in relation to these mottled areas (letters to BN, 28 September and 12 October 1956 (*TGA*)), he is merely using a fashionable term, not suggesting a tachist influence on BN's work. See, however, Patrick Heron's amusing comments in *Ben Nicholson*, Tate Gallery, 1993, p.231.

79 BN letter to John Summerson, n.d. <April 1955> (*TGA*).

80 BN letters to Helen Sutherland, 4 February 1954 (*TGA*) and Herbert Read, 15 March 1954 (*Read Archive*). In 1956 BN's work was represented in twelve public collections in Britain, twelve in America, and ten in other parts of the world.

81 His only previous submission, *White Jug* in 1922, had been rejected.

82 This topic is treated at length by Jeremy Lewison in *Ben Nicholson*, Tate Gallery, 1993, pp.70ff.

83 BN letter to Herbert Read, 15 March 1954 (*Read Archive*).

84 BN letter to John Summerson, 1 January 1954 (*TGA*).

85 BN, 'Defending Modern Artists', *Daily Mail*, 7 August 1951, p.2 (reprinted in *SIS* 1969, p.39).

86 See Felicitas Vogler, 'Ben Nicholson nel Ticino', in Simone Soldini (ed.), *Ben Nicholson – opere dal 1921 al 1981*, Museo d'Arte, Mendrisio, 1993, pp.130ff.

87 BN letter to Adrian Stokes, 15 May 1964 (*TGA*).

88 BN letter to Herbert Read, 9 March 1962 (*Read Archive*).

89 BN, 'The Aims of the Modern Artist' (interview), *The Studio*, vol.104, December 1932, p.333 (reprinted in *SIS* 1969, p.30). This is not essentially different from the term *idéiste*, coined by G.-Albert Aurier (in 'Le Symbolisme en peinture', *Mercure de France*, March 1891, p.162) to characterize the painting of Gauguin and the Synthetists, whose chief aim was 'l'expression de l'Idée'. Similarly, Apollinaire had described certain Cubist paintings as drawing not on the reality of sight but on that of instinct and intuition (Guillaume Apollinaire, *Les Peintres Cubistes*, Figuière, Paris, 1913, p.24).

90 Helen Sutherland, Notebook 1, October 1926, p.73r (*TGA*, by permission of the Executors of the Estate of Nicolete Gray).

91 *Cf* Aristotle's concept of τὸ εἶδος ἐν τῇ ψυχῇ (*Metaphysics*, VII, 7 = 1032b) – an inner *form* present in the soul of the artist and transferred by his activity into matter. This, and Nicholson's use of the word 'idea', should not be confused with the more familiar Platonic 'ideas' whose history in art is outlined in Erwin Panofsky, *Idea: ein Beitrag zur Begriffsgeschichte der älteren Kunsttheorie*, 2nd edn, Bruno Hessling, Berlin, 1960.

92 Arthur Waley, 'Yūgen', *New Statesman*, 26 March 1921, p.729.

93 BN in exhibition catalogue, Galerie Beyeler, Basel, April–June 1968.

94 Osvald Sirén, *Chinese Painting*, vol.II, Lund Humphries, 1956, pp.132, 141. Similarly Raphael Petrucci, *La Philosophie de la nature dans l'art d'extrême-orient*, Henri Laurens, Paris, 1910, p.137.

95 Geoffrey Grigson, 'Ben Nicholson: The Latest Reliefs', in *Ben Nicholson, Twelve New Works*, Marlborough Gallery, June 1967.

96 BN letter to Geoffrey Grigson, 21 April 1967 (by courtesy of Dr Caroline Grigson).

97 Helen Sutherland, Diary entry for 18 November 1957 (by permission of the Executors of the Estate of Nicolete Gray).

98 BN letter to Herbert Read, 16 March 1961 (*Read Archive*).

99 BN, 'Notes on "Abstract" Art', in Herbert Read (introduction), *Ben Nicholson – paintings, reliefs, drawings*, Lund Humphries, 1948, p.27. Read's explanation (*ibid*, p.16) of BN's alternating, or even concurrent, use of a 'naturalistic style' and an 'abstract style' in psychological terms of affirmation and rejection of the world is not convincing. Similarly, in his *Contemporary British Art*, Penguin, 1951, p.32, the lop-sided emphasis on the abstract to the exclusion of the figurative in Nicholson's work is fundamentally false.

100 BN, 'Notes on "Abstract" Art', *Horizon*, vol.4, no.22, October 1941, pp.272–6 (reprinted in *SIS* 1969, p.33).

101 BN letter to Margaret Gardiner, 28 May <1967> (*TGA*). The letter describes an afternoon six years later, but this makes no material difference.

102 *eg*: *October 1955 (road to Pienza)*, *1958 (Tesserete nos.1 & 2)*, *April 1959 (Racciano from car)*.

103 Somewhat unusual was his request to Patrick Heron 'to be a good chap' and take some snaps of the Zennor coast between Pendeen and St Ives and send them to him in Switzerland. They helped to refresh his memory before he began work on *Zennor Quoit 2* in 1966. (Recollections of Patrick Heron in *Ben Nicholson – a portrait with landscapes*, BBC Radio 3 documentary, 8 April 1994).

104 Quoted in exh. cat., Galerie Beyeler, Basel, May–June 1973.

105 'In a painting it should be as impossible to separate form from colour or colour from form as it is to separate wood from wood-colour or stone-colour from stone. Colour exists not as applied paint but as the inner core of an idea.' BN in the catalogue to his retrospective exhibition, Tate Gallery, 1955 (reprinted in *SIS* 1969, p.40).

106 All the elements of the late reliefs – circles, rectangles, trapeziums, interlocking axe-heads, curves – are already present in the painting *1945 (two circles)*, but not the perfect (or near-perfect) square.

107 BN letter to Herbert Read, 16 May 1962 (*Read Archive*).

108 Herbert Read letter to Felicitas Vogler, June 1967 reported by BN in letter to

H. S. Ede, 24 June 1967 (*Kettle's Yard Archive, University of Cambridge*) and to Geoffrey Grigson, 27 June 1967.

109 For details see Jeremy Lewison, 'The Early Prints of Ben Nicholson', *Print Quarterly*, vol.11, no.2, June 1985, pp.105–24, and for an overall view, Carol Hogben in *Ben Nicholson: the Graphic Art*, Victoria & Albert Museum, 1975.

110 BN letter to Geoffrey Jellicoe, 2 December 1967 (*TGA*).

111 BN letter to Maurice de Sausmarez, 8 October <1968> (reprinted in *SIS* 1969, p.59).

112 Fifty photographs of Italy, Portugal and Greece are reproduced in Felicitas Vogler, *The Quiet Eye*, Thames & Hudson, 1969. See also Felicitas Vogler, 'Reisen mit Stift und Kamera', *Du* (Zurich), no.238, December 1960, pp.39–45 (English version in *SIS* 1969, pp.21–2).

113 BN letter to Geoffrey Jellicoe, 17 April 1967 (*TGA*).

114 BN letter to H. S. Ede, 23 August 1963 (*Kettle's Yard Archive, University of Cambridge*). BN had been introduced to Mark Tobey by Adrian Stokes at Dartington in 1932 (?) (see BN letter to Adrian Stokes, 24 February 1959 (*TGA*)). They met again at Brissago in March 1963.

115 BN, 'The Life and Opinions of an English "Modern"', in conversation with Vera and John Russell, *The Sunday Times*, 28 April 1963 (reprinted in *SIS* 1969, p.51).

116 Separation concluded in divorce in 1977.

117 BN letter to Geoffrey Jellicoe, 23 September 1971 (*TGA*).

118 BN letter to Geoffrey Grigson, 12 June 1972 (quoted in Geoffrey Grigson, *Britain Observed*, Phaidon, 1975, p.203).

119 It is interesting to compare BN's almost identical treatment in his drawing *April 1954 (Yockenthwaite, Wharfedale)* (see Herbert Read (introduction) *Ben Nicholson, work since 1947*, vol.2, Lund Humphries, 1956, pl.70). Both drawings recall BN's 'naive' paintings of Cumberland landscape dating from 1928–30. There is also a powerful earlier drawing of Burnsall Bridge on the Wharfe dating from May 1954 (see *ibid*, pl.90).

120 BN letter to Adrian Stokes, 24 September 1962 (*TGA*).

121 BN letter to Geoffrey Jellicoe, 20 November 1967 (*TGA*).

122 BN letter to H. S. Ede, 12 July 1974 (*Kettle's Yard Archive, University of Cambridge*).

123 BN letter to Jane Grigson, 27 November 1967 (by courtesy of Dr Caroline Grigson).

124 BN letter to H. S. Ede, 4 February 1975 (*Kettle's Yard Archive, University of Cambridge*).

125 BN letters to H. S. Ede, 12 July <1964> and 7 August 1964 (*Kettle's Yard Archive, University of Cambridge*).

126 H. S. Ede letter to BN, 30 September 1964 (*TGA*).

127 Norbert Lynton (*Ben Nicholson*, Phaidon, 1993, p.249) is altogether too gloomy about the fate of this panel. Damaged but not, as he says, destroyed, it languished for many years at Edinburgh University, then was presented to the Tate Gallery in 1995, restored, and put on display at Tate Modern, Bankside, London in November 2000. (Unfortunately this is only one among many such misstatements and inaccuracies in Lynton's book, some of which are tacitly corrected here.)

128 For the same reason it is impossible to imagine that BN could ever have succeeded in the theatre. In 1934 he did make some designs for a ballet by Massine to Beethoven's *Symphony no. 7* – Stravinsky's *Apollo* might have been a better match – but Massine

could make nothing of them. See Jeremy Lewison, *Ben Nicholson*, Tate Gallery, 1993, pp.218–19.

129 BN letter to Geoffrey Jellicoe, 10 April 1968 (*TGA*). In a similar letter to Herbert Read, 2 February 1960 (*Read Archive*), BN specified the date of this incident as 'in about 1917'.

130 Close on two hundred of BN's works on paper were shown in three separate exhibitions at the Waddington Galleries in October 1978, July 1980 and March 1982.

131 See Harry Holtzman and Martin S. James (ed. & trans.), *The New Art – The New Life: the collected writings of Piet Mondrian*, Thames & Hudson, 1987, pp.78, 80.

132 See BN letter to Geoffrey Grigson, 21 April 1967, quoted on pp.88–9.

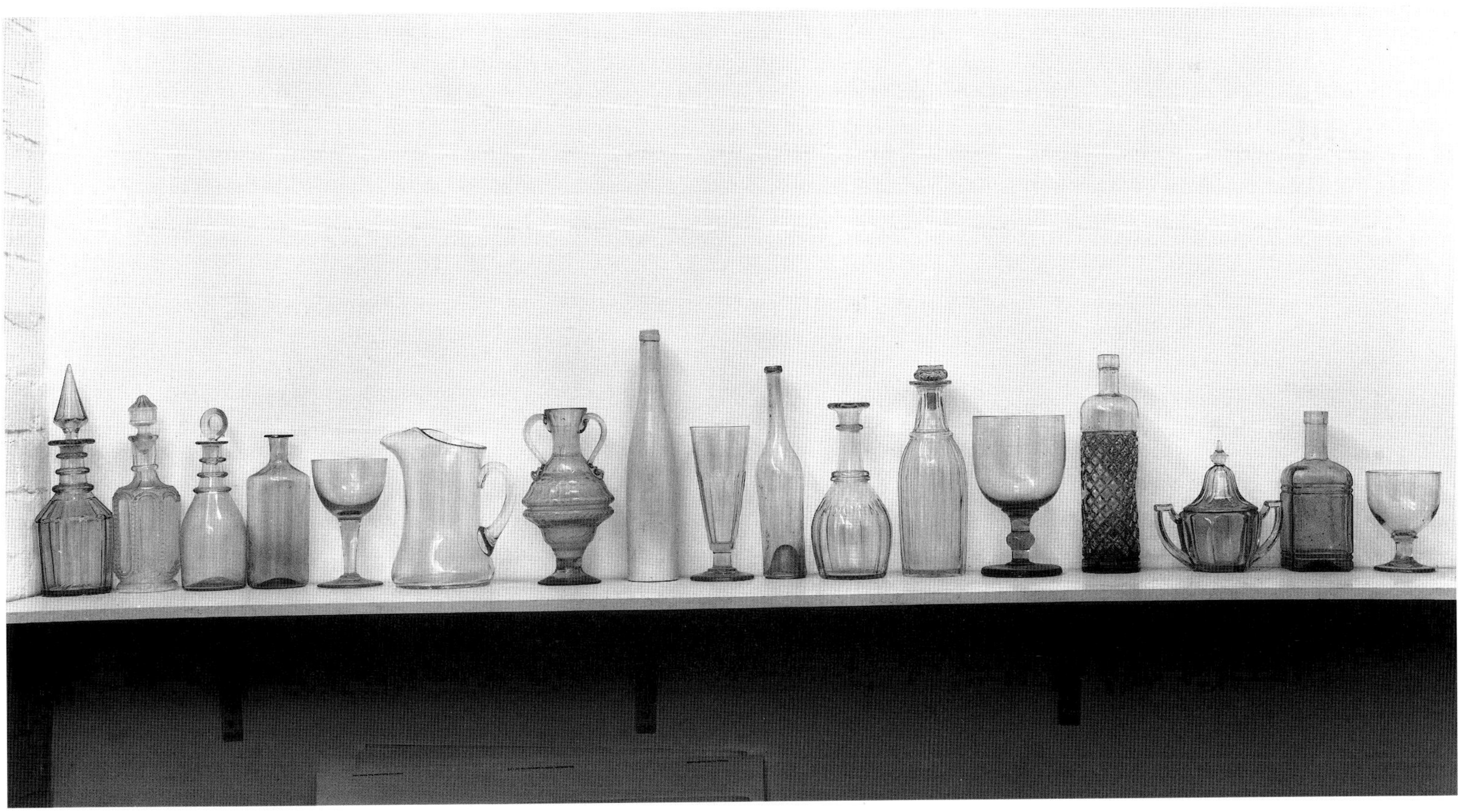

119 Glass objects arranged by BN in his Hampstead studio (photo: James Austin)

BIBLIOGRAPHICAL NOTE

The most comprehensive bibliography of BN to date, though even this is by no means complete, is by Nicola Hunt and Maria White in *Ben Nicholson*, Tate Gallery, 1993, pp. 251–66. Here there is no need to do more than indicate the essential.

REPRODUCTIONS OF BN'S WORK

Read, Herbert (introduction), *Ben Nicholson – Paintings, Reliefs, Drawings*, Lund Humphries, 1948 (reissued in 1955, with some plates substituted and added, under the title *Ben Nicholson – Work from 1911–1948*, vol.1).

Read, Herbert (introduction), *Ben Nicholson – Work since 1947*, vol.2, Lund Humphries, 1956.

Russell, John (introduction), *Ben Nicholson – Drawings, Paintings and Reliefs 1911-1968*, Thames and Hudson, 1969.

All three volumes were produced to a high standard under the artist's supervision, but suffer from a relative dearth of colour plates. This was to some extent remedied by the *c.*360 colour reproductions (many of them, however, too small or too untrue to give an adequate idea of the originals) in Norbert Lynton, *Ben Nicholson*, Phaidon, 1993.

High-quality reproductions are also to be found in some exhibition catalogues, see André Emmerich, New York, 1965, 1974; Marlborough, London, 1963, 1967, 1968, 1970, 1971; Beyeler, Basel, 1968, 1973; André Emmerich, Zurich, 1975; Waddington, London, 1976, 1978, 1980, 1982.

BN'S PUBLISHED STATEMENTS, WRITINGS AND INTERVIEWS

Maurice de Sausmarez (ed.), *Ben Nicholson*, Studio International Special, London, 1969.

WRITINGS ON BN'S WORK

Summerson, John, *Ben Nicholson*, Penguin Modern Painters, Penguin, 1948.

Alley, Ronald, *Ben Nicholson*, Express Art Books, Beaverbrook Newspapers, 1962.

Baxandall, David, *Ben Nicholson,* (Art in Progress), Methuen, 1962.

Harrison, Charles, 'Notes on BN's development and commentary on selected works', in *Ben Nicholson*, Tate Gallery, 1969.

Nash, Steven, 'Ben Nicholson – an historical perspective', in *Ben Nicholson – Fifty Years of his Art*, Albright-Knox Art Gallery, Buffalo, New York, 1978.

Lewison, Jeremy, *Ben Nicholson*, Tate Gallery, 1993.

ACKNOWLEDGEMENTS

I am grateful to Jennifer Booth and the staff of the Tate Gallery Archive for their unfailing helpfulness; to Nigel Farrow for constructive criticism of an earlier version of the text; to Margaret Gardiner for affectionately humorous reminiscences and wise reflections on her long friendship with Ben Nicholson; to the Executors of the late Nicolete Gray for permission to quote from the notebook and diary of Helen Sutherland; to Caroline Grigson for permission to quote from Nicholson's letters to Geoffrey and Jane Grigson; to David Lewis for lively comment as well as practical help; to the McPherson Library, University of Victoria, Victoria BC, Canada, for permission to quote from Nicholson's letters in the Herbert Read Archive; to Jake Nicholson for his invariable patience and courtesy in answering my many questions; to Rachel Nicholson for vetting my opinions; to Cyril Reddihough, Nicholson's oldest friend, for delightful conversations and detailed information, as well as for reading through my manuscript; to Patricia Reed for so generously sharing with me her encyclopaedic knowledge of William Nicholson; and to Felicitas Vogler for vivid evocation of the Ticino years and her own particular insight into the character of Nicholson the man and the artist. Thanks are due also to all those who have allowed me to reproduce works in their possession, though it has not proved possible to trace the present ownership of every work illustrated.

My greatest debt is to Angela Taunt. Over the past twelve years she has been unstinting in her help and advice, sharing with me her unparalleled knowledge, assisting at every stage of the book's long gestation. Without her enthusiasm and generosity it would have been neither begun nor completed.

Photo Credits

James Austin 5, 9, 14, 19, 20, 22, 23, 27, 42, 60, 71, 74, 78, 82, 89, 91, 93, 94, 95, 96, 98, 99, 100, 103, 104, 105, 107, 113–19; Clive Boursnell 110; The Bridgeman Art Library 4; Brian Champion 33; Christie's Images Ltd. 2, 72, 84; David Clarke 32; Prudence Cuming Associates 6, 24, 54, 67, 106, 108; Alberto Flammer 64, 79, 88, 90, 118; Charles Gimpel 52; Lonnie Graham 30; Jane Inskipp 81; William Kuryluk 86; Jonathan Lynch 3, 13; Frank Newbould 10, 40, 43, 46; Simon Nicholson 1; Cyril Reddihough 44; Antonia Reeve 7, 15, 73; Peter Schälchi 25; Glen Segal 18; Studio St Ives 45; Rodney Todd-White & Son 16, 26, 28, 51, 58; V & A Picture Library 31; Felicitas Vogler 109.

INDEX OF WORKS

INDEX